Ripple
Effect

Ripple Effect

A family's story of adventure and faith

Shirley Jamieson

Ripple Effect:
A family's story of adventure and faith
Published by Shirley Jamieson
New Zealand

© 2019 Shirley Jamieson

ISBN 978-0-473-49869-6 (Softcover)
ISBN 978-0-473-49870-2 (ePUB)
ISBN 978-0-473-49871-9 (Kindle)

Editing: Andrea Candy

Production & Typesetting:
Andrew Killick
Castle Publishing Services
www.castlepublishing.co.nz

Cover design:
Paul Smith

All Scripture quotations, unless otherwise indicated,
are taken from the Holy Bible, New International Version®, NIV®.
Copyright ©1973, 1978, 1984, 2011 by Biblica, Inc.™
Used by permission of Zondervan.
All rights reserved worldwide.

ALL RIGHTS RESERVED

No part of this publication may be reproduced,
stored in a retrieval system, or transmitted
in any form or by any means, electronic, mechanical,
photocopying, recording or otherwise,
without prior written permission from the author.

Acknowledgements

My heartfelt gratitude goes to my second cousin, Stewart, in England. In answer to my prayers, he offered to travel to London several times to take digital photos of letters and documents in the London Missionary Society archives. It took time to upload and email them to me too.

This information was the key to unlock the years 1909 to 1924 in my grandparents' lives and it answered many of my questions. Thank you.

> As the rain and snow come down from heaven, and do not return to it without watering the earth and making it bud and flourish, so that it yields seed for the sower and bread for the eater, so is my word that goes out from my mouth: It will not return to me empty, but will accomplish what I desire and achieve the purpose for which I sent it. (Isaiah 55:10-11)

Contents

Preface	9
1. It's a Jungle Out There	13
2. Living with Danger	33
3. New Directions	51
4. Gopiganj on the Grand Trunk Road	59
5. Setbacks and Success	69
6. Archie's Himalayan Adventure	85
7. In Awe of the Mighty Creator	101
8. Joy in Uncertain Times	117
9. A Traumatic Journey	127
10. War: From Gopiganj to France	137
11. The McMillan Children in Wartime London	151
12. Return to India	171
13. Training for the Chamar Teenagers	183
14. Good Times and Sad Times	195
15. Where Now, Lord?	205
16. To New Zealand and Fiji	219
17. Serving God in Fiji	229
18. Mission Ships and a Cruise Ship	243
19. Papua, Pakistan and Fiji	255
20. World War II: A Fijian Perspective	265

21. India 1947: The Political Earthquake	275
22. Grace	287
23. Dispensing Hope	303
References	323

Preface

Several years ago, the idea of writing my grandparents' story dropped into my mind like the seed of a banyan, the national tree of India. It grew fast, and I knew it was something I really wanted to do.

As I collated information – and there was a lot of it – connections and coincidences sprang up like the expanding aerial roots of the tree. These roots form trunks to support the widening network of branches, the way Grace and Archie's story shows the on-going spread – the ripple effect – of God's love.

In writing their story, I began to know them well, discovering what I had missed as a child. A two-week summer visit each year to Tauranga from Whanganui wasn't long enough to form a strong relationship. I could relate to my aunts – Mum's sisters Connie and Lily – and my cousin who lived there too. Connie visited us in Whanganui sometimes and I always looked forward to seeing her.

Mum told me a little about India and Fiji. It seemed unreal – so different from my own life. The Indian curios in the cabinet in my grandparents' home fascinated me. I'd often ask Connie to tell me about them.

I remember Granddad Archie showing me how he wound a long cloth around his head to make an Indian turban. He sent me Indian stamps, with notes on what each one commemorated. Another time, he told me of his precarious adventure crossing the raging Sarju River in the dark. It was his way of sharing his life with me. I was impressed, but unlike him, I didn't feel any connection to India. Not then.

To me, Granny Grace was a sweet old lady who forgot things. I didn't know the brave, resourceful, adaptable woman she had been. She will always be an inspiration to me.

Uncle Frank, Mum's brother, his wife Elzeth and three sons lived in Hamilton. We didn't see them often. Years later, when I was working in Hamilton I boarded with Frank and Elzeth for a while. They were the New Zealand representatives for Elzeth's sister, Elma, and Jack Ringer's mission, the Afghan Border Crusade.

I didn't meet Elma until I was married with three children, and she was a widow in her eighties. I visited her regularly at Meadowcroft, the old cottage her parents had owned. She loved to tell me about the dangers she had faced in her mission work.

Connie and my family met regularly until her death in 1998. She supported all her nephews and nieces, and their families, with love and prayer, all her life.

As I continued writing Grace and Archie's story, I needed to piece together information about each part of their lives from several different sources. I learned about their trials and triumphs, joys and sorrows. Wanting the story to be accurate but personal meant creating most of the conversations from the source material, or using the children's quotes from Grace's notebook.

From the safety of my computer desk, I travelled with them into the Indian jungle, plains and mountains, World War I London and France, New Zealand and on to Fiji. I joined Archie in his trips back to India, then discovered the wonderful work

Preface

Indian missions are doing there now to spread God's love. It is an experience I will never forget.

I hope you will enjoy the journey too.

Chapter 1

It's a Jungle Out There

Kanha National Park in Madhya Pradesh, Central India, is an animal lover's wonderland of diversity.

It is a beautiful place to watch the sun set over the jungle-clad hills, tall grasslands and ravines.

The highlight for many visitors, though, is observing tigers roaming wild and free. The big cats' majestic beauty and savage strength captivate their hearts.

Back in the 1890s this same untamed land inspired Rudyard Kipling to write his famous *Jungle Book* tales. The stories tell of Mowgli the Jungle Boy and his adventures with Sheer Khan the tiger, Bagheera the panther, Akela the wolf and other interesting characters.

Fascinated, ten-year-old Archie McMillan devoured every word of those stories. He didn't know God had exciting plans for him right there in Mowgli's backyard.

Only seven years later, he arrived at the village of Baihar in February 1901. He was joining the small team of missionaries in the Balaghat Mission to the Gonds.

India was part of the British Empire then, and the Madhya Pradesh area was called Central Provinces. Kanha National Park wouldn't be established for another 54 years.

Many of the shy hill tribes had never seen a white man before, and Archie, keen to share the gospel of Jesus, often travelled through tiger territory to reach their villages. He was studying Hindi, reading and writing it every day and practising speaking with the local Gonds. He was also learning about the wildlife.

'A tiger passed this way some hours ago,' one of the other missionaries said to him, pointing out some footprints on the track. 'See, you can recognise the footprint of a wolf by its claw marks. Over here, these soft round pad marks are from a panther.'

Archie memorised each of them. Every year many hill people lost their lives to man-eating tigers, leopards and panthers. To survive, Archie needed to read the jungle like an open book.

One afternoon he saw the fresh paw prints of a tiger in the sandy bed of a stream. Water was oozing up from the sand, filling in the indentations left by the tiger's feet and Archie knew it meant only one thing. The huge cat had just been standing there moments before and was no doubt watching him from nearby rushes or tall grasses.

Praying for protection, Archie backed away, all senses alert.

To his relief, the tiger stayed hidden. It wasn't a man-eater, but there would be several more encounters with the big cats that would leave him in fear of their strength.

Whatever happened, though, Archie knew God was with him.

※

Archie chose to leave everything he knew and loved to travel to India and share the gospel. Several events in his childhood and early teen years convinced him God was directing him to go.

He was born in London on 7 March 1883 and had two sisters, Jessie and Elsie. His full name was Archibald William, but not many people called him that.

John McMillan, his Scottish father, worked for the London and North Western Railway Company. His mother Sarah had been a school teacher before she married John. Archie knew he'd inherited his musical ability from her.

John had met Sarah at a concert. As he watched her entertaining the audience, he was captivated and asked to meet her afterwards. Their friendship grew into love and they were married in 1872.

Archie's Christian upbringing was typical of England in the late 1800s. It was at the other end of the spectrum from life in the Indian jungle.

Sunday morning always found the family at the Clapton Park Congregational Church, and Sunday school dominated the afternoon. Sarah taught more than 100 children aged between five and eight.

Archie was in her class but moved up to the older Sunday school when he was still only six.

'Why can I start now?' he asked.

'It's because you are too bossy,' his new young teacher, J. D. Maynard told him. Archie continued to be disruptive, prompting J. D. to visit his parents one evening to complain.

Sarah greeted him at the door and began listening to the list of his complaints. Then she cut him short.

'You know, Mr Maynard,' she said. 'It's the naughty boys who turn out to be ministers or missionaries.'

It was ironic that, many years later, Archie met up with his Sunday school teacher again in Hoshangabad. Maynard was also a missionary in the Central Provinces in India but with the Friends' Foreign Missionary Association.

Sarah wasn't surprised Archie was disruptive in Sunday school. He wanted to do what was right, but he was a bright, determined, active little boy and couldn't sit still or be quiet for long.

On Sunday evenings Jessie played the organ as the family gathered around singing hymns. Archie sang along too, his clear voice keeping in perfect tune.

'I think you're good enough to join the Band of Hope Choir,' Sarah said to him. 'I'll take you for an audition if you like.'

'Sure, I'll try for it,' Archie agreed.

He was excited when he passed the audition and was accepted into the choir. 'Each year we compete with other choirs at the Crystal Palace!' he told the family.

It meant a lot to him when the choir won the silver shield three years in a row, and he was placed in solo competitions as well.

'Well done, Archie,' John said. 'We are all proud of you.'

John was strict, but Archie knew his father loved him. A kind man, he was often helping people or praying for them.

At church in 1894 they were raising money for the London Missionary Society (LMS) to pay off the debt for the steamer, *John Williams*.

Named in honour of John Williams, an early LMS missionary, the ship sailed to the South Pacific to take missionaries and their supplies to distant lands.

Archie listened to the story, his face alight with interest.

John Williams had first sailed to Tahiti in 1816, then later to other Pacific Islands, telling the people about Jesus and helping them in every way he could. Many of them learned to love him.

Sandalwood traders killed some of the islanders on Erromango in the New Hebrides (Vanuatu) a few days before John and another missionary, James Harris, landed there on 20 November 1839. In fear and retaliation, the cannibals clubbed them to death and ate them.

Five years later, an LMS sailing ship, the *John Williams*, headed for the Pacific. It was the first of several ships with the same name over the years, but by 1894 they'd progressed to a steamship.

'I'll help collect money for it,' Archie said.

By Christmas he'd raised seven shillings and sixpence, winning a book about the mission, the *Story of the South Seas* by George Cousins.

Winning the book wouldn't just become a childhood memory for Archie. It was as though God had dropped a pebble into the pool of his life. The ripples spread until he met George years later, changing the direction of his life. Further on, the ripples reached the South Pacific.

'I'd love to have adventures and live on a South Seas island,' Archie told his family now, his eyes shining.

'Not for me,' Jessie said. 'I'm staying right here in England.' She was ten years older than Archie.

'That would be so boring,' he said. 'I want to travel, see the world – interesting places like India.' He loved Jessie. She had almost been a second mother to him when he was little, but she didn't share his enthusiasm for adventure.

'You should go with him, Jessie,' Elsie said. 'I can just see you charging through the jungle on an elephant.'

Everyone laughed, including Jessie. In their imagination they pictured the trumpeting elephant with Jessie's small figure perched up high, dressed in her frilly blouse, long skirt and Sunday hat.

Jessie never did ride that elephant. It took all her courage to go to India.

At school, Archie's favourite subjects were sports and woodwork, but he achieved well at academic subjects too. Disappointed he had to leave at the end of 1895, he looked for work to supplement the family income.

He was only 12 years old.

He found employment at a wholesale mouldings company and was soon promoted, working in the manager's office preparing estimates and quotes. They were skills, among many others, that he'd need later on.

By the time he was 14, he was sure God wanted him to be a missionary. But where? At a talk about India, he asked to receive their mission newsletter.

Then a couple of years later, he attended a 'lantern lecture,' a talk at the YMCA with photos about Indian missions projected on to a screen.

He approached the visiting speaker at the end of the meeting. 'I'm sure God is directing me to be a missionary. After hearing your talk tonight, I believe it's in India,' he explained. 'I think some knowledge of agriculture would be useful there. What would you advise?'

The speaker thought for a moment. 'Come with me,' he said, indicating for Archie to follow him. 'I'll introduce you to a professor who owns a farm 15 miles from London near Goffs Oak village.'

Within a few minutes of meeting Archie, the professor agreed to take him on. 'I'll see to it that you learn all you need to know about farming,' he said.

Archie moved in with the family, and getting up early, he milked the cows each day, delivering the milk by pony cart to a dairy.

Apart from attending church on Sundays, he joined the senior group of the Christian Endeavour Society. This group trained young people in Christian leadership, held Bible studies and prayed together.

It didn't take long for Archie to notice one of the young women. Grace Waller was pretty. Her large, soft brown eyes sparkled with intelligence, fun, and depth of character.

Over the next few weeks, their friendship grew. He told her he planned to preach the gospel in India and about his family.

He met her parents, Josiah and Elizabeth, and her brother and three sisters. Lilian was married to Jesse Collyer, but Florence and Louise were both single and, like Grace, still lived at home.

Grace's brother, Josiah Henry, whom everyone called Harry, was married to Helen and worked for a printing company. No one knew it then, but God had big plans that would intertwine their lives with Grace and Archie's in unexpected ways.

'Father's family came from France originally,' Grace explained to Archie. 'They were Huguenots who fled to London from persecution many years ago. Each generation continued with their family's silk weaving business, but Dad joined a lithographic printing firm.'

'Printing sure is a big break away from silk weaving,' Archie commented. 'But thinking back to the Huguenot refugees, it must have been tough for them settling in a new land.'

'Yes, it would have,' Grace agreed. 'Life can still be really hard at times now though, can't it? Before I was born, four of my sisters and a brother all died in early childhood from illness. The heartbreak for my parents was unimaginable.'

'That's tragic,' Archie said. 'Our family lost two little girls too.'

꽃

India was never far from Grace and Archie's conversations. After praying together many times, asking God what he wanted them to do, Grace came to a decision.

'I believe God also wants me to go to India,' she told Archie.

'Grace, that may mean we could be together, working with the same mission.' Archie's eyes lit up. 'I do hope so.'

Grace smiled. 'I wonder if it will be in Bengal? Mother's brother Henry emigrated there when he was 16. He has indigo plantations.'

'Maybe,' Archie considered.

But it didn't work out that way at all.

One Saturday in August 1900, Archie biked back home to Clapton Park to attend a church garden party. The minister chatted with him for a while, telling him some interesting news.

'A friend of mine, John Lampard, is back here in England on leave from his mission work in the Central Provinces in India,' he explained. 'He asked me if there was a young man from my church who'd join him working among the hill tribes.'

'Did you give him my name?' Archie asked.

'I certainly did.' The minister smiled. 'There would be no harm in going to see him right now. It might lead to something.'

'Thanks, I will.' Archie leapt on his bike and raced off down the street.

He impressed John Lampard in the short conversation they had. 'I think you are just the sort of young man God will use in our mission,' he told him. 'Tomorrow I'll be giving the children's talk at your church and would love to meet your parents after the service.'

'I'll be there to introduce you.' Archie shook John's hand as he left.

He was spending the night at home, leaving at 5.00 the next

morning to bike back to Goffs Oak to milk the cows. Racing home once more, he changed into his Sunday suit and joined his family in church for the 11.00 a.m. service.

※

As soon as he could, Archie told Grace the news.

'It's pioneering work with jungle tribes,' he told her. 'And I can't wait to go. I'm going to leave from Hull, sailing on the *Othello*. It's a cargo ship but it takes a dozen passengers as well.'

'That's wonderful,' Grace smiled but sadness was there too. 'When will you leave?'

'January.'

'I'm going to miss you so much, Archie.'

'I'll miss you too. I love you, Grace.' Taking a deep breath, he leaned forward and gently held her hands in his. 'Would you consider applying to the mission too? I'd love to ask you to promise to be my wife someday. But the mission has a regulation that women coming out to marry staff need to serve for two years first. It's to see if they can stand it. Jungle life is too tough for most European women.'

Grace looked into his eyes, seeing the intensity there, the enthusiasm for adventure, and his love for her. 'Oh Archie, I love you too. Whatever happens I always will.'

'I'll love you forever, Grace.' Archie pulled her close and their kiss held the promise of enduring love.

※

Archie's first step on to the subcontinent of India was in Bombay (Mumbai) on 14 February 1901.

John Lampard had organised friends to meet him. Staying in their home for five days, Archie experienced life in the chaotic rush of an Indian city.

Young though he was, he impressed his new friends. They asked him to preach in the Baptist church on Sunday evening.

Early on Tuesday morning, he set out for the jungle villages that would be his home for the next few years. Travelling for a week, using a variety of transportation, he arrived at Baihar in the Balaghat district tired and aching. For the final two days he'd bumped and jolted over rocky tracks in a bullock cart with no springs.

The Balaghat Mission to the Gonds had mission houses in three villages: Baihar, Khursipar and Nikkum. On a map, they were placed like three dots to form a triangle. Archie had learned that the Lampards were at Baihar and other missionaries, the Williams, were at Nikkum.

After he'd settled in, the Lampards showed Archie around their small school and farm at Baihar. One of the missionaries was supervising work on another building for the orphanage. It needed to be finished before the monsoon season arrived in June.

'We'd appreciate your help with both the farm and the building work,' John Lampard told him.

'I'll enjoy that.' As he worked, Archie knew he'd be learning a lot too.

'Two tribes live scattered through the jungle – the Gonds and the Baigas,' John continued. 'They are the aboriginals of India, and were probably driven into the forest by invading Aryans many hundreds of years ago.'

'There are other villages in the jungle?' Archie asked.

John nodded. 'Oh, yes, you'll see them when we take you to visit them.'

Nothing could have prepared Archie for jungle life. The Gonds lived in groups of huts made from mud and bamboo. There weren't any windows so the inside of the huts was blackened by smoke. A framework of plaited bamboo placed over the doorway at night didn't always prevent a leopard from entering.

The narrow, stony village streets, stinking with rotting refuse, turned to mud in the rainy season. Men wandered about wearing a narrow cloth tied around their lower bodies. The women wore saris, with brass, pewter, and glass jewellery clustered around their necks, arms, ankles and toes.

As Archie got to know some of the villagers, he was impressed by their courage and strength. Every day they lived among tigers and panthers. Sometimes the large cats killed them – or their cattle and goats.

One of the Gonds Archie met was attacked by a tiger springing on him from behind.

'It ripped at my shoulders with its claws,' the man told him, 'but I punched it hard in the stomach with my elbow.'

'What happened then?' Archie asked, amazed.

'The tiger fell off to catch its breath so I ran.'

Like most Gonds, he was a man of few words, but Archie could picture the attack in his mind. Looking at the deep scars on the man's shoulders he knew that although he was young and athletic, he wouldn't have stood a chance with that tiger.

Since he was British and entitled to carry a gun, he felt a measure of security. The weapon would be useless, though, as tigers attack from behind.

The Baigas lived in more remote areas of the jungle than the Gonds and often ran away when they first saw Archie.

One tribesman who had never seen a European before stood

still, pointed to Archie, and told his son, 'Look, God has come to our village.'

Like the Gonds, the Baigas' huts were also constructed of mud and bamboo. Furnishings and household goods were made from materials from their jungle environment. The people slept on plaited bamboo mats and had earthenware pots, kettles and pails.

Archie watched as the villagers used split bamboo to make fish traps and baskets for collecting berries and sifting grain. They made disposable plates by weaving grass with a creeper.

They were almost completely self-sufficient, except for axes which they traded goods for. At that time, the British were beginning to construct roads into the jungle. For many centuries the Baigas had moved from place to place, cutting and burning areas of the forest and planting their millet in the ashes just before the rainy season each year.

The British outlawed the practice in most areas. They took timber and minerals to the Indian plains for their own use and the tribesmen complained the British thieves were stealing their jungle.

Baigas knew no other way of farming. The jungle was their source of materials to make practically everything they needed. Without it, the way of living they'd developed over centuries could disappear.

Archie, being young and British, couldn't understand why they didn't welcome the challenge to adapt to a different way of farming. He thought it would improve their lives and tried to help.

'If we breed our British hens with yours,' he suggested, 'it will make a strong new variety. They'll lay big eggs and the stock will be immune to local diseases as well.'

'It wouldn't work,' they said.

'Why not?' he asked, remembering what he'd learned about breeding stock on the farm in England.

'Well,' they responded, 'how could it possibly work? Your English hens wouldn't understand ours.'

The idea of a breeding programme ended right there.

※

In September 1901 at the end of Archie's first experience of a monsoon season, several of the missionaries and their families became ill with malaria, some with the added complication of blackwater fever.

It meant their red blood cells were bursting, causing rapidly progressive anaemia accompanied by the misery of high fever, jaundice and vomiting. Urine turned dark red or black. Kidney failure and death often followed.

Nowadays blackwater fever is not common. It's probable that in those days it was an autoimmune reaction caused by the interaction of the malaria parasite and quinine, the medication used for malaria.

That knowledge was unavailable in 1901, and the mission was almost at a standstill.

'You're the only one not ill or caring for those who are,' one of the missionaries said to Archie. 'So we'll leave you in charge of the mission.'

'Sure,' Archie said. 'What would you like me to do?'

'Supervise the Gond teenagers working on the mission farm, teach at the school, and please take the Sunday church services.'

Archie was only 18 years old. He'd been learning Hindi for seven months and could read and write the Hindi script but could only converse at a basic level. 'I'll do my best,' he said.

It was hard work, but he was surprised and pleased to find that with no other English speakers around, his Hindi improved at a faster rate.

Slowly the missionaries regained their health. Often Archie went with two of them to tell the jungle villagers about Jesus. As it was the dry season, they could use a bullock cart, bumping and lurching along the rocky tracks.

In the evening Archie tied a sheet onto two bamboo poles. He and his friends lit a lantern to project translucent pictures about the gospel story onto the sheet. As he showed friendship and kindness, some of the Gonds became his friends and slowly began to take in the gospel story.

The British were building schools, and there was a mission school at Baihar for the children at the orphanage. Only about 1 in 500 Gonds could read.

As Archie learned more about the way of life in the jungle, he moved into a mud bungalow in the village of Khursipar. A young Christian Baiga named Yohan came in April 1902 to cook for him and accompany him on his mission trips.

Archie knew Yohan and his sister had been brought up in the mission orphanage but didn't know much about him.

'Did you come from near here?' he asked, interested.

'No,' Yohan said. 'My sister and I were born in a tiny grass hut a long way from here.' In 1897 a terrible famine had hit his remote area. Cholera followed in a deadly wave, killing hundreds. 'Our parents were most seriously ill. They told us to travel through the jungle and find the Christian teacher who was giving out food. We left after they died.'

'It must have been a dreadful time for you,' Archie said. 'Weren't there other family or friends you could go to?'

'Our family had all died or gone away, Archie. It was a terrible time, but the teacher cared for us. He told us God in heaven loves us and how his son Yishu died for our sins.' Then he grinned. 'I like to tell others how good God is to me.'

'As we travel together, we can both share the good news about Yishu,' Archie said.

He knew he had found a loyal friend.

❦

Hira Singh could read.

Archie was pleased when he found out. He'd begun teaching teenagers at the small school in Khursipar and telling the Gonds about God. Hira was interested to learn.

'Would you like to read the story of Yishu?' Archie handed him a New Testament in Hindi.

'Thank you,' Hira said. 'I will certainly read it.' Some time later he came to see Archie. 'I've read the book,' he told him, 'and I believe what it says is true. I want to follow the God in heaven and to be a Christian.'

Archie felt a deep sense of joy. 'Let's pray,' he said.

Hira was the first person he led to Jesus in India.

Hira's family's fierce opposition battled his decision, but he stood firm in his new faith.

At last his father decided to try a different tactic. A reward might change his son's mind.

'If you return to our gods,' he told him, 'I'll give you two wives, some cattle, and land too.'

Hira recalled the image of the village priest grovelling on the ground to see if he could pick up a rupee in his mouth. If he succeeded it meant Bagh-dev the tiger god would send a tiger to kill another villager despite the fowl they'd sacrificed.

'No thank you, father,' he said. 'God in heaven makes a big difference in my life every day. He gives me peace. I'll never turn back to the old ways.'

His contented smile told it all.

※

Archie knew his mother Sarah was dying in faraway London. Letters took weeks to arrive from England. The nearest post office to Archie was about 50 kilometres away, a trek through swollen rivers and jungle. Archie knew a telegram could be waiting there for him.

He was not able to make the journey, probably due to illness, so Yohan offered to go. He brought back the sad news that Sarah had passed away on 5 September 1902.

Archie read her final message to him. 'The way to reach the jungle tribes for Jesus is to love them.'

Archie's grief was sharp. He had expected to see his mother again when he was back in London on leave in a few years' time. But it was not to be.

Needing the comfort of talking to fellow missionaries, he headed off to see the Williams at Nikkum and spent some time with them.

A tall Gond and his son offered to accompany him on his return journey to Khursipar. It was fortunate they did. Reaching the second river, the Banjar, they found it was now in full flood.

'Let's go back,' Archie said.

But by then the other river had flooded too. Retracing their steps to the Banjar, they trudged along the bank to find the best place to ford. The water raced past them in a torrent.

'We can try crossing here,' the Gond said.

Archie waded out.

In midstream the water rose up to his chin. The bamboo pole he shoved into the sandy bed of the river for balance was no help at all.

He felt the pressure of the current slide his feet along the sand. 'Help!' he yelled.

The Gond, used to crossing flooded rivers, forced his way over to Archie and helped him to the other side.

'If you hadn't come just then, I'd have been swept away – drowned,' Archie said, thanking him.

He was thankful to God too. He thought of his father, grieving for the loss of Sarah. It would have devastated him to lose his son as well.

A picture of his mother's face came to mind. He could almost hear her voice repeating her advice to him: 'The way to reach the jungle tribes for Jesus is to love them.'

He would always remember those words.

※

A few months later, Archie visited the Williams at Nikkum again, this time to celebrate Christmas.

'Stay on for the weekend,' they said.

'I think I will,' Archie told them. 'Actually, I don't feel very well.'

It was an understatement; in fact, he had blackwater fever.

Everything seemed to swirl around him, dimming into blackness, and he slid to the mud floor of the verandah of their house. No one could rouse him.

Several people, including Yohan, set out to carry him the 22 kilometres to Baihar.

'If he dies before we're halfway there, we'll take him back to Nikkum to bury him,' they decided. 'But if he dies on the second half of the journey, we'll bury him in Baihar.'

Archie was unconscious for nine days. Somehow the missionaries got enough water into him to keep him alive, with advice from a doctor in Bengal. He was weak for months afterwards.

In May 1903 Archie travelled to Darjeeling to recuperate, staying three months to regain his strength.

He travelled back by train to Lamta, the nearest railway station to Baihar. His friend Hira Singh was at the station. He'd driven a bullock cart all the way to meet him.

Hira didn't talk much on the return journey. Archie was comfortable with that. He'd learned by experience that Gond men are often quiet. Then Hira broke the silence.

'I'm ready to be baptised,' he said.

'That is wonderful news to come home to,' Archie told him. 'I'm sure John Lampard could do it at Baihar tomorrow.'

After Hira's baptism, Archie wrote in his diary:

> In the Baihar church that afternoon he testified to having the eyes of his understanding opened by reading the New Testament. He has endured the blast of 11 months of persecution already so we have no fear that he will prove unstable: he is full of promise. This may be the beginning of great things here!

Later, Hira went to another part of Central Provinces for further education and training as an evangelist. In a letter to Archie, he wrote about the future wife he hoped to find.

> One who is to be my wife must be a woman who will treat

guests and visitors with every respect and must be a real help to me in my work for God.

Back in his own area, he fell in love and married Manna Bai, a girl from the Baihar orphanage, and they settled in Hira's village of Khursipar. They invited 250 people to a Christmas party and told the story of Jesus' birth and sang bhajans – songs written mostly by Indian Christians and set to their own music.

The day impressed many of the people and encouraged Hira to continue talking to them about God.

Archie was away for a few months as he was needed in Baihar, and the Williams were staying at Khursipar. Mrs Williams sent a villager with a letter to Archie, letting him know several more Gonds had given their lives to God and were baptised.

It was wonderful news.

Chapter 2

Living with Danger

Back in England, Grace Waller had been studying at a Bible College during 1901 and 1902.

The news that she was accepted by the Balaghat Mission filled Archie's heart with joy.

Impatient, he longed to see her.

After weeks of travelling, she arrived in Baihar and began helping Mrs Lampard in the orphanage. She was learning to speak, read, and write Hindi. Like Archie, she had a natural talent for picking up the language and speaking it with good pronunciation. When competent enough, she taught at the mission school.

She and Archie were engaged on 16 July 1903 on her mother's 64th birthday.

Archie was stationed in Khursipar. Taking the gospel story to the villages, he sometimes rode a horse or travelled by bullock cart. In the rainy season he waded barefoot through the muddy jungle tracks.

In one remote village he shared his plans for the next day with the villagers.

'I'll be going on to Dhamingaon tomorrow,' he said.

'What is the use of going there?' asked a man. 'There's no one living there; it's desolate.'

'But I went there myself a few months ago and held a meeting in the headman's courtyard,' Archie protested.

'Yes, that may be,' the man continued, 'but in the meantime, Satan has harassed them most extensively. They have all gone. There isn't one family left there now.'

Archie was shocked. 'What on earth happened to drive them away?' he wanted to know. He leaned forward to listen.

'Satan came into their houses night after night and took away basketfuls of grain. They could hear him,' the villager explained. 'He carried the baskets to the river, spilling a little now and then.'

'Hmm, I'll definitely go and see them,' Archie said. 'Where are they?' He didn't believe the burglar was demonic but thought it unlikely any sane villager would wander through the jungle at night. Tigers and leopards would be delighted.

The dozen families of Dhamingaon, led by the headman, had moved to an area about 32 kilometres away and built new homes. The villager gave Archie directions to the new location.

When Archie arrived there, he listened to their strange story. Despite his scepticism he could understand the jungle villagers' fear. They believed hordes of evil imps roamed through the air. Slapping a hand over their mouths whenever they yawned, they made a desperate attempt to prevent one entering their bodies.

They believed the evil spirits haunted the dense jungle and streambeds and hid among boulders and in ravines. They believed evil was present when anything happened that didn't have a natural explanation they understood.

When entering a village, Archie often saw a heap of grain on the threshing floor, surrounded by a narrow line of white ashes. A tiny light burned nearby, fuelled by an oil-soaked rag in a clay saucer, and a few thick sticks were poked into the ground.

'What is this for?' he had asked when he first saw it.

'I couldn't finish threshing all my grain before sunset,' a man explained. 'These ashes, light and sticks prevent evil spirits from stealing it.'

'Would they do that?'

'Of course, if they could.' The man was surprised at Archie's ignorance. 'Many more bhoots (evil imps) come out at night, hunting for anything they can get.'

It was a great opening to share the love of God.

※

After two weeks in the jungle villages, Archie caught up with local news when he returned to Khursipar.

'A leopard came at night and killed our pig,' the Gond villagers told him. 'We saw him eating it early in the morning so we shouted and threw stones at him.'

'So he's gone?' Archie asked. 'You haven't seen him since?'

'He'll be dead,' a man said. 'My friend was sure he saw him fall into the Malajkhand Cave.'

Falling straight down into the jungle-clad hillside and home for countless bats, the cavern was only about 450 metres from Archie's home.

'Alright, then, please get ropes and lower me into the cave to look,' Archie decided. 'I'd really like to get some leopard teeth and claws as a memento.'

'The cave is haunted, a bad place,' the oldest villager warned him. 'Bhimsen the rain god has lived there for many years.' He shook his head at Archie's foolhardy plan. 'No one has ever gone in there. It's too dangerous.'

Archie knew about many of the jungle people's gods by now. He knew the village pujari (priest) sacrificed goats or fowl to

Bhimsen. Each village sacrificed to the god they said ruled it, so the rains would come to water their crops.

They made sacrifices to their chief god Burha-dev for blessings on home and family; sacrifices to Mata, the Hindu goddess, to stop her anger spilling over them with smallpox. And there were sacrifices to Bagh-dev the tiger god and Nang-dev the snake god, but people were often attacked and died.

'No evil spirits will harm me, you'll see,' Archie said. 'Why do you say the rain god lives there?'

The storyteller waved his hand and pointed. 'See that hill? In days gone by, when Bhimsen was enjoying a meal of rice and fish, his sister came unexpectedly. He was, of course, furious she had interrupted his meal, so naturally he refused to eat. The hill is his rice which turned to stone where he threw it in anger.'

'And what happened to his fish?' Archie asked.

'The fish? They turned to stone too,' the man continued. 'You know the rocks piled up on the footpath by the cavern entrance?'

Archie nodded.

'Well, they are his fish.'

Archie smiled. He was intrigued by the local myths and legends but he wanted to show the people that the God of heaven was true and could be trusted. 'I still would like to look down there,' he told the old man and the other villagers who gathered around him. 'I know my God is stronger than any evil.'

'Alright, we will help you,' they finally agreed.

Together they found ropes and helped Archie descend into the darkness.

'Throw down some burning grass,' he called up to them. 'I can't see a thing.'

By the flickering light he could make out two other large caverns leading off the main one he was standing in. Copper streaked the walls and a strong smell from the long habitation of bats filled the air. That was all.

'Nothing here,' he called up to the men and they pulled him up to the surface. 'Thank you for your help,' he said. 'There's no leopard and no evil spirits there either. Don't be afraid of the cave anymore.'

'Your God must be powerful,' the oldest villager said in awe. 'No harm came to you.'

They gathered up the ropes and began heading down the hillside.

'Yes, he is all-powerful,' Archie said as they walked. 'Remember, I've told you God in heaven sent his son Yishu to save us from sin and the fear of evil spirits. He loves you, each one of you.'

'Yohan, your Baiga cook told us that too,' someone said. 'He reckoned that's why he's not afraid of the Rabda Pat pool now.'

'So he told you about our swim that day?' Archie asked.

'Yes.'

The day was still clear in Archie's memory.

The Sone River zigzagged its way through rugged mountains before it disappeared into a narrow ravine only about three metres wide.

Emerging again, the deep river snaked its way on through the steep jungle hills. A pool had formed in one of the bends of the river. It was reputed to be the home of a demon, Rabda Pat.

Gonds and Baigas trekked through the jungle to the pool every year to sacrifice a pig or goat at the water's edge. Sometimes they presented rice, and after eating part of it, fed the rest to the fish.

Crystal clear near the shore, the water darkened to black in the centre. The jungle folk said it was bottomless. Not one of them dared swim in it, fearing Rabda Pat would drag them down, down, down, to the lair where he lived.

They would never be seen again.

If anyone managed to escape from the pool alive, the demon would take on the form of a tiger and seize him onshore.

Archie and Yohan had been on a mission outreach trip when they joined some villagers trekking along a jungle track. That afternoon the temperature had climbed to 40 degrees Celsius and they were all hot and tired when they came to the pool.

It was the first time Archie had seen it. 'Oh, wonderful,' he said. 'I'm going in for a swim.'

'No, sahib,' pleaded the villagers. 'You will die.'

As they told him the legend, their voices trembled, and their eyes grew round with fear.

Yohan spoke up. 'I'm not afraid of Rabda Pat,' he said. 'I'll swim with you.'

He and Archie enjoyed their dip, cooling off in the clear water while the villagers prepared to flee at the first sign of danger.

Climbing back up onto the bank, Archie noticed something that may have triggered the legend. Judging from the size of the footprints, he estimated the resident crocodile was at least three metres long.

'Sahib, see what the pujari from Karamsara has done to us!' The distressed people of Khursipar gathered around Archie.

'What's happened?' he asked. It was obvious there was something really wrong.

'He has sacrificed a fowl to Bagh-dev, the tiger god, because several people in his village have been eaten by a tiger,' they explained. Horror was evident in every face in the group. 'And he buried the fowl in *our* jungle to lure the tiger away from them and over to us.'

Archie always felt a mixture of sadness and anger when he heard a wild animal had killed someone. Trying to tell the villagers that tigers weren't controlled by Bagh-dev was met with cynical smiles.

He thought for a moment. 'If you believe that the tiger will come here, why not dig the fowl up and bury it again in front of my bungalow?' he suggested. 'I have a gun.'

'No, no, we must not do that,' the villagers all agreed in panic. 'We cannot risk the tiger attacking you.'

The tiger didn't come, but not far away, a panther killed several men. A number of cattle met the same fate.

A messenger ran to alert Archie. 'Come, sahib,' he pleaded. 'Bring your gun. The panther has just killed another cow.'

Knowing the panther would return, several men helped Archie set up a machan, a platform in a tree above the remains of the cow.

Archie waited.

It wasn't long before the panther arrived and Archie shot it.

He never hunted for sport the way many British men in India did. The British Government encouraged it, paying a reward for shooting panthers, leopards, wolves and tigers. They called the wild carnivores 'brutes'.

Archie admired the beauty and power of the big cats. One morning he and Yohan went for a walk up a steep jungle track a few minutes from his home. Halfway up the hill, they stopped to catch their breath.

Casually glancing up into the tree he was standing under, Archie was startled to see a leopard crouched along a branch. It stared at him with large green eyes.

Archie stared back. He always carried a gun with him in the jungle, and now he held it ready in case the leopard sprang to attack.

Then, out of the corner of his eye, he saw a slight movement in the grasses a few metres away.

Another leopard.

Archie and Yohan stood still and silent.

Waiting.

Minutes passed. Without warning, the first leopard jumped down from the tree in a graceful curve and joined his mate in the grass. Together, they wandered off up the hill.

'Well, we can relax now,' Yohan said. 'Those leopards must have eaten well yesterday.'

'They probably killed the mother of the baby gazelle I came across yesterday evening,' Archie commented. 'I guess I saved her life.'

He'd caught the little gazelle and brought her home to care for her. Naming her Rani, Hindi for 'queen', he kept her for nearly two years. She soon learned to trust him and became a delightful pet.

Grace and Archie were married on 12 April 1905, standing under a bower of flowers and green leaves in the little church in Baihar. It was the first European wedding in the jungle.

No family members were there, but they were surrounded by Indian and missionary friends. After the service everyone walked the short distance to the mission bungalow for the wedding reception.

For their honeymoon they travelled to the west coast of India and on to Bombay and then to Agra. They visited the huge bulk of Agra Fort and the ornate palace, but the Taj Mahal was the highlight.

As they stood taking in the scene by the long waterway leading up to the perfect symmetry of the building, Grace smiled up at Archie. 'When I die, would you build a beautiful memorial to me like the Taj Mahal?' she asked.

'Your memorial will always be a beautiful place deep in my heart,' Archie said, slipping his arm around her shoulders.

'That's exactly what I wanted to hear,' she answered, her eyes shining.

Together they wandered down the walkway and into the building before they headed back to their accommodation.

In the following days their journey brought them to Landour, a small hill station in the lower Himalayan ranges. The British often stayed there to escape the heat of the plains.

The track up to the town was considered too steep for British ladies to climb. Grace was carried up the hills in a dandy, a sedan chair.

The dandy had forward poles that triangled from the centred seat to attach to the middle of a crossbar. The seat of slatted wood was softened by cushions, and sides prevented the passenger falling out. Attached to the sides of the seat, the rear poles tilted upwards and were attached to the centre of the rear crossbar. This design meant passengers could still sit in an upright position as the four porters shouldered the crossbars to carry them up and down the steep winding tracks.

Grace turned to Archie walking beside her dandy. 'I wonder what the British Raj would think if they saw me in a bullock cart bumping over the rocks along our jungle tracks?'

He grinned. Grace was tougher than she looked in her frilly blouse, long skirt and broad-brimmed hat.

Landour was a pleasant place to stay during the following few weeks.

'You know, the name Landour doesn't sound very Indian to me,' Grace commented as they wandered through the town bazaar.

'It isn't,' Archie said. 'Someone told me it was derived from Llanddowror in Wales.' The British often named places in India after their home towns. 'At least this version of the name is a lot easier to spell,' he added, laughing.

Back in Khursipar after the honeymoon, they moved into a little cottage with trellis work framing the veranda. Wedding gifts from England nestled in with Indian furniture and other household items.

Their long wait to have a home together was over.

Now Grace often joined Archie and Yohan on jungle trips. They loaded up a bullock cart with bedding, tents, food, cooking pots, books, straw for the bullocks, and Archie's concertina. Grace climbed in and they headed off.

Bullock carts were sturdy transport, not easily overturned on the rocky tracks, but it could happen without warning.

Once, descending the bank at a river crossing, a cart wheel lurched down into a mud hole, tipping Grace out.

'Archie!' She shouted in shock. Her dress was caught in the wheel, dragging her towards the swollen river.

Yohan began pulling on the reins to stop the bullocks charging down the bank while Archie ran back to Grace.

'I'm coming!' he called as he struggled up the bank, squelching in mud and stumbling over boulders.

The bullocks began lumbering into the water. Yohan yelled at them and pulled on the reins again.

They halted.

Grace was lying at the water's edge, muddy and shaken.

'Thank you, Lord,' Archie whispered. He bent down, freed

Grace's dress from the wheel and helped her up. 'Are you alright, darling?' he asked, wrapping his arms around her.

'I will be soon,' she said, trying to smile. Let's keep going.'

Archie settled her back into the cart, and they pushed slowly through the river, bumping over the track towards their destination.

※

Travelling the jungle roads could be a life-threatening experience. Most tigers ignored people but if they ventured near human habitation, they'd attack bullocks and other livestock.

Man-eating tigers were different. They lurked beside roads in the bushes and tall grasses. Their strategy was to leap out and attack someone walking alone or the last person in a group.

Not far from Grace and Archie's home, a man and his son were riding in a bullock cart when a tiger leapt out.

The bullocks fled in terror, bumping and lurching down the sloping road. The tiger bounded after them for more than one and a half kilometres before they met two men driving another cart from the opposite direction.

The men yelled and waved their arms at the tiger. It stopped, then wandered off into the jungle, growling in frustration.

It was a fortunate escape for them but not for another man from Khursipar. The day after he'd been to Archie's gospel meeting, he set off to go to market. By nightfall he still hadn't returned.

The next day, Archie formed a search party. They walked down the road for about 20 minutes, investigating places where a tiger might wait in ambush.

'Look,' someone pointed out footprints where a tiger had sprung from behind a bush. 'This is where it happened.'

They followed the trail through the tall grass on the opposite side of the road. There were only a few tragic remains left of their neighbour.

Another day, a man came running into Khursipar to find Archie.

'Sahib,' he said, his breath coming in gasps. 'A tiger dragged my friend away… We were taking bullocks to market yesterday…'

'I'm so sorry,' Archie said to the traumatised man. 'We'll go as soon as we can.'

He set out down the road with a small group of men. A track of beaten-down grass alerted them to where the tiger had dragged his victim. They followed the trail for a few minutes.

Every muscle tensed for action, Archie was prepared to shoot on reflex. They knew the tiger could leap out at them at any moment from the tall grass.

'Look, crows!' someone said suddenly, pointing. 'In that tree over there.'

They all knew what it meant.

'Let's fan out, make as much noise as we can, and head for the tree,' Archie suggested. He had learned that technique from the villagers. If the tiger was still there, the racket would drive it into cover. From there, it would watch, deciding whether it was best to retreat or attack.

The men advanced. Below the tree they found the remains of the man's body.

'I'll wait here for the tiger's return,' Archie said, his face grim.

'Right, I'll stay with you,' a Baiga offered.

In quiet sadness for the deceased villager, they built a machan platform out of a creaky old string bed frame, fixing it in the branches of the tree about four metres up. The other men returned to the relative safety of the road, leaving the two men alone.

They waited in silence, barely moving.

About half an hour later a magnificent tiger and tigress came wandering to the tree from behind them.

Archie couldn't shoot from that angle, and it was pointless to move to a better position. The slight sound would send the tigers into hiding. Looking down from over his right shoulder, he watched them.

He wrote about the experience later:

> One of the two handsome animals stood erect, all alert, truly regal. The other, the tigress, lay down at full length and, licking her paws, began washing her face in true cat fashion. Perhaps we had interrupted them from their gruesome meal? Then I had an unusual thrill, for they both started purring at delight at having found their meal had been left undisturbed.

The tigers then disappeared into the tall grasses, their striped coats camouflaged among the shadows.

By sunset, the tigers hadn't returned.

'Come and escort us out to the village!' Archie and the Baiga yelled to the waiting villagers.

'It's too dangerous,' they yelled back. 'Stay where you are!'

They headed back home.

It was a cold, hungry, uncomfortable and sleepless night for the two men sitting in the tree. The sun was well up when they descended and trudged home.

Grace ran out to meet him when she saw Archie coming.

'Come in and sit down, dear, there's hot food waiting,' she said.

While Archie was eating, he told her what had happened.

Grace listened. 'I spent a lot of the night awake too, praying for your and the villagers' safety.'

'You're a wonderful wife to me,' Archie said, the gratitude in his voice overlaid by weariness. He yawned. 'Maybe I'll have a nap later but I have a few things I must do first.'

He had only been home for five hours when a messenger arrived at the door. He had bad news.

'Sahib, please come,' he pleaded.

Archie listened as the worried man spilled out his fear. The day before, while Archie watched the tigers by the tree, a herdsman had not returned home to his village 16 kilometres away.

'His buffaloes came back on their own,' the messenger explained. 'One of them is missing as well.'

'I'll certainly come,' Archie decided at once. 'It will take a short while to get everything packed in the bullock cart, but I'm sure my wife will organise something for you to eat while you wait.'

He went inside and told the news to Grace. 'I'm sorry,' he added. 'I know how you worry about me, but I feel I must go. If there's anything I can do to save people from this awful danger, I'll do it.'

'I know,' she said, sliding her arms around his neck. 'That's one of the things I love about you.'

She began organising food for the messenger and some for Archie to take with him. She put in some extra warm clothes in the bag in case he spent another winter's night out in the grasslands.

'Take a rug too,' she said when he came in after hitching the bullocks to the cart.

'Thanks,' he said, kissing her gently goodbye. 'And Grace, thanks for being so understanding about this.'

It was late afternoon when Archie reined in the cart at the messenger's village. A group of men joined him and the search began.

About five kilometres down a track they came across the dead buffalo. The body of the herdsman was not far away. It was yet another sad loss of life.

Archie noted the sun was already setting.

'I'll wait here overnight,' he said, beginning to unload what he needed from the bullock cart.

'If you're going to do that, the best place to build a machan is up in those thick bamboos,' the village headman said. 'The tiger would find it hard to climb up there.'

They didn't take long to fix up the platform. This time Archie had brought a chair; his body was aching from weariness by now. The Gond headman stayed with him while the others left with the bullock cart for the village.

'Come back for us in the morning,' Archie called after them as they hurried away.

'We'll be there,' they answered

The two men sat in silence.

Would the tiger return to its kill as darkness deepened the sky?

Archie knew he wouldn't be able to get a shot at it until the moon rose at about 11.00 p.m.

The darkness became intense.

Stealthy footsteps crushed fallen leaves.

Then to the men's horror, they had to listen as the tiger feasted on the herdsman's body. After some time, they heard it walk off, passing close by in the darkness, its footsteps fading into the distance.

All was quiet.

The hours dragged by. It was Archie's second night without sleep. Finally, dawn came but the village men didn't arrive until hours later.

Relieved, the two men climbed down from the machan, grateful to stretch their legs and go home after 16 hours in cramped conditions.

That was the only occasion on which I have sat in a tiger's dining room, Archie wrote later. And I am not anxious to do so again.

Tigers didn't enter the villagers' houses the way leopards, panthers and cobras did. These animals were feared more than any tiger.

'Archie, listen to this,' Grace said, looking over to him as he was writing a letter. She'd been reading the fatality statistics from wild animal attacks in 1904. One figure had shocked her more than the others.

'What is it, dear?' he asked.

'Nearly 22,000 died just from snake bites alone here in India last year.'

'That's a shocking number,' he said.

'Yes, it's tragic.'

'Always stay alert, dear,' he said putting his pen down, 'especially when I'm not here.'

'Don't worry, I do,' she said.

A few mornings later Grace was teaching her class of little boys on the verandah when one pupil interrupted the lesson.

'Memsahib,' he said. 'I just saw the end of a snake sliding into your house.'

'I think it will just be a little one,' Grace said, 'but we'd better go and hunt for it.'

They began searching the house, looking behind furniture and checking under beds.

'There it is.' A small boy pointed into the box room.

A section of tail was poking out from behind a storage chest. 'Right,' Grace decided. 'We can kill it quickly if we all push the box hard against the wall.'

They gathered around Grace as she leant against the crate. 'Now, push.'

With their combined strength they shoved at the chest.

'Good work,' Grace said, standing up.

'Can we see it, memsahib?' the boys asked.

'Yes, of course. I'll pull the crate away from the wall and throw the snake outside.'

She leapt back at the sound of an angry hiss. A large cobra, its head held erect and hood inflated, stared at them poised to attack.

'Get out of here, *now!*' There was a rush out the door and Grace shut it firmly behind them.

'Mr McMillan will be home soon,' she told them when they were all settled back on the verandah. 'I think we'll let *him* deal with that snake. It's a bit big for us.'

'Will he shoot it with his gun, memsahib?' one of the boys asked.

'He will deal with it,' Grace answered. 'Now let's thank Yishu that we are all safe.'

Chapter 3

New Directions

In March 1906, Grace and Archie sailed to England. It was time for a break away from the jungle and to see family once again.

Archie's sister Jessie had never married and had been caring for John since Sarah died. His younger sister Elsie was 20 and still living at home.

Grace's sisters, Florence and Louise were still single and living at home at Goffs Oak with their parents.

That year saw a new direction in Grace and Archie's lives. The death of the widow who supported them financially meant they had no income.

'I believe God still wants us in India,' Grace said. 'We both speak Hindi well and will always love the people.'

'I agree,' Archie said.

They committed their future to God and were waiting for his direction. Archie was writing a book about his work. *Jungle Pioneering in Gondland* would be published later that year.

'A long letter has arrived from Yohan in Khursipar,' he told Grace as he opened the mail one morning. It was a mammoth task getting mail to and from the jungle. 'He says he received my letter,' he added.

'That young man couldn't be a more helpful friend and helper to us,' Grace said. 'He lives out his Christian faith in all he does.'

'Yes, I hope we can return. It will be so good to see him again.'

The next mission mail to arrive later in the year brought sad news. Yohan had drowned while bathing in a river.

The news hit them hard.

※

As they hadn't been able to find someone else to sponsor them to return to the Balaghat Mission to the Gonds, Archie wrote to John Lampard. With sadness, he and Grace resigned from the mission.

'We can continue to keep in contact with all of them at the mission and encourage them,' Archie said to Grace as he sealed the letter.

'Yes. God hasn't finished with us yet,' she answered in Hindi. They often switched from English when on their own. 'He has plans. We just need to find out what they are.'

'You're right. I think I'll approach the London Missionary Society, the LMS.' He had been interested in the mission since he'd won *The Story of the South Seas* as an 11-year-old. He still had the book and would always keep it.

'Definitely write to them. It may well be where God is leading us.'

The LMS secretary's return letter asked Archie to come for an interview with the board in their London head office.

It was a pleasant surprise for Archie to find out one of the interviewers was George Cousins, the author of his book.

Archie answered countless questions, and the interview seemed to be going well.

Towards the end, George leaned back in his chair and looked straight at Archie. 'Mr McMillan, will you please tell us what you would do if you were praying in public in India. Would you think in Hindi or in English and then quickly translate?'

'I'd think in Hindi.' Archie's response was immediate.

Turning to the board, George said, 'That, gentlemen, is enough.'

The others smiled in agreement. Archie and Grace could take up work in North India, but it would be a while before they could go.

A large sum of money had been gifted in a will to the LMS for new mission stations. A deputation from the board was going to travel to North and South India in 1907 and report to the directors with their recommendations.

To make the best use of the waiting time, the LMS paid Archie to attend a course on tropical diseases at Livingston College in London.

'This will be so helpful to me,' he said, reading the course information out to Grace. 'It says that, "Livingston College is intended to teach missionaries: (a) How to care for their own health and the health of their fellow missionaries when far from qualified medical aid, and (b) How to deal with the more simple diseases of the natives of the country in which they will be working".'

He went on to explain that he could begin after Easter 1906 and study until the midsummer break in July 1907. Although courses started in October, students were permitted to enrol for the longest course in January or April in exceptional cases. There were courses for six months and three months as well.

'I should attend one of those courses,' Grace commented. 'It would be sensible for me to do the same one as you.'

'No. Not that one, not any of those,' Archie told her. 'They're only for men. It wouldn't be appropriate to have women in the class with the kind of topics we will be discussing.' Noticing her frustrated look, he added, 'There is a course of 16 lectures on tropical hygiene you *could* go to. The next one starts in June.'

'I'll think about it,' Grace said, and changed the subject. It was ridiculous, she thought. A woman needed the same amount of skill as a man in similar circumstances, and most Indian women wouldn't go to a man for treatment.

After Easter, Archie headed off to the college. He hadn't wanted to leave school so young and now he had the opportunity for further study. He drank in knowledge like water and radiated enthusiasm when he returned home in the evening.

'We're studying anatomy, medicine, tropical diseases, elementary midwifery, dentistry and dispensary work,' he told her.

'That's a very comprehensive course for you then,' Grace said, trying to keep the frustration out of her comment without success. They both knew that no Indian woman having difficulty in labour would go to a man for medical aid; their husband would rather let them die than live with the disgrace. 'But what about the Indian women?' she demanded. 'Who will care for them?'

'You're right. There's a huge need for women doctors and medical staff. Hopefully they'll agree to train them in future, but there will be a lot of people I can help now.' Archie paused, thoughtfully then said, 'Grace, it would make sense for me to pass on to you some of what I'm learning in class. Would you like that?'

'Oh, yes, yes I would.' Grace's heart lifted, and she smiled at Archie.

'That's settled then,' he said.

When he started the course, he'd told her a little about the men in his class. 'There's a German missionary on leave from South India, and three Boers from South Africa. Another German is going to Central Africa.'

Grace nodded. 'And who else?' she asked.

'A Frenchman, and a young chap going to China. Another is going to West Africa.'

There were others going to Ceylon (Sri Lanka), South India, Central America, Southern Rhodesia (Zimbabwe), North Africa and of course Archie going to North India.

With such a diverse class there was always interesting conversation at the midday mealtime, accompanied by spontaneous laughter. On the dining room wall was the motto: DO IT HEARTILY.

It was meant to be a spiritual encouragement but all the students made sure it applied to meals too.

Archie told Grace about it one evening after dinner. 'And I've got a funny story to tell you too,' he said.

She looked up from her knitting.

'One of the German students who is still learning English was asked to speak at a local Sunday school. He hesitated before asking to be excused, saying, "Because I might use bad language".'

Grace laughed.

Deep contentment filled her. It was good to see Archie so happy. It was wonderful, too, being close to family again for most of this year of 1906. In a few days they'd be celebrating Christmas together.

There was also another reason for her happiness. 'Archie…' she began.

'Yes, dear?'

'You're going to be a dad next year. We're going to have a baby.'

Archie leapt up to hug her, nearly knocking her knitting flying.

'Oh Grace, that's wonderful news.' He looked down, noticing for the first time what she was working on. 'You're making a wee jacket.'

'Yes,' Grace's smile glowed.

'I'm going to be a dad,' Archie said in awe, and kissed her. 'When are you due, dear?' he added, standing up. 'You must take things easy now. Can I get you anything, Grace? A cup of tea?'

'That would be lovely, dear, but I'm not due till August next year!'

'Time goes fast,' Archie said. 'I'm just so grateful you're here in London and not in the Indian jungle. God's timing is perfect.'

※

Frank Archibald McMillan was born on 17 August 1907 on his Aunty Elsie's 22nd birthday.

Three weeks later, Elsie married James King. Archie would have been there to celebrate but it is doubtful Grace attended with baby Frank. Most women had bed rest for two to four weeks after birth in those days.

Archie began lectures at Harley College that autumn to train as a minister. He finished the course at Easter 1908 and his ordination was held in his home church in Clapton Park. His father, John, took part. It was a special service for the family.

Reverend Harries was still the minister of the church. He had known Archie since he was ten years old and had arranged for him to meet John Lampard of the Balaghat Mission.

Several directors of the LMS were present. One of them asked Archie about his Christian life and beliefs. It was then time to talk about his new work in India.

'Mr and Mrs McMillan are going to the hardest part of that

very hard field, India,' a director began, 'a field which at the present time is causing great anxiety because of movements that are going on there – intellectual and political movements.'

Archie and Grace had already seen the amazing difference Jesus made in the jungle people's lives. This was a strategic time for the message of Jesus to reach the Indian people.

The speaker continued. 'They are to be stationed in Gopiganj in the Benares district in India. Our friend will need infinite patience; he will need infinite grace; he will need a love that triumphs over all rudeness and all obstacles; he will need a faith that is constantly laying hold upon God.'

Archie nodded in agreement. He'd heard about the LMS missionary nine years before who had tried to share the gospel in Gopiganj and given up. A Brahmin had constantly shouted him down and disrupted his meetings so often that the missionary had returned to Benares (Varanasi) in defeat.

Now, Archie concentrated on the speaker again.

'It is a condition which calls upon our sympathies to the last degree and which calls forth our prayers. May God help us to remember him when he is away and to pray for him constantly.'

They would both need prayer support and letters of encouragement, Grace thought. She knew from experience how invaluable letters from home could be.

She was hardly mentioned in the director's speech. In India she'd be concentrating on caring for baby Frank. The LMS policy meant that missionaries' wives with children under the age of five didn't serve as missionaries themselves. Grace vowed to support Archie every way she could.

She and Archie had made a decision. They wouldn't employ an ayah (Indian nanny) for their children or send them away to England for schooling which was a common practice of the

British in India. They wanted to care for their children themselves. This would have a great impact on family decisions in the future.

Archie had taken notes during his ordination address. He added his own comments:

> The ordination prayer offered by Mr Harries was fervent and uplifting and it included an earnest reference to my wife:
>
>> 'We thank thee for his partner in life. We thank thee for her profound sympathy with him in this work. We commend their child to thee. May he be spared to grow up to become a good man. And now, Mother, may Christ be with thee, speak through thy lips and extend His kingdom through thine instrumentality. Amen and amen.'

This is the only part of the prayer Archie included in the memoirs he started to write in 1967.

Chapter 4

Gopiganj on the Grand Trunk Road

Archie, Grace, and 14-month-old Frank sailed for India on 24 October 1908. Five other new recruits for the LMS and a missionary returning from furlough sailed with them. The McMillans were the only ones moving to Gopiganj in Uttar Pradesh in the northeast.

After about six weeks on board ship there was a mixture of excitement and relief when they stepped on to dry land. The following day, the McMillans set out on the 650-kilometre train journey northwest from Calcutta (Kolkata) to Mirzapur.

Known for its beautiful carpets and brassware, Mirzapur was only 29 kilometres from Gopiganj. The Ganges River flowed over fertile lands close by, and the LMS had a mission compound and secondary school in the city. The McMillans would be staying with the missionaries there until after Christmas.

The train chuffed a rhythmic beat as it swayed gently along the track. Frank curled up on the seat next to Grace, leaning his head on her lap as he drifted into exhausted sleep. India was a whole new world for him.

In fact, starting a mission would bring many new trials and experiences to all of them.

Together, Grace and Archie prayed: 'Lord, we know you can provide for all our needs. Overrule the opposition to the gospel in Gopiganj we pray, and give us the ability to win people for Jesus.'

Grateful that they'd have other missionaries not too far away, Grace voiced her thoughts aloud to Archie. 'It will be so good to have the friendship and support of the Mirzapur missionaries.'

'Yes, I'm looking forward to meeting them,' he said. 'They'll introduce us to our LMS missionaries at Benares and at the hospital in Kachhwa* as well.' Kachhwa was going to be a support base for Grace and Archie's new mission. Doctor Robert Ashton and his wife had opened the LMS medical mission there back in 1893. It had been temporarily closed for three years, but the hospital had reopened in 1897.

Over the years, Doctor Ashton had helped many of the lower castes, performing cataract operations, other surgeries and administering first aid.

At first, he needed to teach the people that ointment wasn't for eating and neither was the prescription form. The people had learned to respect his advice and they trusted him. He was planning to hold a clinic every week at Gopiganj once a dispensary was built.

Archie's London course in tropical diseases meant he'd be treating many cases himself. A trained dispenser would be joining him from the start.

The days sped into weeks for the McMillans. Their stay at Mirzapur was soon over and visits to the Benares and Kachhwa LMS compounds established lasting friendships there too.

The missionaries told them of the months of painstaking negotiations trying to purchase the land for the mission in Gopiganj.

'To begin with, there was a dispute about who the land actu-

---

* At this time, the name of the village was spelled 'Kachwa'.

ally belonged to,' they told Archie and Grace. 'We often travelled over there to try and sort through the tangle. Eventually everyone was satisfied with the deal and we were able to buy the land.'

When the McMillan family arrived in the busy market town of Gopiganj on 31 December, there weren't any buildings on the mission's new property on the Grand Trunk Road. Archie pitched their tents under some mango trees and they settled in as best they could.

News of their arrival travelled fast. The local people showed friendship and curiosity as they crowded around to see what the English family looked like.

Some wanted to hear the music Archie played, some came for medical treatment and others were drawn to talk to little Frank. High caste and low caste, business owners and landowners, Hindus and Muslims – they all came. Grace and Archie welcomed them and shared the gospel with everyone who would listen.

'Namaste,' a middle-aged Brahmin landowner greeted Archie as he approached the tent not long after they arrived. 'I'm Ramswarup.'

Archie returned the greeting with a smile. 'And I'm Archie McMillan,' he said. He invited Ramswarup to stay awhile, and they sat down together under the mango trees to talk. 'I've come here with my wife and son to tell people about the God of heaven,' Archie explained to the Brahmin. 'He loves us all so much he sent his son Yishu to earth to tell us.'

'I am interested to talk about this Yishu,' Ramswarup leaned forward, his expression intense. 'Nine years ago, a missionary came here from Benares and set up his tent right here, like you, under the trees.' He paused, frowning.

Was this the man who disrupted those gospel meetings? Archie wondered. He prayed each day for wisdom and guidance when talking to people and here was a God-given opportunity. 'You talked with him?' he asked.

'I shouted him down constantly,' Ramswarup admitted. 'He left Gopiganj in defeat.' He sighed. 'But I regret that most sincerely now.'

Archie could hardly believe what he was hearing. Here was a Hindu Brahmin actually apologising for ridiculing the gospel. He sat in interested silence, waiting for Ramswarup to continue.

'Some of the things he said about Yishu have stuck in my mind,' Ramswarup explained. 'I keep thinking about it and wonder if what he said could be true. But I find it impossible to believe that there's a God who loves everyone, even Untouchables.'

Archie knew that, as a Brahmin, Ramswarup belonged to the highest caste in Indian society. They believed if an Untouchable came anywhere near their food or water, it would be contaminated, making it inedible or undrinkable.

God was the only one who could change Ramswarup's heart.

'You are welcome to come to my meeting tonight,' Archie said. 'I'll show pictures on a screen, talk about Yishu and sing bhajans.'

'I shall come,' Ramswarup promised. 'I am a pandit, a teacher. I have studied the ancient Hindu writings, religious rituals and law intensively. I get much enjoyment from discussion.'

Later, during the meeting, Archie was pleased and relieved to find Ramswarup was keen to listen. He asked intelligent questions and discussed different points with Archie but was never disruptive.

Archie talked to Grace after the meeting. 'To think God has been working in his life for the last nine years.'

'It's so encouraging.' Grace smiled at him. 'It means even

when we think we haven't touched someone's life, the message of the gospel is still dropping seeds. They can grow if the person is searching for the truth.'

'Yes, and we'll pray he finds it,' Archie said. 'He's a leader in the community and people listen to what he says. I like him.'

***

The new dispenser, Babu Shahadat Masih and his wife were sincere Christians. It wasn't long before they became firm friends with Grace and Archie, and Frank played with their five children. Shahadat impressed Archie with the way he shared the gospel in a clear, concise but powerful way.

Archie cycled to nearby villages to offer help wherever he could. He employed a cook to give Grace more time to visit women in their homes.

'The women are all so shy,' she said to him after her first few visits. 'But I'll keep on showing them kindness and I'll invite them here too.'

'I'm sure they'll come when they know you a little more,' Archie encouraged her.

He was right. Grace often had visitors. They gathered under the mango trees, chatting in a friendly circle while their children played close by. Grace talked to them about Jesus and they listened.

Grace and Archie knew that living in tents was only possible during the dry winter months. Building a home and accommodation for staff needed to start soon. Archie drew up plans for all the buildings for the mission site and organised a bricklaying contractor from Benares (Varanasi) to come near the end of January 1909.

The Grand Trunk Road was an ideal situation. It stretches across India from Varanasi in West Bengal to Peshawar in present-day Pakistan, and on up to Kabul in Afghanistan. Work on the road had begun long ago during the Maurya Empire in the 3rd century BC. Many centuries later in the 16th century, the emperor Sher Shah Suri organised for it to be repaved and extended.

There was always something interesting to see.

Local farmers' bullock carts laden with grain, milk or homespun cloth made their slow way past. Camels stacked with carpets from Mirzapur headed to market. Covered carts pulled by camels rumbled by, filled with passengers.

Hindu pilgrims streamed past to bathe in the Ganges River, believing it to be the goddess Ganga. Returning pilgrims trudged past carrying pots of the 'holy water' on their shoulders.

And still they came. Silent mourners crept past to a Muslim funeral. A boy wandered past with his goats. A Hindu wedding party, vibrant with colour and sound hurried by, and then came a sad, half-starved pony pulling an overloaded cart as it struggled on.

Archie snapped a photo of a sadhu as he caterpillared past, stretching full length on the road, and then hunching up to repeat the process. It was a slow, painful journey to bathe in the Ganges River to wash away his sins.

While travelling through India, Archie and Grace had often seen sadhus. In Hindi, sadhu means good man or holy man but from what they could see, sadhus were far from happy or holy.

Sadhus consider themselves to be dead; many attend their own funeral during initiation rituals to follow a guru, vowing a life of austerity. They serve for many years before setting out on their own.

With no family life and denying all sexual desires, they own only the clothes they wear (if any) and a bowl, relying on the public to supply food. Some sadhus dispense cures to the local community, claiming to be able to remove the curse of evil eyes or bless a marriage. Others sit naked on beds of nails, hold their arms in the air until they atrophy, or perform other acts of self-destruction. Some constantly pray and chant.

As practising yogis, they are dedicated to achieving 'moksha', finally ending their cycle of death and reincarnation. They believe that by meditation of their inner selves they can reach Brahman, the all-powerful god.

Shaiva sadhus are devoted to the god Shiva. They smoke hashish regularly, claiming their god also smokes it constantly. In some Indian districts, the highest quality hashish is often made by the local sadhus.

'That information doesn't surprise me at all, considering Shiva is the god of destruction,' Archie commented to Grace as another sadhu walked by, holding a conical clay pipe.

※

Not far from the mission, a twice-weekly market sold a variety of produce and at the mission compound there were paddocks for their own house cow, Daisy. She became devoted to Grace, affectionately resting her head on Grace's shoulder.

The McMillans kept hens brought from England and the family dog, Jack, probably came with them on the ship as well.

Progress on building their home crept along with deliberate slowness. The contractor proved unreliable and there was one unnecessary delay after another.

It was now the spring of 1909. When the monsoon rains

came, building work slowed almost to a standstill as the melting heat of summer sapped everyone's energy.

Brahmin friends, realising the problem, made them a kind offer.

'There's an empty house on our indigo plantation. You are most welcome to move in, no rent to pay,' they told Grace and Archie. 'You would like this?'

'Thank you, it is very kind of you,' Archie said, accepting the offer. The house was some distance from the mission site but it was a welcome roof over their heads.

By April, when their bungalow still hadn't risen above its concrete foundations, Archie decided he needed to take responsibility for overseeing everything. It would save money as well. The monsoon was only two months away.

The rail link between Gopiganj, Mirzapur, Benares and Allahabad was now completed and its new station opened for travellers.

'Do you want to see a train, Frank?' Grace asked him.

'Twain. Puff puff,' Frank said. 'See twain.'

The family stood watching as the first passenger train into Gopiganj pulled up to the platform. Archie took a photo.

'Twain.' Frank shouted. 'See twain!'

'You're going on a train with Mummy soon,' Archie told him. 'It will be too hot for you here in summer.'

'Go now?' Frank asked.

'No, not today. Soon.'

At the end of the month, Grace set out with 20-month-old Frank on the long journey to Almora in the foothills of the Himalayas. She was five months pregnant and needed to escape the burning 40-degree summer heat of the plains.

At the station, porters loaded the piles of luggage she would need into the waiting train.

Archie, holding his little son, stood on the platform close to Grace. 'Take care, my dear,' he said. 'I'll be missing you and wee Frank the moment the train leaves, but you'll be in good hands in Almora.'

'I will be fine, love,' Grace said with confidence.

It was comforting to both of them to know the doctors and nurses at the LMS mission hospital in Almora would keep an eye on her through the last months of pregnancy and during the birth of the baby.

'Bye-bye, Frank.' Archie handed him to Grace and put his arms around both of them as he kissed her goodbye.

'I love you Archie. I'll write soon as I can.' She stepped away, ready to board the train.

'Bye-bye Dadda,' Frank waved. 'Bye-bye Dadda.'

Archie stood watching as the train disappeared from sight, Frank's baby voice echoing in his mind. 'Bye-bye Dadda. Bye-bye Dadda.'

※

Grace and little Frank changed trains at Benares, and again hours later at Bareilly Junction where they boarded the narrow-gauge railway. They'd be travelling all night until they reached Kathgodam in northern India early in the morning.

From there, the long trek began, riding in a dandy up the steep mountain tracks, four porters shouldering the corner poles. Other porters trudged with them, carrying the luggage strapped to their backs.

Partway up the hill track, they stopped for a rest at a guest house, or dak bungalow.

Grace settled Frank down to sleep and wrote to Archie. It

would be months before she saw him again and she was missing him already.

When it was time to leave, she began packing everything away ready to continue the journey. Frank trotted around with her, dropping things into the wooden trunks.

Then she realised her letter to Archie had disappeared.

'I can't find the letter I wrote to Dadda,' she told Frank as she searched everywhere in the room. 'It's gone.'

'Dadda gone,' Frank said.

'Yes, Dadda gone and the letter gone,' Grace answered. The only place left to look was the open fireplace. There, crumpled up among the rubbish was the letter.

'Here it is!' Grace turned and knelt down to Frank. 'Did you put it in there?' she asked.

'Help Mummy.' His eager little face grinned up at her.

Grace knew he'd seen her throw rubbish in the fireplace and had tried to help clear up too. She couldn't be angry with him. 'Just Mummy puts things in the fireplace,' she said, ruffling his hair. 'Alright?'

Frank nodded. 'Mummy,' he said.

Outside, the porters were waiting. Grace settled on the dandy's cushioned seat and a porter lifted Frank in to sit beside her.

After two more days trekking up the mountain, stopping at dak bungalows for rests or overnight, Almora came into view at last. The town lay astride a mountain spur at 1,675 metres, buildings dotting the hillsides.

It was midday by the time they reached it. The incredible panorama of snow-clad mountain ranges delighted Grace.

There was a warm welcome waiting for them at Snow View, the LMS mission compound. Tired though she was Grace knew she was among friends.

Chapter 5

Setbacks and Success

In June, Archie began working on the partly-built servants' quarters and stable blocks at Gopiganj. Making use of the lessons he'd learned in woodwork classes at school, and experience as a teenager in the joiner's business, he finished the roofs before the monsoon arrived.

Now the dispenser Babu Shahadat Masih and his family and Archie's cook could live in the servants' block until the Christian workers' houses were finished.

Each year in northern India everyone expected the rain to start on 15 June. That year was no exception. Archie had to halt all outside work on the family bungalow and other buildings for the next three months until after the rainy season. He continued working on the inside of the buildings instead.

In helpless frustration he watched the 50,000 sun-dried mud bricks made on site in winter and spring by the contractor's men ooze into piles of mud.

At last the stables were habitable too. Pleased, he shifted from his friends' house on the indigo plantation and moved in at the beginning of July.

It was far from luxurious but it would be satisfactory for Grace, Frank, and the new baby when they returned home.

In July, LMS missionaries met in Mirzapur for their Benares

District Committee (BDC). Archie attended the two-day meeting, along with missionaries from Benares, Kachhwa, Mangari, and of course Mirzapur.

Everyone was concerned about the extreme shortage of funds. A typed request for urgent aid was sent to LMS headquarters in London. The only alternative they could see was to close one of the missions and that was unthinkable.

The money gifted to establish the mission compound at Gopiganj was specifically earmarked for a new mission and couldn't be used for day-to-day expenses.

The financial situation was particularly unsettling for Archie and Grace. They'd only just arrived a few months back.

Would the Gopiganj mission station fold before it had even opened?

※

A few weeks later, there was some wonderful news to cheer Archie. Baby Lily Grace was born on 8 August 1909 at Snow View, Almora. In joy, he travelled up to the Himalayan town to see his new baby daughter, grateful that both Grace and Lily were doing well.

'Dadda.' Frank came running to meet him when he saw Archie arriving at the mission compound. 'Dadda.'

Archie swung him into his arms and held him close. 'I've missed you so much, son. Let's go and see Mummy, shall we?'

Frank nodded. 'Lily Bubba too?'

'Yes, I want to see Lily Bubba too.'

Grace was still resting in bed. When Archie entered her room with Frank wriggling and chatting in his arms, she felt hot tears sliding down her face. 'Oh, Archie … it's … so wonderful … to see you.' Through the tears, her face was alight with happiness.

Frank slid out of Archie's arms. 'Dadda, look at Bubba.'

Archie leaned over to kiss Grace gently on her wet cheek. 'I love you,' he whispered. He looked down at the tiny face peeping from the shawl in Grace's arms.

'Do you want to hold her?' Grace asked.

Archie lifted the tiny bundle into his arms. Pride, joy, and love filled his heart. Scenes of the desolate rain-soaked building site at Gopiganj disappeared from his mind.

He was the father of a little boy and a baby girl.

He had the dearest, bravest wife in the world.

God was so good to them.

One of the missionaries caring for Frank came into the room to take him for his afternoon sleep. Archie and Grace were left in peace to talk.

'I can stay for a few days with you, dear,' he said to Grace, 'so I'll be here for Frank's second birthday on the seventeenth.'

'We'll make the most of our time together then,' she said.

Archie left at the weekend but only ten days later he had an urgent message to return to Almora. Grace was seriously ill.

There is no record of what was wrong or how long Archie stayed, but he eventually returned to Gopiganj, leaving Grace in Almora to recover.

She was well enough to travel in October, and packed their crates for the long journey back to Gopiganj. Her final task before they left was to lock the boxes.

The keys had vanished.

After searching without success, Grace began pulling items out of the crates in frustration. There, halfway down a box, she found the keys.

She sighed in relief. 'Thank you, Lord.'

Two-year-old Frank was standing close by. He smiled as

Grace lifted out the keys. 'I help Mummy,' he said, pride shining in his eyes.

Grace thought of the screwed-up letter in the fireplace on the journey up to Almora. Frank hadn't intended to be naughty, she realised, and now she had the keys she could see the funny side of the situation.

'Yes, you do try to help Mummy a lot,' she said, laughing, giving him a hug. 'But next time remember we need the keys out here so Mummy can lock the boxes like this.'

'Alright,' Frank said as he watched her.

'Want a ride, young boy?' A hill porter called out to him, helping him climb onto the seat of a backpack carrier and hoisting the straps over his shoulders.

'Look, Mummy. Me up high!' Frank shouted.

'You are up high,' Grace said, holding Lily cuddled warm against the chill mountain morning. She climbed onto the dandy. The hill porters lifted the poles. Others had already loaded the boxes bound with leather straps onto their backs. They set off down the mountain.

⁂

Now the rainy season was over, Archie was busy overseeing the building project at Gopiganj with welcome advice from Doctor Ashton. The LMS Benares District Committee approved his decision, knowing he wouldn't be able to do itinerant work in other villages over winter while he concentrated on establishing his mission centre.

Archie had been studying for language examinations, along with some of the other missionaries in the area. He achieved 82 percent for Hindi in 1909. His third year Hindi and first year Urdu studies could wait until the end of 1911. Completing the buildings was more important.

The incompetent, deceitful brick contractor from Benares returned to work at Gopiganj. Archie couldn't risk a lawsuit by releasing him before his contract ended. Instead, he employed a number of local bricklayers and they began another production line in competition.

Archie's men made 200,000 bricks. The Benares contractor, realising he was no longer the only option and his contract wouldn't be renewed, speeded up his output.

In November, Archie journeyed to the jungles at Gorakhpur near the Nepalese border to buy roof beams and several hundred poles straight from the sawmill. He organised it all to be railed to Gopiganj, saving hundreds of rupees.

He was now employing several carpenters. As many of them were illiterate, he needed to check angles on door and window frames and make sure the walls were straight.

Apart from the McMillans' home, they worked on another bungalow, the dispensary including wards for 12 inpatients, blocks for five families of Christian workers, two blocks for servants and another two blocks for kitchens. The list didn't include the stable and stores block the family was now living in, or a church and school which they'd build at a later date.

The buildings all needed wide eaves to keep rain off the mud brick walls covered with a thick coating of plaster inside and out.

Due to a shortage of tiles, the two bungalows and the dispensary had thatched roofs made from grass from the Kachhwa area.

Termites were a problem on the site. They could hide in the thatch and make their way down the walls, eating through the house. Archie learned a good way to prevent trouble was to mix copper sulphate with the mortar in the top course of bricks in the walls.

He worked nine-hour days over autumn, through the winter of 1909/1910 and through the spring. Often the temperature was in the mid-30s. He loved the work but it was exhausting.

Again, there were delays – an outbreak of cholera, festivals, and then the masons went on strike. Archie had reprimanded them over their filthy language.

'This is a mission site,' he explained, his tone firm. 'I won't allow words like that spoken around here. This place is dedicated to the glory of God.'

The men dropped their tools, refusing to work. Knowing Archie was way behind schedule, they waited for him to back down.

He didn't.

Days passed.

At last the men returned to work, amazed that Archie would rather let them go than compromise his beliefs.

※

Excitement filled the McMillan home.

The year's supplies had arrived from England and Frank never knew what might be hidden in the large crates. They had travelled as cargo on the SS *Caledonia* from England all the way to India, and were then transported to Gopiganj.

Frank watched as the boxes were opened to reveal tools, bolts of material, clothes, books and even toys. To him there seemed an unending supply of new things.

'How did it come?' he asked as each item was unpacked.

'On the *Caledonia*,' Grace told him.

Six-month-old baby Lily was lying nearby, waving her arms and laughing, shaking her new rattle.

'Oh, sweetie,' Grace picked her up. 'You're happy now your new front tooth has come through, aren't you?' She pointed it out to Frank. 'Look, there it is.'

Frank stared at it thoughtfully. 'Did it come on the *Caledonia* too?' he asked.

※

Another missionary, Ellen Stevens, had now joined the McMillans to help the local women. As there wasn't a bungalow ready for her, she was camping in a tent over winter, the same as the McMillans had done the year before. It was dry and temperatures ranged from 7 to 27 degrees, making it reasonably comfortable.

She would move into the stable block, or Equine Villa as one of the LMS missionaries called it, when the McMillan bungalow was finished. Archie promised it would be before the summer heat shot up to around 40 degrees.

At last the McMillans' home was ready for them in March.

Grace was thrilled. 'It's so cool in here. And there's so much more space for the children too.' She wrapped her arms around Archie and looked up into his face. 'Thank you so much. I'm so proud of you, Archie. You've worked long, hard hours for this and you've been under real pressure for months and months.'

'It's been hard for you too but you've been so patient about it all, never nagging.'

'Why should I nag? You did everything you possibly could through all those many difficult situations. And you've worn yourself out, dear. I won't take the children to Almora this year. I'll stay and care for you.'

'Would you really?' Archie was deeply touched by Grace's kindness. 'Maybe when the humidity gets unbearable in July you could take the children to Baihar to stay with the Lampards in the jungle. It's somewhat cooler there and they've given us an open invitation to visit when we can. You know they'd welcome you.'

'I'd love to see everyone there again, but what about you? You need a break more than I do.'

'I could come towards the end of the monsoon season and escort you and the children home in September.'

Grace considered the idea. 'I guess we could go. I'll let the Lampards know. But will you take care of yourself without me here?'

'I'm absolutely sure; I'll be fine. What about your brother, Harry? He'll be due for a holiday by then. Maybe he can travel with me to Baihar.'

'Harry? Oh, I do hope so.' Grace's face broke into a delighted smile. 'I'll write to him and ask.'

Harry had arrived in northeast India the year before, in 1909. After only one day to consider it, he had decided to leave England to take up a position in Calcutta (Kolkata) to be manager of a printing company owned by two wealthy Sikh brothers.

His wife, Helen, and three adult children stayed back in England, not wanting to move to a foreign country at short notice.

The company had contracts with the British Indian Government, printing forms and documents for the Post Office, the British Indian Army, the Indian Army, and the Public Works Department. They also contracted for the Bengal-Nagpur

Railway, and did a lot of commercial, educational and jobbing printing.

When King Edward VII died on 6 May 1910, the British Indian Government ordered all their officials to use stationery with black borders. Forms already printed didn't have borders of course. In a frenzy of activity, workmen hand-rolled black edges on rows of papers lining the floors of the long corridors and verandahs.

Grace often talked to Frank about Uncle Harry. She told him he was living in India too and he would see him one day.

In May, Halley's comet shone a clear, bright trail in the night sky. Grace and Archie pointed it out to Frank.

'There are two Uncle Halley comets,' Frank said.

'Uncle Harry comets?' Grace asked.

'Yes. Two Uncle Halley comets,' Frank nodded.

Archie grinned, hiding laughter. 'There's only one Uncle Halley comet,' he told him.

'I see one out the back door and 'novver one when I go out the front door,' Frank said, sure of his facts.

'No, it's the same one,' Grace explained.

Frank thought for a moment. 'Oh yes, that is the same one, and this one is 'novver one.'

❧

Now at Baihar, Grace told Frank about the jungle and tall grasslands and about the animals that lived there. He listened, wide-eyed, when she talked about tigers.

'I'm not afraid.' Frank ran off, coming back with his toy gun. 'I'll go into the jungle. And won't the tigers be frightened when they see me coming with my gun.'

Grace sat down and pulled him onto her knee. 'You can have lots of fun pretending to hunt tigers here in the house,' she said. 'But *never* go into the jungle.'

'Why?' Frank asked.

'Mmm…' Grace paused a moment then said, 'Because some tigers hurt little boys. So, promise?'

'Yes, Mummy.' He wriggled off her knee. 'Pow, pow, pow!' he yelled as he charged out the door.

※

Archie and Harry's arrival at Baihar was a mixture of joyful reunions and meeting new friends.

More visitors arrived one evening, so Archie and Harry opted to sleep on the verandah. They brought out their bedding and began arranging it on the floor.

'Have you everything you need?' Mrs Lampard came out to ask.

'We're fine, thank you,' Harry said. 'By the way, I can hear jackals screeching out there. Do you think there are any other large, four-legged creatures close by?'

'Yes, there are,' she answered. 'Just a few weeks ago, a tiger snatched our cook from our mission compound. He was sleeping in the stock room with his family when the tiger rushed in and carried him away. It was terrible.'

It was not a comforting thought for the two men as they settled down for the night on the open verandah.

'I think we'd better keep our guns right next to our beds tonight, Archie,' Harry said.

'We definitely should,' Archie agreed. 'And I'll put the hurricane lantern on the steps.'

Harry stayed awake for hours, listening to the sounds of the jungle at night, imagining every rustle in the bushes meant the tiger was preparing to attack. Eventually he slipped into sleep, wakening to sunshine, the raucous cawing of crows, and the constant chattering of myna birds.

Later in the morning the others headed to market, leaving Harry sitting reading in the peaceful shade of a tree.

He was disturbed by a Gond woman running into the compound towards him. 'Sahib... there in jungle... big animal... big eyes... big mouth! I run... run... to tell you!' she shouted in fright, her breath coming in gasps.

The image of a tiger shot into Harry's mind. He leapt up and grabbed his gun, running off in the direction the woman had pointed.

Climbing a steep hill, he looked back now and then to keep the mission compound in sight. The bungalow now appeared as a tiny doll's house far below.

He lost sight of it as he descended into a sandy gully. Then, beside a large boulder, he saw fresh paw prints left in the sand.

The tiger was on the other side of the boulder.

Harry, gripped by fear and sudden panic at how alone he was, realised his gun gave him pitiful protection.

What if the tiger charged and he missed?

What if he only injured the tiger as it leapt on him?

His heart thumping, Harry stepped backwards, expecting an attack at any moment as he retreated.

It did not come.

In relief he headed back to the mission compound but his confidence dived as he passed a cairn along the pathway. The inscription stated that a government official had died there, gored by a wild boar.

Everyone was back at the bungalow when he returned and he told them of his foolhardy adventure.

'You definitely had a narrow escape,' John Lampard said. 'The tiger living up that hill is the man-eater.'

A short while later, a hunting party set out. They shot the man-eater and carried the large body back to the mission compound. The men placed the dead tiger on the verandah where Harry and Archie had slept the night before.

The grand opening of the Gopiganj mission compound was at the end of that year on 29 December 1910. Crowds of people poured from the town and nearby villages to see it. Missionaries and Indian Christians from Benares, Mirzapur and Kachhwa came, and an elephant gave rides to visitors.

In his opening speech, Archie gave glory to God for his amazing provision.

Doctor Ashton announced to the crowd that the dispensary would open on 2 January. He or another missionary, Doctor Evans, would hold a weekly clinic but Archie could attend to many of their medical issues at other times.

It was a day of triumph.

In early March 1911 the LMS District Committee met at Benares. Everyone was deeply concerned. A letter from the LMS Board of Directors in London suggested the possibility of reviewing the feasibility of the whole or part of the mission in their area. The reason given was that there weren't many converts in the Benares district after years of sharing the gospel.

In South India, however, the news was encouraging; many were receiving Jesus as their Saviour.

The possibility of leaving was a shock for Grace and Archie. Their mission station had only just opened.

Archie and the other missionaries wrote out a statement for the LMS Board. They declared they needed all the mission stations because of the large population in the area. It would take years to reach everyone. Their area and the Calcutta district were more opposed to the gospel than other places but why give up now? God would give them the victory.

The review never eventuated. Thankful, the missionaries continued to pray and share the good news about Jesus. They were a united team. Kathleen Morris had now joined Grace and Archie at Gopiganj to work with the women along with Miss Few, now that Miss Stevens had returned to Mirzapur.

It didn't take long to travel by train from Gopiganj to Benares. Apart from board meetings, the McMillan family occasionally met up with the Lenwoods, who were LMS missionaries there, and attended events in the city.

It was an honour in 1911 when the Maharajah invited them, along with other guests, to his palace one afternoon.

A crimson carpet ran up the centre of the hall to the front where the Maharajah sat on his throne. Seated on chairs placed along each side of the carpet, the guests talked quietly together and waited for the ceremony to begin.

Before Grace could stop her, Lily wriggled off her knee and ran along the carpet, stopping in front of the Maharajah. To his surprise, she dropped her doll into his hands, turned, and ran back to Grace. He was left sitting on his throne, wearing his official robes and holding a doll. A smile began creeping over his face at the awkward situation, and then he burst out laughing.

'Go and get your doll,' Grace whispered to Lily. 'I don't think the Maharajah needs her.'

Lily raced off and snatched the doll away in case he decided he wanted it after all. Everyone was laughing by now.

'Don't worry, we've never heard the Maharajah laugh so much,' several people told Archie and Grace when they apologised afterwards.

Everyone agreed Lily had brought a light touch to a formal afternoon.

※

In autumn, the festival of Ram Lila lasted for several days in Benares. Archie joined the crowds of people watching the actors dressed in bright costumes and masks to enact the legend of Ram and Sita. He was intrigued as the story unfolded.

Ram was an Indian prince tricked into banishment in the jungle. His devoted wife, Sita, went with him. One day, she saw a golden deer and pleaded to Ram to capture it for her.

He raced through the jungle, but as he reached it, the deer changed into a demon. In fear he ran back for Sita, only to discover she'd been kidnapped by the demon king Ravana, a creature with ten heads.

Hanuman the Monkey King vowed to help Ram, organising an army of monkeys and other animals to search for Sita.

Finding out she was held captive on an island, the animals built a causeway of rocks, sand and grass.

With Ram and his brother Lakshman, they crossed over and a fierce battle began.

At last, Ram shot Ravana with a magic arrow and killed him.

It meant Ram and Sita were then free to go back to their own country. Oil lamps shone in the windows of all the houses to welcome the couple, and Ram was crowned the rightful king. He and Sita lived happily for the rest of their lives.

At the end of Ram Lila was Diwali, the festival of lights. An effigy of Ravana was burned, to the great satisfaction of the crowd. To the Hindus it meant good had triumphed over evil.

The story was an interesting opening for Archie to share the gospel with everyone he met. 'God's son, Yishu came to the world to seek the lost, and save those trapped by evil. We cannot free ourselves; Yishu took punishment for all our sins,' he explained. 'Give your lives to him. He will spread his light into your hearts because he loves you.'

During the winter months the McMillan family set out along the Ganges River to reach villages inaccessible by road. They hired an open sailing craft, loading it with tents, camping gear and all they'd need for several weeks. Archie shared the gospel message wherever they went and treated people with illnesses and injuries.

Chapter 6

Archie's Himalayan Adventure

Grace and the children spent the summer months in Almora again, and Archie made his way to the Himalayan town to join them in the autumn. It was precious to be reunited with his family, spending time with them and playing with the children.

He and Grace stood on the verandah, snatching a few minutes alone while the children had an afternoon sleep. Taking in deep breaths of cool mountain air and the amazing view, Archie felt the stress and heat of the plains slip away.

'It would be hard to believe a mission station could have a grander view than this,' he said in awe. Kumaon, the Himalayan area of India in which Almora is located, has its own share of snow-clad peaks. From the distant northwest stretching far across to the northeast, they could see the snow-capped summits of Tibet and Nepal. 'How amazing it would be to go right up to them.'

'Now you're on holiday, why don't you go tramping?' Grace suggested.

'I guess I could,' Archie said, weighing up the possibility. 'I'll organise a couple of hill porters and climb up to the Pindari Glacier. That book I borrowed about trekking says the round trip can take thirteen to eighteen days from Almora. But I reckon I can do it in eight.'

'Don't push yourself too hard and take unnecessary risks, dear.' Grace thought back to their years in the jungle. Whenever they returned home from travelling, Archie's eyes held a fixed look for a couple of days, after the constant high alert of watching for attacking predators. It was as though he didn't dare blink.

Archie drew her close and kissed her. 'I'll be fine, love. I just don't want to be away from you and the children any longer than that.'

'We'll be here to welcome you when you get back.' Grace smiled up at him. 'It's early September, a perfect time to go, and the monsoon seems to be easing off early.'

On Wednesday morning, 6 September, Archie set out, heading north with a hill porter and his friend and helper, Subaran Singh. Grace and the children waved goodbye at the entrance of the mission compound.

'I want to go with you, Dadda.' Frank trotted after him.

Archie turned. 'Not this time, son,' he said. 'It's too far.'

'But I can see the snow,' he persisted. 'I can walk there too.' It was a 120-kilometre trek but Frank couldn't understand that.

'Alright, you can walk a little way with us,' Archie said.

Almost a kilometre down the road Archie had to tell Frank to head back home.

Frank burst into tears. 'I want to come with you,' he sobbed.

'I know,' Archie said. 'When you're bigger, you can tramp up to the snow with me. How's that?'

'Okay Dadda,' Frank sighed.

Archie watched as the solitary little figure set off back along the road.

※

The day before, Archie's cook, Bideshi, and another porter had gone ahead, carrying half of the supplies in a tin box, to arrive in Loharkhet before him. Archie and the other two expected to catch up with them on Thursday after hiking 78 kilometres.

'It will be a faster trek if they go before us,' he'd explained to Grace when she asked. 'They can take their time carrying the heavier loads.'

Subaran shouldered a satchel containing a waterproof cape, an umbrella, lunch, Archie's camera, photographic plates and a thermos flask. Archie had bedding rolled into a waterproof groundsheet. Binoculars swung from his neck.

The porter walking with them had the second tin box strapped to his shoulders. In it was the other half of the food, changes of clothing, medicines, bandages, and a pocket case of surgical instruments. Archie had included two small books and a pair of slippers.

This tin box, coated with a black lacquered finish, brought back childhood memories to Archie. Scenes flashed in his mind of his mother, Sarah, packing that same box for the train journey to the Welsh seaside town of Rhyl. Those family holidays had been fun.

His father would love to know about the adventure he was having now. Archie decided to write notes about his trek, and when he arrived back in Gopiganj, he'd write it up as a diary. It would be a gift to John for his birthday in November.

In his mind, Archie checked over the list of food packed in the two tin boxes. It included nine loaves of bread, biscuits, cakes, flour, tea, cocoa, salt, Bovril, breakfast cereal, tinned milk, cornflour, rice, lentils, rolled oats and bacon. In fact, enough for at least eight days and some extra in case of delay through bad weather, sickness or fatigue.

There should be plenty.

Archie, Subaran and the porter were now following the track from Almora up Kalimat, a forested hill. The name meant black soil. It was a good description; the soil here was seamed with lead.

Reaching a pine-clad ridge at nearly 1,830 metres, they continued along the top. Views down to cultivated valleys far below peeped in and out of sight as the trail snaked its way through the trees.

They passed the LMS school in the little village of Dinapani, cut across the ridge and descended several hundred metres through thick forest into a valley.

Several villages nestled on the surrounding hillsides among pomegranate and plantain trees.

'Listen,' Archie said to the others. 'This valley laughs and sings.' The river was tumbling over its rocky bed in joyful harmony. Golden rice ready for harvest whispered in the breeze.

'It is indeed a lovely place,' Subaran agreed.

'I've never seen a more fertile or prosperous area than this.' Archie stopped for a moment or two taking in the vibrant scene. 'God is such an amazing Creator.'

The hill porter was waiting a few steps ahead. 'There is no place more beautiful in the world than these mountains,' he said.

'I think you could be right,' Archie said, catching up to him.

They walked beside the river for a while. Here and there, farmers had diverted the water to flow over a waterwheel attached to a mill for grinding corn.

After crossing the river at a ford, they climbed a steep hill, passed the Takula dak bungalow and dipped down into a shady area. A stream chattered over smooth stones.

'How about stopping for lunch here?' Archie asked.

'Good idea,' the others agreed. It was 1.45 p.m. and they'd walked nearly 21 kilometres in just over four hours in steep terrain.

Forty minutes later, they set off to climb to a pass at 1,676 metres. Another steep descent led them down to massive pine trees in a narrow valley.

There seemed no way out of the valley. A precipitous cliff loomed ahead of them.

'We have to go up *there*, Archie?' Subaran pointed at the offending cliff face.

'I guess so. I can't see any other way.'

It was a 1-in-7 climb to the top and Archie's flask of water was soon empty. Further down the track, a spring bubbled up nearby.

'I doubt typhoid will be a problem here,' Archie said, filling his flask. 'I'll take the risk, anyway.'

The water was cool and clear. Refreshed, they continued on.

'I read that it was near here that the English first experimented with growing tea in India,' Archie commented. 'They gave it a good trial but found the moist, humid air of the Darjeeling and Assam mountains was better.'

'Yes, but the Dewaldhar Tea and Fruit Garden is still here,' the porter said.

Rounding a curve in the track, they passed the entrance. It seemed a remote place for a plantation, Archie thought.

The chill wind dug icy fingers down his neck and he pulled up the collar of his jacket.

As they descended down a steep track into a valley, each step jolted his knees and his toes rubbed raw against his boots. The twisting path, coated thick with pine needles, formed a slippery slide, but the chill wind was left behind and the air seemed thick and warm in the valley.

'Stop a moment while I take my jacket off,' Archie said.

He looked around him. The sunset glowed pink in the western sky, but as the moon rose, the colour faded, darkening the wide rushing mass of the Sarju River. To Archie, the now inky slate-coloured river turned ugly, threatening danger.

The hill porter pointed to where the river swirled against the bank beside the road. 'No one knows how deep that is,' he said. 'The river has many pools like this but it's well stocked with fish. They're big fish, too.'

It was getting dark when they reached the town of Bageshwar at the confluence of the Sarju and Gomti rivers.

'There are many old temples here,' the porter told Subaran and Archie. 'Some are one thousand years old.'

'That's interesting,' Archie said. 'Tomorrow we'll be able to see the place in good light.'

Drained of energy, they crossed the suspension bridge over the river, grateful that the dak bungalow guest house was close by. They had tramped 39 kilometres in nine and a half hours. Relieved, Archie pulled off his boots. The dak bungalow cook brought them a good meal and they enjoyed every mouthful.

The three men talked as they ate, the porter telling the others a little about the town. 'There's a midwinter fair here every year,' he said.

'Doesn't it get snowed out?' Archie asked in surprise.

'No, this valley is warm.'

Archie didn't consider an average of -2 to 0 degrees Celsius to be warm. Compared with other parts of the Himalayas, though, he guessed it was. He found it an intriguing place. Bageshwar had been an important town in the Kumaon area before Almora became the capital in 1568. As the porter had said, there were many ancient temples.

There was even a post office. Before he settled for the night, Archie wrote to Grace to let her know he'd reached the historic town.

Archie and the others set out at sunrise the next day. The morning was cloudy and cool. The carved shop fronts on the stone-paved streets reminded him of Almora.

He looked with interest at the different tribal groups buying, selling, or exchanging goods. Leather-clad Tibetans, Dhanpuri, and militant Garhwali dressed in pinned-up blankets mixed with sturdy Dotiyal, a tribe from Nepal.

The Kumaon Bhotiya tribespeople wore homespun woollen coats tinted in a variety of plant-based dyes. They were nomadic shepherds, trading wool and salt between Tibet and India.

As they walked past, Archie listened as the different tribal groups chatted to each other in the languages of the mountains.

Leaving the town behind, they walked along the valley, coming to a gorge. The Sarju River roared in anger through the narrow shaft below.

Partway through the gorge, two ropes were slung across the chasm.

'Do we cross over on those?' Archie asked the hill porter.

'Oh, no,' he answered to Archie's secret relief. 'That's a privately-owned bridge. We can't use that.'

Further on, the gorge opened into a valley. People were cutting rice and laying it on plaited bamboo mats while others trod on it to remove the grain.

Oak trees and wild roses grew nearby but the track was open to the sun bursting through the clouds with the bright enthusiasm of midmorning. Archie felt his arms and neck beginning to burn.

They searched out a shady area for a late breakfast. Always

loud in the background, the Sarju River charged over huge boulders in fury.

As they set out again, a large lizard waddled from the river across in front of them and disappeared into the bushes. It was more than a metre long, its grey-brown skin covered in dark speckles.

'Wow, what was that?' he asked the porter.

'A bis-cobra lizard.' The porter stopped walking and turned to face Archie and Subaran.

Archie knew that 'bis' in Hindi meant twice. 'Why is it called that?' he asked, surprised.

'Well, its name means it is twice as dangerous as the cobra. It bites or spits poison. Very dangerous.'

'Thanks for the warning.' Archie eyed the bushes. All was still now. 'I think we'll leave him alone today then,' he said, smiling as they set off down the track again.

Hidden in a fertile valley in the mountains, Kapkote village was a beautiful place.

'This is a perfect place to stop awhile,' Archie told the others when they arrived at lunchtime. 'Actually, I know of someone here – he's an LMS preacher – Babu Armar Singh. We'll find him after we've had something to eat and a rest.'

He slid off his boots, soaking his sore toes in the cool Sarju River while Subaran cooked their meal.

Later, talking with Babu Armar Singh and his wife, Archie learned they'd lived in the village for 18 years.

'It's grand the message of Jesus is preached so far into the mountains,' he said in encouragement. 'You are so isolated from other mission workers out here though. Do any LMS staff ever visit you?'

'Oh yes,' Babu Armar answered. 'Once a year someone comes, and I visit the LMS station in Almora once a year too.'

'That's not often,' Archie commented.

'No, but we're sure God wants us here,' he answered. 'He gives us times of blessing, like your visit today.'

'I pray that God will continually bless and keep you,' Archie said as he left.

He looked around the lush valley and the surrounding mountains, comparing the remoteness to the busy Grand Trunk Road in Gopiganj. The realisation hit him of how much Babu Armar and his wife had sacrificed for Yishu's sake. He didn't think he'd be able to take the isolation.

The three trampers set out in mid-afternoon, reaching a fork in the path an hour later. One track led over the Milam Pass into Tibet. They needed to take the other.

'I've heard there are only two months of the year when it's possible to traverse the full length of the Milam Pass,' Archie said.

'That is right, sahib,' the porter said, 'and it is for mountain people only. It is difficult and dangerous for others.'

'Sahib, Pastor Rawat of the Hindustani Church in Almora – where you preached last week – he came from around here, didn't he?' Subaran asked.

'Yes. Years ago, he was a student at the LMS high school in Almora and became a Christian. He's been the principal of the school for a long time now as well as pastor of the church.'

Archie thought of the two LMS women missionaries now in Almora who had lived in this wild backbone of Asia, sharing the gospel of Yishu with the Bhotiya people. One of the women, Miss Turner, had lived among them for three years.

The Bhotiya shifted to different altitudes according to the time of year, moving lower as winter advanced. She would have moved with them.

He felt a sudden surge of pride in being part of the LMS team. 'Yishu shall reign here in these giant mountains,' he said with conviction. The wind caught his voice and the echo bounced across the valley onto the surrounding rocky crags.

The track led them away from the Milam Pass road, and across the river. Past the village of Khar they climbed a ridge with a view of a valley on one side and the Sarju on the other.

Thunder rumbled among the mountains.

'The storm is not far away,' the porter warned them.

It was now 5.00 p.m. Would they reach shelter at the Loharkhet dak bungalow before dark, before the storm hit?

Archie doubted it. 'Look!' he pointed to the river 100 metres below them.

A torrid flood of red swirling water was roaring downstream from heavy rain higher up in the hills.

'Just as well we crossed the river when we did,' Subaran said.

The others agreed. A flood like that could sweep away a rickety bridge in moments.

'We need to cross the river again,' the hill porter said. 'Let's hope the bridge is still there.'

A while later heavy rain began to fall. Angry fingers of lightning stabbed across the sky and thunder boomed, reverberating over the mountains.

At the river crossing the three men stood and stared. There was nothing but red, swirling, foaming water.

'The bridge has gone,' Archie's frustration and disappointment mirrored the thoughts of the others. Through the rain, they could just make out the track on the other side of the Sarju.

'So, we're stuck between the two river crossings.' Subaran was wet and miserable. He must have been mad, he thought, to agree to come with Archie into the mountains at the end of the monsoon season.

'Looks like it. No, wait a minute…' The porter began walking along a narrow footpath. 'This is going in the right direction. Shall we try it?'

Lightning flashed, followed by thunder rolling through the mountains.

'It's a great deal better than waiting here,' Archie commented as he joined him. Subaran followed.

But the footpath came to an abrupt halt in front of a huge boulder.

'I think we've come to the end of the trail. That boulder must be higher than a hillman's house.' Archie wasn't often discouraged but he felt it now. He was responsible for the others; the trek had been his idea alone. 'Lord,' he prayed. 'Please guide us, show us where we need to go.'

Then they saw it. Underneath an overhanging rock near the boulder, a rough-hewn ladder clung to the cliff.

'Thank you, Lord.' As Archie climbed, a waterfall cascaded over him from above. 'For the ladder, that is, Lord,' he added, managing to smile, 'but not the shower.'

At the top he could see past the boulder. A second ladder descended on the other side of it. 'There's a way over,' he called down to the others. 'But I think it would be impossible carrying your heavy load,' he added to his porter.

He re-joined the others and they discussed what they should do.

'Sahib, I'm willing to stay here while you and Subaran go on to find help,' the porter suggested.

'Are you sure?' Archie was doubtful. He was uncomfortable leaving his helper stranded and alone.

'The rain is falling on me whether I wait here or go with you,' the porter reasoned.

'If you're sure,' Archie finally agreed. 'We'll be back as soon as we can. Namaskar – goodbye.'

Soaking wet, Subaran followed Archie up and down the ladders. They weaved their way around boulders, sloshing through shallow pools close to the Sarju on their left.

A narrow path emerged through the rocks, leading up a precipitous slope. It was their only option. Slipping and stumbling over rocks, with water showering them from countless waterfalls over the track, they struggled upwards. The path soon disappeared underwater. Trees dripped overhead.

Dusk was falling.

With each step, Archie's concern for the porter grew. At the point of suggesting to Subaran they turn back, they broke through the trees and entered a field.

It was now almost dark.

The rumbling thunder faded into the distance and the rain eased.

'Look, houses!' Subaran shouted. 'Hey, anyone there?'

Two men came out to meet them and relief flooded over them as the villagers offered their aid when they heard what had happened. They wasted no time in making a decision.

'I can go and find your porter,' one of the villagers said.

'I'll go with you,' Subaran said, at once. It was good knowing he now had somewhere dry to come back to for the night.

Archie reached for Subaran's gear. 'I'll take that for you, then.' The light from the villagers' lanterns shone on his watch. It was now 6.45 p.m. He turned to the other villager. 'Is there a bridge where we can cross the river near here to reach Loharkhet?' he asked.

'Yes, certainly I can show you,' he said.

'That's so kind of all of you,' Archie said, grateful. 'Thank you.' He thought of the first porter and Bideshi, his cook, waiting to greet them at the Loharkhet dak bungalow. Thoughts of the comfort of a hot dinner, a warm bath and dry clothes made him smile.

Feeling encouraged, he waved goodbye to Subaran as he disappeared after the first villager into the semi-darkness.

The second villager headed off towards the Sarju. Archie followed. They were scrambling over stones along the edge of a river bed when they heard someone calling out.

They turned.

Archie could make out the entrance of a low cave in the cliff face. He bent down to look in. Just visible in the twilight was the outline of a tin box. A man sat next to it. 'Namaste?'

'Sahib!'

It was the first porter. Archie's heart sank. Visions of a hot dinner waiting for him at Loharkhet vanished into the night.

'Sahib, you found me. I'm so pleased to see you,' the man said excitedly. 'It was the flood; I could not cross the river.'

Archie realised the porter must have carried his heavy load the same way he and Subaran had come after they'd left their porter by the boulder. It had been a herculean effort.

'Where's Bideshi?' Archie asked now, anxious for his friend.

'He did not carry such a big load and walked faster. He crossed the river before the bridge was washed away.'

Relief filled Archie's heart. 'Come with us now. This villager says we've not far to go.'

A few minutes later they came to a tributary of the Sarju. A torrent of dark water rushed past them.

'The bridge is right here,' the villager told them.

Stretched above the water were branches and reeds strapped on to two pine logs, forming a rough horizontal ladder. It was only about 60 centimetres wide. Somehow, they all crossed, the porter shouldering the heavy box.

Relief was short-lived. A second torrent with a similar bridge was waiting a short distance away, but edging their way over, they crossed it as well.

'The Sarju is close now,' the villager said.

Archie couldn't see it, but he could hear it dashing and swirling in the pitch darkness in the depths of the chasm. As predicted, there was yet another horizontal ladder daring them to cross.

Later, in daylight, Archie could see the chasm walls dropping down to the raging Sarju more than 15 metres below.

Now he crept his way step by step in the darkness to the other side. The villager was there waiting. Archie breathed a prayer of relief as the porter, balancing his heavy load, stepped off the last branch onto solid ground next to him.

'Thank the Lord Yishu,' he said. He turned to the porter, 'If you'd slipped, you couldn't have swum to shore with that box on your back.'

'Just as well neither of you fell,' the villager commented. 'No one could live in that torrent. They'd never find your body either.'

'Awful thought,' Archie said. 'I wouldn't want to try crossing this at night again.'

'It's just a steep climb and you're at Loharkhet.' The villager set off up rocky path ahead of them.

The last one and a half kilometres of the trek was a 245-metre climb up a rocky track. At the end of a long day, it was tough going.

Bideshi was at the bungalow when they arrived. He grinned, surprised and pleased to see Archie had made it through the storm. 'Sahib, I didn't think you'd get here tonight. The rain, it was very heavy.'

'We didn't think we would get here either. The bridge was washed away in a flood,' Archie explained. 'This kind villager here showed us another way through.'

'That is good, but where is Subaran Singh? And the other porter?' Bideshi asked.

'My neighbour is showing them the way across,' the villager said. 'I'll wait for them to arrive and then go back home with him.'

'You're welcome to have a hot drink and something to eat while you wait,' Archie said.

Bideshi hurried about, lighting a fire, heating water for tea and a bath for Archie. It was then he noticed the blood all over Archie's trousers, from his knees to his ankles. 'Sahib! What happened to you?' He pointed in horror.

Archie rolled up his trouser legs to discover the 24 leeches he'd brought along with him on the journey. It took an hour for the bleeding to finally stop.

Bideshi had prepared a hot meal by then. Hungry, the men concentrated on eating, talking little. There was plenty left for Subaran, the second porter and the other villager when they arrived exhausted at 10.00 p.m.

The two villagers left for home, taking the heaped gratitude of the five trampers along with them.

Their kindness would not be forgotten.

Archie unrolled his bedding from the waterproof sheeting. He couldn't believe it – everything was dry. Too tired to care even if it had been a little damp, he fell asleep.

Chapter 7

In Awe of the Mighty Creator

Friday morning brought dull skies, and a fine mist wafted over the mountains. Archie, Bideshi and Subaran set out to climb another 1,200 metres up to 2,780 metres before lunchtime.

As they'd be returning to Loharkhet in four days, they left some of their food and gear at the bungalow. It meant the two porters were carrying lighter loads for the steep climb and higher altitudes. They would follow the other three at a slower pace.

It began to rain and, as expected, the temperature dropped the higher they climbed until it was bitterly cold.

Off to their right, the Sarju River raced down the mountainside. Archie knew it joined the Gogra River on the plains to reach the mighty Ganges River at Patna, 1,609 kilometres from where he stood.

Water running off the pathway at his feet drained into the Pindar River which flowed into the Ganges at Haridwar at the foot of the Himalayas.

The Hindus believed Haridwar to be one of the four places Garuda, the celestial bird, accidentally spilled drops of the elixir of immortality from the pitcher he was carrying.

Every three years a huge number of sadhus gathered at one of the four places for the rituals of Kumbh Mela. Thousands of pilgrims came for the rituals as well, bathing in the river to wash away their sins. It was Haridwar's turn every 12 years.

'It would depend on which way a puff of wind blows if a raindrop lands in the Sarju or the Pindar, or not at all,' Archie commented.

Subaran knew Archie used everyday situations to explain spiritual truths. He said, 'So, sahib, if we don't have a strong faith in God, it means we can be swayed by all kinds of different ideas and may end up in the wrong place.'

Archie was impressed. 'That's great insight, my friend,' he said.

Encouraged, Subaran trudged up the pathway in a burst of energy. It was only a short distance to the top now.

At the summit they passed a cairn at the side of the path. The tribesmen of the hills always added a stone to it and tied a piece of rag to a bush each time they passed that way. Before continuing on their journey, they'd repeat: 'The almighty lord and Nanda Devi have conquered (all our difficulties for us) and are our guides.'

Nanda Devi is the second highest peak in India. According to Hindus, it is the dwelling place of Parvati the bliss-giving goddess, and the 'almighty lord Shiva' is the creator and destroyer who dwells in Mount Kailash in Tibet.

'The porters will add a stone to that cairn when they come past,' Bideshi said.

'No doubt,' Archie answered. 'But I'm thankful it's God in heaven who has the power to help us, not a god who lives in rocks, snow and ice.'

They continued talking about it as they scrambled down a zigzagging path to the Dhakuri bungalow nestled among pines 800 metres below.

'Sahib, you say God is holy,' Bideshi said, 'but if so, I don't see why he'd want anything to do with people.'

'I can understand why you'd think that,' Archie told him, 'but God is also love.'

He thought of Ramswarup the Brahmin back in Gopiganj. Now, after talking with Archie many times, he was reading the Bible and taking it to heart. He hadn't decided to become a Christian yet; it would mean a huge disruption to his family if he did. No one would marry his daughters.

None of the missionaries had heard of a Brahmin becoming a Christian in all of the Benares district before. To Hindus, it was unthinkable.

Archie had faith that everything was possible with God.

※

The Dhakuri bungalow, built on a small piece of level ground on the mountain slopes, derived its name from the word dhakur, or sheep pen, in the language of the mountains.

A Bhotiya man in charge of the bungalow came out to greet them. Dressed in a homespun blanket clasped by ornamental pins, one on each side of his chest, he welcomed them inside, his wrinkled face beaming.

It only took a few moments for Archie to decide he liked him. The old man had the merry eyes of a Gurkha, encouraging Archie to laugh along with him as he talked.

'You are my first visitors,' he told them. 'I was appointed three months ago to look after this bungalow, and you are the first to stay.'

'Do you live here on your own?' Archie asked him. There were no other houses nearby.

'No, no, I cannot live *here*.' He rolled his eyes. 'The bears are too dangerous. I live near Loharkhet with my family and when I heard you were in town and heading for Dhakuri, I hurried with my son to arrive before you.' He stopped talking and another smile lit his face. 'Now what can I get you? What can I give to my first visitors?'

After leaving them for a short while, he came back, presenting Archie with an edible gourd.

'Thank you,' Archie said. 'It's very kind of you.'

'You are welcome.' The Bhotiya man touched Archie's feet in a gesture of hospitality. 'How long do you wish to stay?'

'The three of us would like to continue on as soon as we can today, but my porters will need a good rest here before heading off again,' Archie explained.

The Bhotiya's son spoke for the first time. 'I could go with you, carrying one of the loads as far as Khati if you like.'

Archie smiled his thanks. 'That would be wonderful. We'll only need to take one box.'

The three travellers were still wet through from tramping in the rain. Someone lit a fire and they crowded around, grateful for the warmth as they ate, sipped hot drinks and chatted with the Bhotiyas about their families.

The hill porters arrived. They dumped their tin boxes on the floor and settled by the fire to enjoy a rest and a meal while Archie and his two friends prepared to leave.

'Are you ready to go?' The Bhotiya's son swung a tin box over his shoulders in one easy movement and adjusted the straps.

They stepped into the rain. It had eased a little but Archie took care not to slip down the steep clay track into a valley. The Bhotiya, surefooted as a Himalayan tahr, impressed him as he trotted ahead as if he were carrying only a light load.

Khati, nestled between Nanda Devi and another majestic mountain, was the last village before the glacier. The view was spectacular now that the rain had cleared. At the western edge of the valley, there was a 150-metre sheer drop down to the foaming Pindar River.

The men headed straight for the unattended dak bungalow; a change of clothes was a priority, food a close second.

After a brief rest, the young Bhotiya left for home.

Archie was sorting out his gear when Bideshi came running from the kitchen, which was housed in a separate building at the back. 'Sahib, this is terrible. I cannot cook in there.' His face screwed up in disgust.

'What is it?' Archie asked.

'Come and see.'

Archie followed him to the doorway of the kitchen. It was obvious the last visitors hadn't cleaned up before they'd dashed south at the onset of the rains in June. Now the whole room was a hopping, moving mass of fleas.

'I think we'll leave them to it,' said Archie, shutting the door fast. 'Come into the bungalow. I'm sure we can make other arrangements for cooking tonight.'

Early in the morning, they set out through thick, dark forest along the bank of the Pindar River. Archie dipped his hand into the water. The icy chill seemed to bite into his bones. 'That's freezing!' He grinned, wiping his hand dry on his clothing.

'Too cold for any fish, I reckon' Bideshi said.

They were tramping through a narrow gorge hundreds of metres deep. Waterfalls were everywhere, splashing down the rocky walls. Two or three of the falls appeared to be dropping from the sky, caught by gravity and then hurled straight down in a giant chute towards the earth.

A wooden bridge built by the British brought them across to the right bank of the river. The foaming torrent, charging around enormous boulders, thundered in their ears, blocking out their voices.

Not far along the track they found ripe blackberries in the forest.

'I can't believe it,' Archie said. He hadn't seen any since leaving England, and he popped some in his mouth. 'Mmm, they're good. On the way back, I'll collect some to take home to Grace.'

Picking handfuls of the berries, the men snacked while they continued walking.

Sometimes they passed caves in the rocky walls of the gorge where the Bhotiya shepherds kept their sheep at night. It wasn't long before some shepherds came towards them, leading their flock through the forest. The sheep, so different from the English varieties Archie knew, had long silken white wool and wide curved horns.

Dwali, the second to last dak bungalow on their journey, perched on a high strip of land between the confluence of the Pindar and Khuphini Rivers at 2,438 metres above sea level.

As they approached, Archie saw several smashed windows and door frames that had been clawed into shreds in places.

The man in charge of the bungalow came out to greet them. 'I am sorry about the damage,' he apologised. 'The bears are curious, fearless and aggressive. They try to break in.'

'Don't worry, we won't be here long.' Archie thought of the Dhakuri bungalow. The smiling Bhotiya in charge there was concerned about bears as well. ' I'm surprised that bears live so high up in the mountains,' he added.

'They roam around up here during the warmer months,' the man told him. 'But in October they go down into the valleys to find somewhere to hibernate over winter.'

'So, do you come all the way from Khati to look after this place?' he asked.

'Yes. It's too isolated for anyone to want to live here. Only the British come all this way to see the glacier.'

'The beauty of the mountains is so inspiring.' Archie stood quietly for a moment, taking in the dramatic scene around him. 'I think breakfast out here on the verandah would be just great.'

A while later, the porters who had been walking at a slower pace arrived with the rain.

The valley was now choked in cloud. Archie, Subaran and Bideshi set out for the glacier. It would be a steep climb up to 3,260 metres in less than five kilometres.

They hadn't gone far when Archie shouted, 'Look! A snow-bridge.'

Wider than the length of a rugby field, Archie estimated it to be between three and a half and six metres deep.

'I haven't touched snow since I came to India,' he said, reaching down to lay his hand on the hard-packed snow.

Bideshi held some in his hand and stared at it. 'This is amazing, amazing,' he repeated in awe. He put a little in his mouth to taste.

'I guess you haven't had the chance to see snow before, living in Gopiganj,' Archie commented.

'No, never.' Bideshi threw down the snowball and waved his hand, indicating the massive snow-bridge. 'Oh, if only I could afford to bring my relatives to see this field of snow.'

'I know it's not the same, but I'll take photos and you can show them to your family when you're back home.'

'Thank you, sahib.' Bideshi grinned. 'I will be telling the story of our journey to family and friends for many days to come.'

At times as they crossed the snow-bridge they heard the Pindar River rushing below them. Large blocks of frozen snow, the size of small houses, lay scattered like rocks along a coast.

Further on, flattened rhododendron bushes clung to the rocky slopes around them. They'd be covered by four to eight metres of snow in winter, and then in March and April, avalanches would plough over them. Archie wondered how they survived.

When the men reached the Phurkia bungalow at about 3,260 metres above sea level, the clouds suddenly cleared. *They're pulling straight up as if invisible giants have called them away,* Archie thought.

The man in charge came out to greet them. 'I guide you to guleseer tomorrow,' he offered.

'To the glacier? Thank you,' Archie said.

Bideshi lit a fire, and as they dried their wet clothes, Archie began reading through the bungalow visitors' book.

'Climbers have noted that clouds often shroud the glacier after 9.00 a.m,' he told the others. 'I think we should leave here at dawn tomorrow.'

'That's fine with us,' the men said.

Archie dived back into the book.

The list of flowers visitors had found growing in the area surprised him: rhododendron, including the yellow variety which was only found growing at altitudes of about 3,500 to 4,900 metres, honeysuckle, lilac, rose, Michaelmas daisy, geranium, balsam, wild thyme and begonia. The list continued; buttercup, purple crane's bill, blue gentian, anemones, dandelion, blackberry, strawberry, purple columbine, orchids, bluebells, raspberry and currants.

A strong homesickness for England flooded over him. 'I'll go for a look around outside for a while,' he said.

Within a stone's throw of the bungalow he found 17 different kinds of flowers in the natural alpine garden.

Subaran followed him outside. 'Is everything alright, Archie?'

'Yes. Thank you, Subaran.' Archie stretched out his arm, indicating the floral beauty. 'Aren't the colours exquisite? Many of these flowers grow in England and it is so special for me to see them here.'

'It is God's gift for you in this remote and majestic place.' Subaran bent down and picked one of the flowers, touching its delicate petals. 'Isn't it amazing they grow at such high altitudes?'

Archie nodded. 'To think that for about nine months of the year they are buried deep in snow, and then they gladly burst into flower to greet the sun. I shall never forget this afternoon.'

At sunset the 7,620-metre high snowy peak of Nanda Devi at the top of the valley glowed with golden light.

'Wouldn't it be wonderful if cameras could take colour photos?' Archie said. As the colour faded into dusk, the peak stood out clearly against the sky.

'If I set the exposure of the film for seven minutes, I can take a photo now.'

Archie knew that in poor light, his camera needed a long time to absorb enough for a photo. Typical of those used at the time, his camera used a thin strip of film treated with a special light-sensitive chemical that changed when sunlight struck the film. The more light was exposed to the film, the brighter the photo would become.

As he ate dinner, the moon spread its silver light over the mountain. Archie set the camera on a chair on the verandah and left it set for 20 minutes.

He'd need to wait until the film was developed to find out how clear the photos were but he was hoping for a good result.

During the night, the freezing air shivered him out of sleep a couple of times. After stoking the fire, sipping warm cocoa from his thermos flask and adding extra layers of woollens over his clothes, he peeped out the window at the moonlit mountain. In the isolated stillness, the only sound he could hear was the continual rush of falling water.

Peace.

Curling back in his blankets, he drifted into sleep.

Archie was awake again before 5.00 a.m. It wasn't long before they headed off into the chilly darkness, their guide leading the way. Climbing soon warmed them and they watched as dawn began sliding into the sky.

Nanda Devi reflected various shades of delicious pink, lemon and rich gold – beautiful colours after the crisp silver of the night.

They passed the site of the first Phurkia dak bungalow that had been swept away by an avalanche several years before and came to the rushing Pindar again. Deciding it was too dangerous to cross, they climbed along the edge to a snow-bridge.

'This is crazy, but I can hear dogs barking,' Archie said, stopping partway across the bridge.

Their guide pointed. 'There is a flock of sheep. Look, over there on the bare mountainside.'

Reaching the further side, they could see a small hut made of stones. Two or three shepherds, woken from sleep, called from inside to silence the dogs.

The track now ascended slowly through the wide valley. Large boulders swept down by avalanches lay everywhere.

Some time later, more dogs began barking far away on the slopes across the Pindar River. A shepherd called out to Archie's guide, his lilting voice covering the long distance.

In Awe of the Mighty Creator

The guide answered in a different singing tone.

'What did he say?' Archie asked.

'He asked why you are here,' the guide explained, 'and I told him you want to see guleseer.'

Not far ahead, the track rounded a hill and Archie stopped in amazement.

There, in front of them was the glistening white river of ice.

'It's incredible,' he whispered. All those days walking in the rain had been worth it.

'Better to see up there,' the guide said pointing to the moraine.

The view expanded as Archie climbed the 60 metres to the top.

On his left, the sun shone on a row of pure white peaks rising sheer above the glacier. To his right, ominous mountains in shadow seemed to close in on him. A dull roar alerted him to a massive wall of snow thundering down the slopes.

To the northeast, Nanda Kot rose 6,861 metres into the clear sky. Like Nanda Devi, this mountain was worshipped by the Hindus who believed it was a fortress for one of the forms of the goddess Parvati. Archie saw it as an awe-inspiring creation of God.

The glacier, an enormous weight of ice, sloped down between Nanda Devi and Nanda Kot. Huge ice crags towered over the higher part, and columns of ice were topped by boulders lower down.

Curving behind him was the snout of the glacier, a huge cavern of ice. The Pindar River tumbled from the entrance and Archie felt a sense of wonder. The water, after travelling a long distance, would eventually be only about three kilometres from Gopiganj.

In the solemn loneliness, surrounded by the grandeur of the massive mountains, Archie felt the presence of the Creator.

Many hundreds of years before, ancient people had stood in awe, as he was doing now, but they had deified the mountains rather than the one who created them. Archie could almost understand. In his imagination he could picture the pure white giants silently conversing with each other.

He wrote in his diary for John, his father:

> It was like being in another world. A feeling came over me that I have never experienced in the reading of a book. The still small voice (of God) seemed to speak to me out of the silence. I wanted to stay on. As I looked upward at the glittered splendour of sparkling snow 10,000 feet above me, I seemed truly to have reached the Great White Throne. What a cathedral!

Inspired, he headed down from the moraine, looking around for the rest of the party.

Bideshi and the others were trying to light the spirit stove to boil ice to brew tea. They'd nearly used a box of matches and still the stove refused to cooperate.

'You're sure it was methylated spirits you brought for the stove?' Archie asked.

'Yes sahib. Look for yourself.'

It was with a mixture of disappointment and amusement that Archie found they'd filled the stove with olive oil.

There would be no hot drinks for anyone that morning.

'I'll go onto the glacier for a bit,' he said.

He walked cautiously out onto the ice with hobnailed boots and his iron-spiked alpine staff. The glacier seemed more massive now he was down on the surface, making him feel like a tiny speck on the river of ice.

The glacier was about three kilometres long and about 400 metres wide. Sweeping down from 4,260 metres, it extended down to 3,650 metres.

The cold was intense and Archie's feet began to ache. A drizzling rain began to fall and mist closed in around them. It was time to go.

Back in the Phurkia dak bungalow, Archie wrote in the visitors' book, capturing the enjoyment of his glacial experience. His was the first party to reach the glacier so early in autumn. The last party had to turn back in May on account of heavy snow drifts.

It didn't take long to pack, and they headed down to Dwali. Archie rested on the verandah, entertained for an hour by two little brown field mice playing together three metres from his chair.

The following morning on their trek to Dhakuri they met a large man in charge of several porters. They were a road crew, working to repair damage from landslides and wash-outs – not an easy task in the Himalayas.

The supervisor stopped to talk to Archie.

'I'm a descendant of Malak Singh Buda,' the man told him with pride. 'He built the Pindari track to the glacier in the 1830s. It was George Traill, the British Commissioner of the Kumaon district back then who wanted it made.'

'Your family has done a great job,' Archie congratulated him. 'It was an incredible experience for us, visiting the glacier.'

The man smiled. 'Thank you. The commissioner had hoped the track could reach all the way from Almora as far as Tibet, but that wasn't possible. The terrain is too rugged past the glacier.'

'I can believe that,' Archie said, thinking of the steep mountains and the eternal snows. 'I hope all goes well for you today,' he added in parting.

An hour later further along the track, he was amazed to meet a postman coming towards him.

'Where are you going way out here?' he asked in disbelief.

'Well, actually, I have a letter for you,' he answered casually.

To Archie's further astonishment, the postman handed him a letter from Grace.

It was addressed to Loharkhet Post Office, but the postmaster had given the letter to the postman in case he met up with Archie along the way. Archie tucked the letter into his pocket to read at leisure.

When they reached the Dhakuri bungalow, their Bhotiya friend came out to meet them, still full of smiles.

'I have a gift for you,' he told Archie, handing him a carved walking stick. 'My son made this especially for your memsahib when she walks in the hills near Almora.'

'Thank you,' Archie said with real gratitude. 'I will tell her of your kindness.'

'You are most welcome,' the old man said.

Up until then, Archie hadn't felt any fatigue or aches and pains from tramping, but on the next stage of the journey the steep drop down to the valley below juddered his knees. That evening, he rubbed them with a mixture of turpentine and mustard oil to relieve the inflammation.

From there on, the journey was uneventful. They crossed the horizontal ladder bridges over the Sarju River between Loharkhet and Bageshwar in daylight with no problems.

At Bageshwar, after talking with the others about the final stage of the trek, they came to a decision. The porters and Bideshi would take two days to reach Almora while Archie and Subaran would walk the 39 kilometres in one day, hoping to reach Almora by dusk.

As he was descending the Dewaldhar Pass near the Fruit and Tea Gardens, the muscles above Archie's right knee cramped in pain again. After he had soaked his knees in the cold water of a stream, the pain eased and they continued on their way.

A Brahmin overtook them, heading for Almora at a fast pace.

'Please will you leave a message at Snow View to tell them the sahib will be home by sunset?' Archie asked.

'Certainly,' the man answered and hurried on down the track.

At sunset, close to Almora, Archie saw three figures coming towards him, one tall, and two short. Grace and the two children were coming to meet him.

'Dadda!' Frank shouted, and he began to run.

Chapter 8

Joy in Uncertain Times

Over the winter months of 1911/12, the family was together in Gopiganj. Archie continued his mission work, tending the sick and injured, prescribing medicine and telling the people about Yishu.

Not long after he'd returned from Almora, he began telling a local sadhu about his trip to the Pindari Glacier.

'It was amazing being there, looking out over the huge river of ice and the majestic mountains,' he said. 'God is an incredible Creator.'

'Many pilgrims go to Badrinath in the mountains,' the sadhu answered. 'There's a fountain of milk there. *That* is amazing.'

'Have you seen it?' Archie asked.

'No.'

Badrinath, on the bank of the Alaknanda River in the Indian state of Uttarakhand near the Chinese border, was surrounded by superstition. A mythical fountain of milk, Archie thought, was a poor substitute for the grandeur of the Pindari.

Winter was the best time of year for the whole family to go on camping mission trips. One time during a mission trip to Kachhwa, a sudden storm blew up, rocking the tent.

'We'll pray the tent holds,' Archie said, after hammering the pegs in again.

The next morning all was still.

'The storm's gone,' Frank said, peeping outside. 'And the tent didn't blow down. God and the pegs held it up.'

Grace and Archie looked at each other and burst into laughter.

'What's so funny?' Frank asked, puzzled. 'You prayed God would hold it up.'

※

Despite financial difficulties, the LMS Board in London decided to continue work in the Benares district.

There was a little money left from the development of the mission station in Gopiganj. As the benefactor had stipulated that funds were only to be used for developing new mission stations, Archie built an outpost at Sahsepur, near the Madhosingh Railway Junction, roughly halfway between Gopiganj and Kachhwa.

It was a thickly populated area.

The Maharajah of Benares had gifted land for a school on one condition – that if the LMS no longer needed it, the land would be returned to the State. He also donated money for the school building if the LMS would fund the rest.

At the LMS Benares District Committee (BDC) meeting in February 1912, Archie reported that he was looking out for a smaller plot of land to build housing for a schoolmaster, another Christian worker, and visiting missionaries. Building would start soon after land was purchased.

Two months later, Grace and the children were back in Almora. Grace was busy each day caring for the two children, and she was pregnant again.

Frank, Lily, and another missionary's little boy often played together. As well as the LMS compound, there was a British boarding school and military quarters in the hillside town.

An army captain who often visited the missionaries stopped as the children ran up to him.

'I'm going to shoot you,' Frank said, holding up his toy gun. 'Bang! Bang!'

The captain, playing along, slid to the ground under a tree, feigning death.

Lily burst into action. Dressed in her nurse's outfit, she ran to give him first aid. Holding up a can of water, she tipped it over his face. She danced in delight to see her patient instantly leap back into life.

In mid-August Frank started school as a day pupil at the large British boarding school.

Archie had already arrived in Almora to spend three weeks with his family. A few days later, baby Vera Jessie was born on 20 August.

Grace and Archie were thrilled with their wee daughter.

'She will be a little friend for Lily now Frank's at school,' Archie said, looking down at baby Vera asleep in his arms.

'Yes.' Grace's eyes filled with tenderness. 'I can tell she's going to be an active wee girl from the way she kicked.'

Archie laughed. The time spent with his family was precious. It would soon be over.

He left for Gopiganj at the beginning of September but at the end of the month he returned to escort his family home.

The clinic at Gopiganj was always busy. Archie found the tropical medicine course he'd taken in London was invaluable. The patients paid just under cost for medication, and Doctor Evans, the LMS missionary from Mirzapur, was now coming once a week to see to the more difficult cases.

The Lenwoods, the LMS missionaries in Benares, had left India. Frank Lenwood taking up the position of secretary for the LMS Board in London. Grace and Archie missed them. The older couple had been a great support. They had similar views on how to handle issues and laughed at the same things.

'Remember when we visited the Lenwoods in Benares when Frank was three?' Grace reminded Archie.

'Yes?'

'And Mrs Lenwood called Frank to come outside and see the water running around the garden.'

'Oh, that's right. He piped up and said, "Yes and it hasn't any legs!" Smart boy, our Frank.' Archie grinned but then he became serious. 'I'm certainly going to miss Frank Lenwood at our BDC meetings. He really knows how things tick here, and has a lot of local knowledge, like Doctor Ashton does.'

At the next meeting on 13 November, the committee wrote to the LMS Board regarding the need for a new girls' school by the Gopiganj bazaar. Land had been offered free and the committee members, including Miss Few and Kathleen Morris who were now stationed at Gopiganj, had seen and approved of the site.

The Maharajah of Benares had again gifted money towards the building fund. Wanting to make improvements for the people in his district, he could see how the LMS schools and clinics were making an impact for good.

※

The year 1913 proved to be full of challenges as well as rays of hope.

Archie's second year Urdu examination results came back;

he'd achieved overall marks of 77.2 percent for the oral and written sections.

Mr Mukerji, the Indian honorary pastor of the Hindustani Church in Benares, was now serving a three-year term on the BDC. It was a step in the right direction. Indigenous churches were one of the committee's most important goals.

There was bad news for Miss Few though. Plagued by illness and exhaustion, she was diagnosed with dry pleurisy and possibly the early stage of tuberculosis. She left for England in early April.

To replace her, Alice Gill from the LMS mission in Benares joined Kathleen Morris and the McMillans in Gopiganj. Living in a smaller town suited her after the fast pace of an Indian city.

Archie had built a dispensary as well as the new school at the outpost near the Madhosingh Railway Junction.

He wrote a long letter to the LMS Board, letting them know his news. He applied for a grant to pay the dispenser and for the necessary medications. The LMS Board was short of funds but Archie hoped and prayed that Christians in Britain would donate money during mission talks in May.

In his letter, he wrote that he and Grace felt sure God had led them to Gopiganj. They fitted in well with the other LMS missionaries in the area; they were a great team, worked well together and enjoyed each other's company.

Everyone was aware of the challenges of preaching the gospel in that district. Benares was a centre for Hindu pilgrims and steeped in tradition, but Archie was hopeful. His Brahmin friend, Ramswarup, was now ready for baptism, and his adult son was interested, but his wife was holding fast to her Hindu beliefs.

Archie longed for an indigenous church community in

Gopiganj, independent of foreign aid. The little church meeting on the mission compound was mainly filled with missionaries, their families and Christian employees.

He concluded his letter to the board with family news:

> The children do bring additional responsibility and expense but to the parents they are more than worth it. It gives us a real home out here and lightens many a burden to have their love and hear their laughter.*

※

Lily was now almost four years old. Her precious doll was with her most of the day. At night, she fell asleep cuddling it in her arms.

The outer body of the doll had come from England – probably on the *Caledonia* – and it had been stuffed with Indian cotton wool on arrival at Gopiganj.

Both the older children knew that.

To Frank, it raised an intriguing question, a trick question Lily wouldn't be able to answer. 'Does that mean she's an English doll or an Indian doll?' he asked her.

'Both,' she answered without hesitation.

'She can't be both.' His voice held all the scorn of two years' seniority.

'Yes, she can. Same as you.' Lily stood firm.

Frank despised playing with dolls. He'd hoped to trick Lily and it wasn't working. 'No, she's not,' he said, annoyed.

---

* 24 April 1913 letter in the LMS Archives, School of Oriental and African Studies, London.

'Of course she is the same as you because you were born in England and then you've been filled with food over here in India.'

Overhearing them, Grace smiled. She loved to hear the amusing things the children said.

That year, Grace and the children spent what they hoped was the first of several summers in Nainital. Hidden in the mountains, only 62 kilometres from Almora, the town crouched against the wild beauty of rocky heights, and dipped down to a Himalayan tal, or lake.

It was a town of dramatic contrasts.

Many British troops, officials, and their families stayed in the town over summer. From yachts racing on the tal and polo ponies competing on the recreation grounds, there was always something to watch.

Near the lake, the layered conical roofs of the temple of the goddess Naina Devi stood out against the backdrop of rugged peaks.

Grace and Archie knew the Hindus believed Nainital to be one of the 64 places where pieces of the goddess Sati fell to earth when the god Shiva carried her body. They said her eyes (naina) fell to make the lake at Nainital.

There were also some Christian churches and schools in Nainital. The McMillans felt it was a good place for Grace to spend the summer with the children, and the military presence of the Seaforth Highlanders created a sense of safety.

When Archie's sister, Jessie, read about the Highlanders in Grace and Archie's letters home, she outfitted a doll in a kilt and tall black highland hat and sent it to Lily.

Lily loved the doll, even taking it to church with her the following Sunday evening.

During the service Grace opened her eyes after a prayer and

looked up to see Frank standing facing the back row where the Seaforth Highlanders sat wearing their kilts. The little boy held the doll up high for them to see.

Not daring to look round in case she couldn't hold back her laughter, Grace tapped Frank on his arm.

'I think they've all seen the doll,' she whispered. 'You can turn around and sit down now.'

Frank was now attending Philander Smith College, high on the hills above the town. It was a steep climb for a little boy, so for safety he was always accompanied by an adult.

At home, baby Vera watched everything the others did, and was delighted when she learned to crawl.

Now she could explore.

While Grace and the children were in Nainital, Alice Gill and Kathleen Morris headed to Almora with two other LMS missionaries for a break. Three of them were staying at the Snow View mission compound but Alice Gill stayed with Doctor Eleanor Shepheard in her home.

Archie was now the only missionary left at Gopiganj. He carried on working in the humid heat of the plains.

※

The letter brought devastating news. Dated 21 May 1913, it came from the LMS Board in London and arrived in mid-June.

There was no mistake. The mission was now deep in debt.

Usually, some of the donations to the LMS were set aside to maintain and run the mission compounds and pay the missionaries and their employees, but now there was a gross shortfall.

The lack of funds affected all the LMS mission stations in India.

The news spread rapidly to the scattered BDC members and their families. Deeply concerned, they prayed wherever they were that God would intervene and that funds would become available so they could continue to share the gospel.

The BDC met in July. They decided that, by using money in hand and spending the chaplaincy fund, they wouldn't need to withdraw from the consolidated grant until the end of September, saving the LMS 4,297 rupees (£300).

The only way they could see to save money was to cut back on educational spending for the school children in their area and curb medical and evangelistic work as well.

They would need to close two of their mission stations. Some of the missionaries would have to leave.

The thought was heart-breaking.

To help solve the crisis, they decided to contact the secretaries of all the LMS district committees in India to recommend forming an advisory committee. If they agreed to the idea, a representative from each committee could meet in September in Calcutta to form the new group. Maybe they could come up with a workable plan together.

The BDC sent a report of their decisions and suggestions to the board in London, along with their prayers. They knew how hard it had been for the board to crush their hopes.

They prayed, trusting in God.

The many obstacles had looked impossible to overcome when Archie was building the Gopiganj mission compound, but God had made a way through them all.

'Father in heaven,' he prayed now. 'Show us the way forward.'

On the last Sunday in August, Archie baptised an Indian and his two sons who had become Christians. It was a triumph. Archie looked forward to the day his Brahmin friend, Ramswarup, would be baptised too. He was now a dedicated Christian but wasn't ready to declare his faith publicly.

He and the other Indian Christians were saving money to buy land and build a church, independent of foreign aid.

Archie was thrilled.

He spent time at the outpost near Madhosingh Junction during the rainy season. Fifty boys now attended the Kathara School there, taught by an Indian Christian teacher, and a Sunday school was held every Sunday. The dispensary was up and running as well.

Archie walked or cycled between villages in the area in spite of the heat and rain. The outdoor life suited him, and he felt fit and healthy. During the dry winter the family would be living in tents again on a two- or three-month tour, sharing the gospel with everyone they met.

Archie wrote to the LMS Board in mid-September. In two weeks, he'd head to Nainital to spend a fortnight with his family then bring them home to Gopiganj.

In early November the BDC met again. In response to the LMS Director's letter advising them of the need to severely cut costs, all the missionaries voted against closing their mission stations. They were doing everything possible to keep expenses low but felt they couldn't pull out unless others were ready to take up the challenge.

Chapter 9

A Traumatic Journey

A few days before Easter 1914, four-year-old Lily developed tonsillitis.

Miserable and in pain, she was often in tears. A peritonsillar abscess formed in the back of her throat and her temperature spiked and remained at a dangerous level.

On Easter Sunday Archie conferred with Grace as they stood by Lily's bed.

'I think we'd better call Doctor Ashton from Kachhwa,' he told her.

'Send an urgent message,' Grace's voice trembled. 'He must operate, do something soon…'

She reached down to sponge Lily's flushed face, speaking to her gently. 'Mummy and Dadda are here, darling. The doctor will come.'

Archie was already leaving the room. 'I'll send a message right now,' he said.

Before antibiotics were available, bacterial infections were dangerous. He and Grace knew there was a high possibility Lily could die.

Robert Ashton arrived that evening, and after examining Lily, he shook his head. 'Her fever is too high. I can't operate, I'm so sorry.' Seeing Grace's face twist in heartbreak, he added, 'Take her up to Snow View at Almora immediately. Maybe the cooler temperatures will lessen her fever and Doctor Shepheard can operate. That's the only hope we have of saving her.'

Together they prayed for a miracle.

'I'll come with you as far as Benares,' he continued. 'We'll get a second opinion from a doctor there.'

Grace and Archie packed half the night for the months Grace and the children would be away for summer. The family and Doctor Ashton left in the darkness of early Monday.

A procession of porters carried their luggage as they trudged by lantern light to the Gopiganj station. Archie and a porter carried Lily, still lying on her mattress.

He bought tickets, organised loading their luggage onto the train, and then settled his family in a carriage.

It was the beginning of their 724-kilometre journey.

Would Lily survive it?

Throughout the day, Archie sponged Lily's hot little face, giving her any comfort he could, while Grace cared for Frank and baby Vera.

When they reached Benares, the doctor at the government hospital confirmed that an operation was the only way to save Lily – but only when her fever dropped. It meant that he, too, could do nothing to help.

Back at the Benares station, the McMillans thanked Robert Ashton for his support before they caught a train to Bareilly Junction. Hour after hour it puffed its way through the heat and dust of the plains.

At Bareilly, Frank and Vera curled up to sleep on their mattresses on the platform until they boarded the narrow-gauge railway at 11.00 p.m. The strong scent of citronella surrounded the family as they dabbed it on to ward off mosquitoes.

A Traumatic Journey

Hours later, their train rumbled into the station. After settling the three children on the seats, Grace and Archie drifted into sleep. Minutes later Grace stirred awake to feel a breeze blowing around her. The thundering of the train as it swayed into the curving track seemed louder too.

Her eyes widened in shock.

The outside carriage door had swung open. Little Vera was sleeping on the seat right next to it.

Any moment she could roll over or the swaying motion of the train could swing her out into the rushing darkness.

'Archie!' At Grace's cry, Archie leapt to his feet, awake in an instant. Grace snatched Vera into her arms while Archie wrestled the door shut.

On Tuesday morning the train steamed its way into Kathgodam station as the sun reached up to shine gold onto the snowy mountains.

The air was cooler here in the foothills of the Himalayas, and the family struggled into warmer clothes on the platform. Trunks packed with piles of household items – bedding, clothes, food and cooking utensils – surrounded them.

Grace, too tired to think, automatically handed food to Archie, Frank and 19-month-old Vera. She set up their portable oil stove to boil more water to cool in earthenware jars for drinking later.

Lily was lying on a mattress on the platform. Her usually expressive dark eyes, now clouded with fever, gave no indication she was aware of her surroundings.

Archie sponged her forehead, looking with concern at her swollen neck. He checked the thermometer.

'How is she?' Grace asked.

'Her temperature's risen again Grace,' he said.

'Oh no!' The fear, trauma, lack of sleep and the shock of nearly losing Vera on the night train were too great. Grace tried to wipe away the tears spilling onto her cheeks but more threatened to fall. Somehow, she held them back, grateful that Frank and Vera hadn't seen her cry. 'Please heavenly Father, please make Lily's temperature drop so Doctor Shepheard can operate,' she whispered.

She knew Archie was praying too.

'Dadda, will we get to the hospital in Almora today?' asked six-year-old Frank, clutching his chapati with both hands.

'No, not today.' Archie answered.

Frank knew Lily was really ill – too ill to argue or even talk to him. But he did not realise how close he was to losing his little sister. He looked over to where his father was now approaching a group of hill porters. Archie would pay them to carry their luggage up the steep mountain track on the next stage of the journey. Two dandies and a child backpack carrier were ready waiting there too.

One of the dandies was for Grace and little Vera. Lily lay on her mattress in another. Frank, knowing what to do without being told, climbed on to the seat of the carrier and a porter lifted him onto his shoulders.

The porters hoisted the dandy poles and began the long slow trek into the mountains. Archie walked beside Lily, holding an umbrella over her to shield her from the sun.

Frank shifted in his seat, holding on to the front edge of the carrier. 'We're going up the mountain, we're going up the mountain,' he chanted. 'I want to walk with you Dadda.'

'No,' Archie answered. 'You couldn't keep up. When we stop, then you can run around.'

'Frank, what can you see over there?' Grace asked to distract him. She pointed to a fertile terrace on the hillside.

'There's a village, people working in the rice fields,' Frank said. He settled down, taking in each new scene coming into view as the track twisted round yet another bend. Streams danced in the sunlight, mighty trees smothered wooded hillsides, and magnificent snowy peaks towered in the distance. He always loved the trek into the mountains.

At midday their party reached the dak bungalow at Bhim Tal, a lake deep in the mountains. Grace and Archie decided Lily was too ill to travel further that day. Her temperature had topped 105 degrees Fahrenheit (40.5 Celsius) and she was delirious.

Archie sat with her during the afternoon and on into the night. Grace took a shift so he could sleep. Frank and Vera needed to be looked after too.

With constant care, Lily's temperature dropped a few degrees.

The following morning, Wednesday, they made good progress. Crossing a narrow suspension bridge over a ravine, they reached a dak bungalow 32 kilometres further on at Ramgarh, 2,100 metres above sea level.

After a rest, the trek continued during the afternoon until they stopped for the night at another bungalow.

One more broken night, anxiety creeping through the slow, dark hours.

Praying.

Hoping.

Yet another morning passed trudging in the mountains, the men sweating in the cool mountain air under the weight of the trunks and dandies.

'Almora!' Archie pointed as the town came into view but it was midday before they reached the doctor's house.

A messenger alerted Doctor Eleanor Shepheard at the hospital that the McMillans had arrived and needed her urgently.

She hurried home and examined Lily.

'Can you operate today, Doctor?' Grace asked hopefully. She was trembling, her voice shaking.

'No,' Eleanor said. She choked back emotion, knowing she'd devastate her friends with her next few words. 'We can't operate at all. The abscess is now too close to the artery and veins in her neck. It is too dangerous.'

'So, is there nothing we can do?' Archie asked. He glanced at Grace. She was stroking Lily's hair, tears rolling unchecked down her pale face.

'Please help her,' Grace was whispering. 'She's made it this far. We've travelled for days…'

'I do understand.' Eleanor was quiet for a moment. There seemed little hope for Lily, but it was better to try something – anything – rather than let her parents stand by helplessly, watching their little daughter die. 'There's one thing we can try,' she said at last. 'I've a sample of a new poultice that I haven't prescribed to anyone yet. It's just possible it could help Lily.'

She showed them how to place the poultices on Lily's neck and they continued applying them over the next few days. The abscess drained and the fever faded.

One evening, Grace and Archie sat together in the mission house sitting room after the children were asleep. Their conversation centred around the trauma of the last two weeks.

'God is so good, Grace. We still have our Lily,' Archie said.

'I don't think I'd have coped at all, Archie, if I'd lost her. Or Frank or Vera,' Grace said. 'Mother and Father lost five little ones and your parents lost two. How did they bear it?'

'A sorrow too deep to express in words,' Archie said. 'I know their faith in God, and the certain belief their children are in heaven waiting for them gave them hope.'

'It did – a great deal – but I know Mother was quiet at times, and her eyes were filled with sadness. Father joked a lot, sometimes too much. I think it was his way of dealing with it.'

Archie nodded. 'I guess we'll never know how we'd react unless we were in that situation ourselves. I pray we never will be.'

'I pray for the children's protection – and yours – every day. I'm determined to trust God whatever happens.'

'Yes, we can commit everything into God's hands. He will get us through,' Archie agreed. 'It certainly was a miracle Lily battled through those days of fever to reach Almora at all.'

'And a miracle Vera wasn't swallowed into the darkness off the train to Kathgodam.' A smile spread across Grace's face. 'I'll always be thankful to God and Eleanor Shepheard.'

Comforted by the knowledge that Lily was out of danger and the rest of the family was well, Archie travelled back to the plains alone ten days later.

The LMS had asked him to take charge temporarily of a mission station at the small jungle town of Dudhi in the Mirzapur district. The previous missionary had left and another mission would be taking it on in September. In the meantime, Archie divided his time between his own mission and Dudhi.

The church at Gopiganj was completed in May before the monsoon rains came. Local Christians, full of enthusiasm, had volunteered their help. Families invited Archie to dinner to give his cook more time to help with the building project. The two women missionaries tied dusters around their hair as they sifted lime for cement.

Now it was a time to celebrate. Archie's joy would have been complete if his family had been there to share it, but love bridges distance and they were with him in heart.

A few days later, though, Archie received an urgent letter from Grace.

Frank was ill with typhoid – or enteric fever as Archie called it.

After the near tragedies with the girls just a short time ago, would they now lose Frank? Archie travelled up to Almora to be with them, sleeping in the same room as Frank to be there whenever he needed him. After the third week of Frank's illness, he left, knowing Frank would recover in time.

'Just watch him though,' Archie said before he set off. 'He might be improving now but he could have a relapse.'

Grace nodded. 'I'm aware of that,' she said. 'Don't worry, dear. He's in good hands here.'

She tried to sound encouraging but she knew how hard it was for Archie to leave.

Frank spent six long, slow weeks in bed before he recovered.

June rains in Almora brought vibrant carpets of flowers smothering the hills in an explosion of colour.

During breaks in the weather, as Frank grew stronger, Grace and the children wandered along the pathways, enjoying the beauty around them.

'Pittie fitties looking at baby,' Vera chanted as she held out her hands to the flowers.

'Doesn't she know 'pittie fitties' aren't proper words, Mummy?' Frank asked.

'She can't say pretty flowers yet. She'll speak better with practice.' Grace smiled down at him. 'That's the way you learned to talk too.'

'She can't say Vera yet either,' Lily put in. 'She says Vela.'

'Like when we say our prayers.' Frank's eyes shone in laughter. 'She stands up in her cot and keeps saying "Baby Vela, Baby Vela" all the time till we say "God bless Baby Vera".'

Lily giggled. 'And then she sits down,' she said, finishing off the story. 'She's so funny.'

Grace bent down to kiss Vera on her soft pink cheek. 'Yes you are, my rose petal.'

Vera wriggled and shook her head. 'No, not rose petal. Baby Vela!' she shouted.

Grace smiled in contentment. She loved to see all her children well and enjoying life in the mountains.

These were heart-warming days.

Chapter 10

War: From Gopiganj to France

Britain declared war on Germany on 4 August 1914.

The Seaforth Highlanders who attended the church in Nainital left India to fight in France, arriving in October. The Indian Expeditionary Force A, commanded by General Sir James Willcocks, had already arrived in Marseilles on 30 September.

Archie felt torn. Opposing convictions of joining up or continuing with God's call to mission work had tugged at him since he'd prepared to hand over the mission work at Dudhi in early September.

The new Australian missionary, Mr Pittman from the Christian Mission had arrived. Archie was amazed to find out they had both gone to the same Sunday school in London. Their childhood homes were only ten minutes walking distance apart.

'I remember your family emigrated to Australia when I was a child,' Archie said, thinking back. 'What an incredible coincidence.'

They knew the Indian Christians at Dudhi were sad the LMS was withdrawing but Archie wanted to show them that Mr Pittman and the other new missionaries arriving soon would teach them the same gospel. They would continue with the work the LMS had started.

At the church service on Sunday 6 September, Archie preached, reading this verse from the Hindi Bible:

> So neither he who plants nor he who waters is anything, but only God, who makes things grow. The man who plants and the man who waters have one purpose, and each will be rewarded according to his own labor. For we are God's fellow workers; you are God's field, God's building. (1 Corinthians 3:7-9)

The following day, Archie officially handed the mission over to Mr Pittman and returned to Gopiganj. He felt confident. Like the LMS, the new mission was going to care for the people and teach at their schools. The Indian people would learn to love them too.

Life as Archie knew it was changing.

Although the war was in Europe, it was beginning to affect missionaries in India. Archie was concerned that LMS funds from England could dry up in the same way funds had ceased coming to the German Lutheran missionaries in Bihar State, and down in Madras (Chennai).

The treasurer of the Indian National Missionary Council had sent out a desperate appeal for money to meet the Lutheran missionary families' personal needs.

Archie wondered if his family would end up in the same predicament. It depended on how long the war lasted; funds were already short.

Doctor Evans from the LMS mission in Mirzapur was taking up the position of surgeon in the government hospital, and a mission teacher was looking for a government position in Benares. Indian Christians were soon to take over church work at the LMS Mangari mission near Mirzapur.

Towards the end of October, Archie travelled to Almora and accompanied his family home.

A public noticeboard in Gopiganj informed people of the latest war news. Grace and Archie read it with concern.

Indian troops took part in the fighting in the Ypres area in France, and in the next few months they fought in several other major battles. They'd been issued Lee-Enfield rifles and with almost no artillery, needed to rely on other corps at the front line.

Their morale was low in the freezing cold. To make matters worse, replacement officers couldn't speak Hindi.

'This is terrible,' Archie said to Grace. 'I want to be there to help in any way I can.'

Grace looked at him in alarm. 'But your work is here in Gopiganj, Archie,' she reasoned. 'It was only this year that we built the church. And Ramswarup…' Her voice tailed off into a sigh of concern.

'Don't worry about him. He's showing great insight into the Bible now,' Archie said. ' The night school he and his sons started last August is flourishing six nights a week in the village nearby. And he's the only one the villagers trusted to hold the money they collected for their new well.'

'I know his faith is strong,' Grace said, 'but Archie, I hope and pray he'll be baptised before we leave. Are you sure you should go?'

'It will be a wrench to leave.' He didn't add *knowing I might never come back*. 'But my heart is with those poor soldiers too. As you know, our furlough is due in 1916.' Archie took a deep breath and plunged right into what he had to say. 'I've been thinking about it a great deal. We'll all sail to England, and later I'll sign up.'

'In an Indian regiment?'

'No. I'll volunteer for the medical corps to support Indian troops in France, interpret for them, or maybe do YMCA work – something along those lines.'

'We'll need to pray together and seek God's protection and strength – commit it all to him.'

Grace had known fear when Archie had gone after man-eaters in the jungle, but this war was death on a large scale. The Germans were torpedoing supply ships from the United States to Britain. Their family could all be in danger when they left India.

She couldn't help voicing her fears aloud. 'The Germans wouldn't torpedo passenger ships, would they?'

'I doubt it, dear,' Archie said.

His words didn't comfort Grace, but although she was afraid, she remembered what she'd decided after Lily's illness. She repeated it to Archie now. 'I'm determined to trust God whatever happens,' she said.

Archie wrapped her in his arms. 'My dear brave wife,' he said as he kissed her. 'That's what I must do as well.'

***

The children, unaware of the adults' concerns, played games as they usually did.

The wide verandah of their home was a favourite play area and Vera was often out there with her toys. This time, she was pretending to pour cups of tea for her doll.

'Mummy, what's this?' Grace heard her call out.

'It's a teapot,' she answered from inside the house, continuing with her sewing.

'Dear teapot, dear teapot,' Vera began repeating.

Curious, Grace walked outside to see. Vera was standing on the path trying to make friends with a peacock.

Grace laughed. 'Oh, Vera,' she said. 'That's a peacock, not a teapot.'

'I want him to have cuppa tea.' Vera's little face was serious. 'But he won't come.'

'I don't think birds drink tea, but have a party with your doll. She will like that.'

Vera smiled and nodded. 'Yes, she likes cake too.'

Grace went back to her sewing, but a few minutes later Vera came inside. The celluloid body of her doll had come apart.

'My dolly's broken.' In tears, she held the pieces up for Grace to see.

'Take it to Dadda, sweetie,' Grace said. 'He'll fix it for you.'

Archie worked on the doll, then handed it back to Vera, the surgery a success.

In wonder, Vera looked down at her doll then back up at Archie. To her, he had performed the impossible. 'T'ank you, Dadda,' she said. 'I go outside now.'

'That's good. Show your doll the flowers in the garden,' Archie said.

A little later, Vera was back, clutching a flower. Archie could see that her small fist had crushed and bent the thin stem.

'Is that for me?' he asked.

Vera nodded. 'Dadda mend it,' she said, holding it up, her face bright with confidence.

'No. Sorry, dear, there are some things Dadda can't mend.' Archie could see the disappointment in her eyes. 'Come on outside and we'll see what Frank and Lily are doing,' he said, picking her up.

Outside, Frank and Lily were jumping around in excited

laughter. They had brought Danny the calf into the garden and harnessed him with a rope to pull their little wooden cart filled with toys.

Danny leapt forward, bounding and bucking, leaving a trail of toys scattered behind him.

Archie laughed, and Vera, forgetting the broken flower, shouted in joy. Grace, hearing the hilarity, hurried out to join the fun.

When Danny slowed down, Archie freed him from the rope and guided him back into the field.

Later, Archie told Robert Ashton about it the next time he visited them in Gopiganj. 'How I wish I'd had my camera,' he said. The doctor laughed.

The McMillan family always looked forward to Robert's visits. He had a great sense of humour.

'Come and get settled in,' Archie said as the two men headed towards the bungalow.

The guest bedroom had an adjoining bathroom. There was no running water and the bathtub and basin were not plumbed but Doctor Ashton was used to that.

He was surprised, though, when he walked into the bathroom this time. The tub, basin, soap dish and chair were gone, replaced with the equivalent doll's furniture.

Suppressed giggles floated down the hall from the playroom.

Gathering up the tiny furniture, he headed down the hall. In the playroom doorway, Frank and Lily began bouncing with laughter, eyes shining in mischief. Behind them, Robert could see the displaced items from the bathroom.

'Oh dear, I must have grown really big today because I can't fit into these at all,' he said, handing them the toys.

War: From Gopiganj to France

On 7 May 1915 the Germans torpedoed and sank the passenger liner *Lusitania* with a loss of 1,198 lives. The Germans often bombed London too. It was a dangerous time for anyone in Europe.

In Nainital, Grace prayed for the affected families and for an end to the fighting. She knew Archie would be praying in Gopiganj.

They were also praying for Ramswarup's family situation. The Brahmin had often talked to his family about his faith in God, but none of them wanted to join him in his new faith.

'I would love to declare my faith in Yishu by being baptised,' he told Archie, 'but I don't want my wife ostracised by the community because of me.'

'Does she want to become a Christian?'

'I've talked about it with her many times. She would follow me into baptism because I am her husband, but she would still hold her Hindu beliefs. That's not what baptism is.'

'No, it's not. God will give you wisdom and show you what to do.'

The situation came to a head when a rumour began spreading through the district. 'Ramswarup is getting baptised a Christian!' Hindus huddled in horrified groups as they passed on the story.

The Brahmin community arranged a meeting, asking fervent Hindu pandits, lawyers and debaters to come and dissuade him.

Archie was away at a distant village when news of the meeting reached him. Leaving immediately with two Indian preachers, he arrived just in time for the gathering.

A large crowd from nearby towns and villages packed together, eager to see what would happen.

The Hindu debaters spoke first, attacking the teaching of the Bible and Jesus' character.

Archie responded, pointing out the flaws in their arguments, and the Indian preachers joined in the discussion.

The debate continued for three hours. The audience, sitting in fascinated silence, listened as the Hindu debaters shouted abuse; in contrast, Archie and the preachers kept their cool.

At last Pandit Ramswarup raised his hand, and the debate stopped. He began to speak for the first time.

'I have listened to both sides of the argument,' he said. 'I've heard the Hindu debaters ridicule Yishu, my Saviour and Friend, and I will not listen to further insults.'

The crowd stared at him in astonishment.

'Yes, I am a Christian. I've been baptised by the Spirit, and tomorrow,' he paused, looking around the room at everyone, 'I am getting baptised by water.'

Calling to his eldest adult son, he gave him the keys to his property and all his money. 'The farm is yours,' he said. 'Take care of your mother.'

He turned and followed Archie and the two preachers out into the twilight to the mission compound.

'Not only was it the way the Hindu debaters ridiculed Yishu that persuaded me to make my decision public,' he told them. 'It was the way you answered all the points raised in a considerate way. You didn't attack the Hindu gods once.'

'We were privileged to be able to support you,' Archie said. 'I think showing them the love of God leaves a far more powerful impression than attacking what they believe.'

'That's what always drew me to God when you talked with me,' Ramswarup agreed.

Early next morning, he was baptised.

Furious Brahmins pledged an oath with the debaters that they would persuade him back within a month.

Then a plot to kill Ramswarup was discovered and it became too dangerous for him to stay.

Archie quickly weighed up the options and made a decision. 'Here, take this train ticket,' he said to him. 'Go up to the mountains to the mission compound for a few weeks. I'll let you know when things have calmed down here.'

'Thank you, my good friend. God bless you,' Ramswarup said, and he was gone.

When he returned months later the death threats had subsided but old friends ignored him. Shopkeepers or stall owners he'd known for years hurled abuse, refusing to deal with him.

Pandits – scholars and experts in Indian law and philosophy like Ramswarup himself had been – came to argue with him, to turn him back to Hinduism.

They made no headway.

'I once was blind to the truth but now I see,' Ramswarup told them all.

Stumped for an answer, they accused him of receiving a large salary from the mission. 'What is the missionary paying you to say these things?' they asked.

'Nothing at all,' he explained.

Incredulous, the pandits left and spread the story through the district. Ramswarup had been a well-off farmer and landowner but now he lived in a one-roomed cottage and grew crops on mission land. It was all because he wanted to be a Christian like the sahib. He must have gone mad.

Archie often visited the low caste villagers in the area. He brought medical supplies, listened to their problems and helped whenever he could. They knew him as a friend, and sometimes Ramswarup accompanied him.

As a Brahmin, they expected Ramswarup to ignore or abuse

them the way all Brahmins did. It made a huge impression when he, like Archie, sat down with them as a friend on the dirt floor. He listened to them and did what he could to alleviate their desperate need.

'I haven't any silver or gold to give you,' he said to them, quoting Peter in the book of Acts in the Bible, 'but I'll give you what I do have.'

He invited them to his home in the evenings, reading to them from the Bible about Jesus and singing Christian bhajans like this one translated into English:

All days do not pass alike.
Sometimes there is sunshine,
Sometimes shade.
Just as the colour of the clouds,
So this world goes on changing.

Whether kings or subjects,
Rich or poor,
This is the common lot of all.
In this world we sometimes have tears,
And sometimes laughter,

Just like the waves of the ocean.
But often men in the middle of this great sea
Forget the pearl of salvation.
Think, O my soul, in this changeable world
Who will have mercy and save you?

The merciful and compassionate Jesus,
He will carry you across this perilous sea.

Make sincere faith your anchor and Christ the shore.
Remain always his faithful servant
And there will be nothing to fear.

※

For Grace and Archie, news of the Indian troops in France was distressing. Many soldiers fled the battlefield before the infantry divisions had withdrawn to Egypt.

The only sections of the Indian Army left on the Western Front were the two cavalry divisions. Sometimes during the war, they served in the trenches as infantry. The Indian Labour Corps was there too.

After many hours of preparation, the day arrived for the McMillans to travel back to England at the end of 1915.

Indian friends gathered at the station to say goodbye. Some of them were crying.

Lily smiled at them. 'Don't cry,' she said. 'We'll be back tomorrow.'

She had no idea it would be three long years before they returned to India.

During the sea voyage to England, they risked the constant danger of German torpedoes. The *Lusitania* tragedy was still fresh in passengers' memories. Some of the people on board often talked about their fear.

'Why are the people afraid?' Frank asked Grace and Archie in childish logic. 'This boat hasn't sunk yet so why should it do so now?'

Grace hid a smile. 'You've got a point,' she answered. 'No, it doesn't help to worry about things that may never happen. Remember, God is always with us.'

'Will we see Grandpa and Aunty Jessie when we are in England?' Lily asked, 'and Aunty Elsie and Uncle Jim?' She knew there were two cousins to meet for the first time too. Ronald was six but Sheila was little, only a year old.

'Yes, we will see them all,' Archie said. It was a joy just to think of seeing his father and sisters. 'We are going to stay in Grandpa's house.'

'And when we get there, we're going to see Aunty Jessie on England's verandah,' Vera piped up. She knew visitors always came onto the verandah in Gopiganj and her family went out to meet them.

'They'll meet us,' Archie told her, unable to hide his laughter. 'But Grandpa's house doesn't have a verandah like our house in Gopiganj. It's different there.'

'Oh,' Vera said thoughtfully. England must be a strange place. She knew Frank had been born there but he said he was too little to remember anything when the family left.

'We'll visit Granny and Grandad in Goffs Oak too,' Grace told the children. She couldn't wait to see them and her sisters and brother. Harry had left India several years before and had gone back to London.

After arriving in England, the McMillans were on furlough for several months. Archie attended an LMS summer school in Cirencester, and the family had a holiday in Hastings with Grandpa John and Aunty Jessie.

Grace was pregnant again.

Archie was thrilled when she told him. 'Our baby's due in April next year,' she said. 'A spring baby. Wouldn't it be wonderful if the war was over by then?'

But the war wasn't over when baby Constance Elizabeth was born on 24 April 1917. Friends and family visited Grace,

War: From Gopiganj to France

bringing her bunches of daffodils. Some brought small bags of potatoes, which were hard to get hold of during the war, and Grace was grateful.

In May 1917, Archie left to serve in the YMCA. He was placed with the Indian Labour Corps in France. As well as speaking Hindi fluently, he knew a lot of Urdu and was invaluable as an interpreter for the British.

A photo of him wearing his uniform and YMCA cap was taken at Albert, France. Behind the British lines for much of the war, the town had a casualty clearing station hospital, receiving the wounded from field ambulances at the battlefront. It was often a tragic place to be.

Among the Indian troops there were about 2,000 Indian Christians in that area and in the Somme. Apart from the Labour Corps, Indians had taken part in the Battle of the Somme from 1 July to 18 November 1916 and were involved in several other significant battles.

Another photo of Archie on a carte postale shows him in an Indian outfit, ready to give a lecture in Hindi in France. His silk turban, made in Benares, was a gift from the church in Gopiganj.

Letters from his family were precious. Archie read them again and again when he was off duty.

Grace's brother Harry was also in France serving in the YMCA. About 20 years later when he wrote his autobiography *Harry: The Unknown Man*, he wrote a little about the Indian troops in the First World War:

> My next charge was Camp Carcassonne, adjoining Camp Santi, an Indian camp. Shiploads of Indian troops left Bombay for France, and in early 1915 Mr E. C. Carter, Secretary of the YMCA in India, also left Bombay with a

large party to work amongst their compatriots in the different fields of war.

Santi was one of the camps established as a result of these reinforcements; and a very fine camp it was, with every convenience and contrivance for Indians of whatever caste.

Some were splendid actors, and among their recreations I used to witness wonderful performances of Indian drama.

So far as the YMCA work in France was concerned, the Indian and the English sections became merged into one, operating wherever there was need, even at times close to the fighting lines.

Like Harry, Archie no doubt moved from place to place as the battle dictated. Harry's report continued:

After a while I took charge of our work at Camp La Valentine. Here we had some of the crack regiments from India including the Punjab Lancers, said to be amongst the finest horsemen in the world.

The YMCA hut was the rendezvous of all castes and always agog with joy and activity. The lower castes used to sit around the gramophone in the larger hall and listen with rapt attention to bhajans in their mother tongue; whilst the higher castes would use the smaller hall for reading, recreation, etc.

Life in this camp was very interesting for one who already had Indian experience; in fact considering the hilly surroundings and the congenial climate in summer, it was like being in India itself; but unfortunately quite a number of those in the lower castes succumbed to the rigours of the severe winters experienced in those parts.

Chapter 11

The McMillan Children in Wartime London

In London, Grace and the children settled into life with Grandpa John and Aunty Jessie.

The Germans bombed the city at any time, day or night.

During a particularly severe raid one night, Grace hurried downstairs to comfort the children.

'I'm alright now Mummy,' Frank told her. 'The loud noise of the gun outside woke me up so suddenly and made me tremble. So I asked God to take all the fear away, and he came *quite* close to me and my trembling stopped at once.'

'So you're not frightened now, dear?' Grace asked, giving him a hug. 'God helps me too so I know we can trust him to be with us.'

She looked in at Lily and Vera. They were both asleep. It amazed her how they could sleep during a raid.

'If the gun goes off outside our house at night and wakes me up,' Lily had told her, 'I just go off to sleep again.'

Vera was too young to understand the damage and loss of life the bombs caused. One day at the beginning of an air raid, she was playing in the garden.

Grace went out to her. 'Come inside, Vera,' she called. It's an air raid!'

'May I finish this game first?' Vera asked. 'When I see one

of the planes just going to drop a bomb on me, then I'll run in quickly.'

'No, come in now, love,' Grace told her. 'Everyone else is inside.'

Grace included the incident in her letter to Archie to cheer him, along with what their little daughter had told her on Sunday. Vera had been to Sunday school, and later at home Grace asked her what she'd learned.

'We had the story about Jesus calming the storm,' Vera said, full of enthusiasm. 'And in the boat were John and Peter Pan.'

※

Later that year, Frank joined the Boy Scouts.

'I'm so pleased the scoutmaster said I could, even though I'm only ten,' he told the family. 'It's because I'm tall.'

'Yes, you're taller than me, now,' Aunty Jessie said. She was just a little lady.

'Well, my grandson's a scout now,' Grandpa said. 'And to think when you went to India you were just a wee bairn.'

Frank grinned at him, not sure of how to answer.

'Yes, he's grown some since then,' Grace said, remembering. Turning to Frank, she added, 'You're really enjoying scouts, aren't you?'

'Yes, I am. On Saturdays we get a cart and buy supplies for that big convalescent home for wounded soldiers.' Frank paused for a moment, proud to be doing something for the war effort.

'You boys push the cart up that long hill?'

'Sure. Then we prepare vegetables and do lots of other jobs.'

'That's a really practical way to help,' Grace encouraged him. 'The soldiers would be pleased to see you boys too.'

Frank nodded. 'Yeah, I talk to some of them and try to cheer them up. And Matron says she wouldn't know what she'd do without us.'

'And she'd be right,' Grace smiled at him. 'I wouldn't know what to do without you either.'

Some weeks later, Frank came home excited. 'Mummy, the scout bugler is going away and the scoutmaster said I can be the club bugler. May I?'

This was something Grandpa, Grace, and Aunty Jessie needed to agree on. Frank would be practising a lot at home.

'Go for it,' Grandpa said. 'What do you think, Grace?'

'It's an honour for you, Frank. Maybe in fine weather you could practise in the garden.'

'It might make the flowers grow tall too,' Aunty Jessie said.

Frank laughed. A few days later he brought the silver-plated bugle home and began practising.

A few minutes later a nurse came over from next door. 'Please tell your boy to stop that noise,' she demanded. 'It's annoying my patient.'

Another neighbour came over with a similar complaint.

Frank's face fell with disappointment. 'So I can't play anymore?' he asked Grace.

'Keep practising,' she said. 'Why not go across the fields behind our house and play under the trees instead?'

'Thanks Mummy, I will.' Frank raced off in relief, clutching the bugle and his music.

Grace could hear him playing in the distance. As the days went by, she noted his steady improvement until he could play well. The scouts had no complaints about the youngest member of their troop.

For Christmas 1917, Archie sent postcards to all the family.

Vera was delighted. 'Look,' she said, holding her card up for everyone to see. 'It's got butterflies on.'

'Yes, two of them have Union Jack flags on their wings,' Aunty Jessie said.

'The other one has got the French flag,' Frank told her.

'And what do the words on the front say, Vera?' Grandpa asked.

'I don't know.'

'It says, ALWAYS MERRY.'

She laughed. 'There are words on the back too. What do they say Grandpa?'

'"In the war area, France,"' John read aloud. 'Then it says, "To my own darling Vera, hoping that you will have a very happy Christmas, and in the future, as in the past, continue to be ALWAYS MERRY, our happy little sunshine. With love and many kisses and hugs from dear, dear Dadda." How's that, sunshine?'

'Good,' Vera said, holding the card and running her fingers over the raised butterflies.

In the short silence that followed, all of them missed Archie, wishing he was with them.

Oblivious to their sadness, baby Connie reached out to pull John's shoelaces.

'Hey, you little rascal,' Lily said, pulling her away. 'Didn't you get anything from Dadda?'

'Dadda,' Connie repeated. 'Dadda.'

'There *is* a postcard here for Baby Connie,' Grace said in surprise as she flicked through the rest of the mail. 'It says, "To my dear little Connie, hoping you will enjoy your teeny weeny self and blow plenty of happy bubbles on your first Christmas Day, with love and kisses from Dad-dad-dad-dad".'

The weeks and months slipped by. Grace and the children moved to Winchmore Hill, North London, to be closer to Grace's parents and sisters at Goffs Oak. Grace hoped it would be safer there, further from the bombing and artillery in South Hackney.

One day when some children came to play with Vera in the garden, a little girl trod on an overhanging flower as she ran past.

Grace watched Vera stop and lift the flower into her hand, holding it for a moment.

'There. Do you feel better now?' she asked gently, laying it down.

※

In the autumn of 1918, Grace's father Josiah became seriously ill and close to death. The family gathered around him.

'I'd love to see Harry before I go,' he pleaded. 'Please send a message to him in France.'

No one knew if the telegram would reach Harry in time or if it would reach him at all. Permission for leave was hard to get and shipping between France and England was erratic, plagued with danger.

The message reached Harry in camp some time later. Applying for leave, he waited in frustration for days for approval from headquarters in Paris.

Permission granted, he hurried home to stay a few days.

Josiah's spirits lifted to see his son one last time. 'Harry, I think I'll be alright now,' he said. 'You get back and help the boys in France. They need you there.'

Reluctantly, Harry left for his camp at Marseilles.

On the evening of 22 October after a busy day in the canteen he trudged back to his room. A telegram was waiting.

Three stark words leapt from the page:

Father passed away.

Harry felt as if he'd been shot. He and his father had been close. Knowing his mother and sisters would be wrapped in grief too, he longed to be home with his wife and family.

Somehow, he continued working at the YMCA until the end of the campaign.

※

At last Armistice Day arrived on 11 November.

In London, bells chimed and bands paraded along the streets, followed by crowds of cheering soldiers and civilians.

A mass of jubilant, patriotic people gathered outside Buckingham Palace roaring, 'We want the King!'

It was a day of wild rejoicing mixed with deep sadness; joy that the fighting had ended but sadness for those who were maimed or who would never come home.

Armistice meant the fighting had ended on the Western Front but negotiations at the Paris Peace Conference continued on for several months.

Still in France, Archie travelled to join Harry at his camp in the south to speak to about 200 soldiers.

'Our lecturer this evening is a much-travelled man,' Harry introduced him. 'He has faced tigers and panthers in the jungles of India, but the bravest thing he ever did was when he married my sister.'

The audience erupted in laughter. Archie thought of his gentle Grace, and laughed with them.

Archie arrived back in London with Grace and the children in Winchmore Hill in March 1919. The Allies' peace treaty with Germany, the Treaty of Versailles, wasn't officially signed until 28 June 1919.

Apart from his service and victory medals, Archie was mentioned in despatches twice.

This meant that on two occasions he'd done an act of noteworthy gallantry or service acknowledged in an official report by the senior commander in the battle field. The notices were published in the London Gazette.

In 1919 he received a certificate and in 1920, an emblem of a bronze oak leaf to pin on the ribbon of his Victory Medal.

※

It would take time for Archie to adjust to civilian life. London was so different now from the London he remembered.

Grace couldn't help but notice Archie was different too. He didn't speak much about the war, but his eyes told her of the haunting memories of horror he had witnessed.

Still grieving for the loss of her father, she reached out to him with love. 'God loves you. And we all love you, Archie.'

'Knowing that kept me going in the dark days of war in France, Grace,' Archie said. 'Sharing the gospel is so important, isn't it? To shine God's love, goodness and message of forgiveness where there's darkness.'

'It's the most important message there is,' Grace said with conviction. 'Now the war is over, I know you want to speak in different churches about our work in the LMS. How about we and the older children dress in Indian clothes for the services? It would create an interest.'

'That's a great idea.'

'Take a break first, relax and enjoy your family for a while, Archie. We could all go to the zoo and other places like that.'

Archie tried to smile. 'I would love that,' he said.

Top: In Khursipar, Archie and Grace share a family letter from London. Bottom: Bullock carts in a jungle river.

Top: In Gopiganj, Frank with Babu Shahadat Masih's family.
Bottom: Archie attends patients at the new clinic.

Ramswarup, Archie's Brahmin Christian friend.

Archie on Pindari glacier, Himalayas.

Photos

The McMillan family, India, 1913. Left to right: Grace holding Vera, Frank and Archie. Front: Lily.

Archie dressed to give a lecture in Hindi to Indian troops in France, World War I. Usually he wore his army uniform.

Top: Porters ready to carry Vera and Connie in a dandy from Nainital. Bottom: Another journey down the mountain. A porter carries Connie in a back pack.

The McMillan family in Auckland. Back, Left to Right: Frank, Lily. Seated: Grace, Vera, Connie, Archie.

Elzeth and Peter with Captain Evans-Hope
on LMS *John Williams V*, Suva.

Grace's brother Harry during a trip to Samoa, 1935.

Top: The McMillan family in Fiji. Back: Archie, Grace, Elzeth, Frank. Seated: Vera, Bruce, Lily, Peter, Connie. Leo in front. Bottom: In Baihar, 1961, Archie with long-time friends. Far right: Manna Bai, Hira Singh's wife.

Archie and Grace in Tauranga.

Chapter 12

Return to India

When the McMillans left the Gopiganj Mission at the end of 1915, the Grant family came to live there instead. John Grant was an LMS evangelist and took over the men's work until November 1917 when the Murphy family arrived.

Several women missionaries, Kathleen Morris, Ellen Stevens, Albenia Waitt, Miss Roberts and Miss Stanyon all took short turns in the women's work of the mission station. One of them stayed until the end of 1919.

Archie heard from the LMS Board in London that they'd received a letter from John Grant. Missionary work had progressed slowly in the Benares district during the war years.

Now they were hoping to start a training school for the Chamar caste in Kachhwa to teach them dairy farming and agriculture. They already had land suitable for a demonstration farm and hoped to start a similar project near Allahabad with an instructor they knew who could teach.

The Chamar people were a low, uneducated caste whose main trade was tanning leather. With more education and a wider variety of skills, they would broaden their knowledge and be free from depending on one trade alone.

Chamars often came to John from villages in the area south of Kachhwa asking for assistance and he was teaching seven boys to read. There were about 3,000 people attending church meetings throughout the whole Benares district but no more had been baptised yet.

Both Doctor Ashton and John Grant were keen for the McMillans to settle in Kachhwa instead of Gopiganj. John wrote that Archie was an evangelist, spoke the language fluently, could sing bhajans (songs in Hindi), play instruments and motivate people. All the missionaries in the LMS Benares District Committee agreed he'd be ideal for the work there and asked the London board for approval.

Archie and Grace talked about the pros and cons of settling in Kachhwa when they returned to India. They prayed for God to direct them.

'If God wants you there, Archie, I would be content to go to Kachhwa,' Grace said. 'The hospital is there and it isn't too far from Gopiganj or Benares.'

'I believe God does want us there,' Archie said.

The LMS London directors also believed it was God's will. That was the confirmation Archie and Grace needed.

The McMillans returned to India as soon as safe passenger shipping was available in November 1919.

Archie and Grace couldn't wait to visit their friends in Gopiganj. Archie especially wanted to see Ramswarup, the Brahmin Christian, and listened intently as he heard what had happened while he was away.

The shopkeepers in the bazaar had shunned Ramswarup after he was baptised, but after about two years they invited him to talk with them. Ramswarup was an empathetic listener. It was well-known by now in town that if a family had differences, he was asked to be peacemaker, and he'd solved many disputes.

Political factions divided the town. Old family feuds erupted, and the courthouse dealt with countless assault cases.

The town degenerated into an armed camp. Special police units arrived to try to bring order but crime escalated.

In desperation, the town officials asked Ramswarup if he would mediate between the leaders of the two factions. A large angry crowd assembled in the Gopiganj mission compound. Armed with sticks and other weapons, they were ready to fight.

Ramswarup stood at the front. 'Lay your weapons on the ground,' he commanded.

Everyone followed his order.

'Now we can begin to talk,' he continued. 'I see there is fault on both sides. The cycle of revenge is pointless. It solves nothing, causing more pain and suffering only.'

A wave of unrest snaked across the crowd.

Ramswarup had prayed before this meeting, and now he prayed again for God to give him the right words.

'There is better way, a way of love and forgiveness,' he told them. 'It is the way to peace.'

The crowd stilled, listening as he talked. Ramswarup spoke with authority.

'I ask now that the two leaders come forward.' He paused as two men joined him at the front. 'Will you agree to end this hatred and violence? Forgive each other?'

The crowd held their breath, watching intrigued.

To their amazement, the two enemies asked each other for forgiveness and embraced.

Everyone cheered in relief, their weapons forgotten.

There would be peace in Gopiganj… for now.

At Kachhwa, the McMillan family gradually settled into their new home. A stairway led up to the flat roof, and in the evenings the family gathered there in the moonlight. Archie told stories and they sang together.

Another place they liked to be in the evening was the chabutra, a raised platform in their garden. It meant they were safe from snakes creeping up unnoticed in the grass.

In many places in the Gujarat and Madhya Pradesh areas, the Indians built a chabutra as a birdhouse, incorporating a high ornate feeding platform. Sometimes there was a covered area for people to sit underneath.

Archie liked the idea of a raised platform without the addition of a birdhouse and built a circular one for his family to enjoy. He'd bought a small portable organ and carried it outside. He or Grace, and sometimes the children, played along as they sang together or took turns singing solo.

※

Archie had brought a bicycle with him when he returned to India, to replace the one he'd left at Gopiganj. It made travelling from Kachhwa to nearby villages much easier.

He often visited the lower castes, or Dalit, to give them whatever help he could. The lowest of those castes, the Musahar, dressed in rags, lived in tumbledown shelters and caught rats to eat. Most of the inhabitants of the village were malnourished, disease was rife, and no one could read.

'It's so sad and frustrating. The name Musahar actually means rat-eaters; it defines them. They're powerless to improve their lives,' he said to Grace when he returned home one day. He slumped down onto a chair. 'The caste system won't let them work or even attend school with others.'

'Keep on with what you're doing Archie.' Grace smiled at him. 'Help them, attend to their illnesses and show friendship and love as you share the gospel. Pray for them. *That* has power.'

From the beginning of January to mid-February 1920, the McMillan family camped at the village of Bahoranpur on a winter preaching tour.

Philemon, an Indian Christian helper, encouraged the villagers to come and see Archie.

'Go and see the new sahib,' he told everyone. 'He will sort out all problems with gali (abuse), or dhamkana (threats). He is most helpful.'

Archie wished he wasn't quite so enthusiastic in spreading that news. Gali and dhamkana happened every day in the villages. He could easily be a fulltime conciliator and have no time left for anything else.

Many of the Chamar men were interested in hearing Archie preach, but a few were actually plotting against Philemon. He had a hot temper and was more of a hindrance to the gospel than a witness. Archie needed to be alert for any dhamkana against his helper.

Still finding it hard to settle after his years in France, Archie hoped for a change, for peace. He had seen far too many dramatic and horrifying events. In 1917 English soldiers at the Somme had said a conclusive military victory was impossible but with different strategies in 1918, they won the war.

He believed the approach to mission work needed to adapt too; that missionaries needed to look at their methods of outreach and change with the times. Then there would be a breakthrough, a harvest of souls for God.

He had met many of the men in the villages as he biked from place to place, talking to them about what it meant to be a Christian. But the women's work was at a standstill. Albenia Waitt and another woman missionary had joined the McMillans at Bahoranpur to share the gospel with the women for a few weeks but they'd left again. John Grant had been there too with his wife and two children, Barbara and baby Colin, but now they'd left as well.

While Grace was caring for two-year-old Connie along with the older children, the LMS stipulated she wasn't to work until her youngest was five. She talked with the women, though, showing God's love and friendship and as women do everywhere, they talked about their children.

The McMillan children thrived in the Indian countryside. Part of the day was set aside for schoolwork for the older three but there was plenty of time for outside activities and exercise.

The London climate hadn't suited Vera. She'd often had a sore throat and poor appetite. Now she was eating well.

'It's lovely seeing her back to being her old vivacious self again,' Archie said to Grace as they watched Vera playing near the tent with the other children. There was colour in her cheeks and her eyes were shining with laughter.

'Yes, it's wonderful,' Grace agreed. 'I was quite worried about her in England.'

Grace and Archie were encouraged for other reasons as well. Five Chamar Christians had been baptised and several more were keen. Soon, seven more were baptised. In addition, Albenia Waitt had organised three Christian Indian women to work in Bahoranpur.

Archie wrote to the London LMS Board to tell them the good news. There were now five student teachers in Kachhwa. Archie was teaching them from the book of Acts in the Bible. They'd already studied the gospels. It was a special time.

Their faith was real.

To hear them pray, Archie wrote, takes me back in memory to happy days among the village Christians of Balaghat jungles.*

At Kachhwa, Doctor Ashton was continuing to perform surgery, many of them cataract operations. He'd be leaving on furlough soon; his wife was already in Britain. Only one of their five children was still at school there. Two were working, one was attending business school, and their son Frank had scholarships for medical school.

Like many other missionaries serving overseas, it was an immeasurable sacrifice for the doctor and his wife to be separated from their children for years at a time.

꽃

In mid-March Grace and the children travelled to Nainital in the Himalayan foothills before the summer heat reached the plains.

---

* Quote from Archie's letter of 26 January 1920 held at the SOAS LMS Archives, London.

They rented a cottage from American Methodist missionaries, meeting up again with mothers and children they hadn't seen since before the war. It was good to have friends close by.

Poplar Cottage was a perfect name for the house in Nainital – it was surrounded by poplars on the steep slope above the lake. Years before, a hotel on that same slope had been swept away by an avalanche.

'That's why people planted the trees,' Grace explained when the children asked. 'It should be quite safe now.'

One night a storm raged. Lightning charged across the sky, and rolling claps of thunder echoed across the mountains.

It didn't wake the three older children, but Connie, too frightened to sleep, ran to Grace for comfort.

'Come on,' Grace said, giving her a hug. 'Let's watch the lightning from the back window. We can count how long it takes before we hear thunder after the lightning flashes. That way we can tell how far away the storm is.'

As they watched, rocks loosened by the downpour bounced down the hill and thumped against the house. One large boulder rumbled to a standstill outside their back door.

Thankful to God there was no further damage, Grace settled Connie to sleep and crawled into her own bed. The storm had worn itself out and all was quiet.

The possibility of an avalanche stayed in the back of Grace's mind. Panic struck a few days later when her Indian cook began calling through the house: 'Avalanche! Avalanche!'

'Where? Where?' she demanded, leaping to her feet in fright.

'In the dining room, memsahib,' he answered, puzzled. 'Always the family 'ava lunch there.'

Situated at 2,286 metres above sea level, Philander Smith College was a 300-metre climb from Poplar Cottage. Frank set out from home early each day, climbing at a steady pace. He needed to be at school by 7.45 a.m. and it didn't pay to be late.

Rounding a bend in the path one morning he stopped dead in his tracks, not daring to move.

From its perch on a rock, the leopard stared back at him.

Was it a man-eater? People died every year from leopard and tiger attacks in the area.

After a few seconds' prayer to God for safety, he walked boldly past, keeping an eye out for an ambush from the rear.

Nothing happened. He made the most of the story, though, when he told his school friends about it.

Frank knew that Jim Corbett, a wildlife hunter in the area, had attended his school years before. It was called Oak Opening High School then.

Jim Corbett was born in 1875 in Nainital, the son of the postmaster. At the age of ten he learned to use a gun and shot his first wild animal. His skill as a tracker and hunter became well-known as the years passed by. Often, he hunted down man-eating tigers, risking his own life.

Now in 1920, tigers still sometimes killed people or stock. The local milkman arrived late at the McMillan's home one morning. He didn't have much milk either. 'I am most sorry,' he explained. 'A tiger, it chased some of my very good cows down a cliff. Jim Corbett, he is coming soon.'

'Sorry to hear that,' Frank told him. 'Mr Corbett will get it.'

He didn't know that Jim would exchange his gun for a camera in future. Capturing great photos of tigers and other wildlife was a joy to him and he advocated for conservation. In 1936 a national park was established to the west of Nainital at a lower altitude in the Kumaon hills. In 1955 it was renamed the Corbett National Park.

Forty years after that, Nainital Zoo opened to the public. Both the zoo and the park aim to protect the wildlife and biodiversity of the hill region of Uttarakhand, and they play a key role in educating the many tourists who visit.

Frank's school is still there in the mountains. Like the national park, it has changed names. It is now called Birla Vidya Mandir but is still a residential secondary school for boys.

Lily and Vera's primary school, Wellesley School, was down near the tal, or lake. It is now apparently part of the campus of the Dev Singh Bisht University.

One day at Poplar Cottage, Lily and Vera came up to Grace as she sat near a window reading a letter. The girls each carried an unsteady pile of dolls along with their dolls' beds, clothes and a tea set.

Lily spoke first. 'Mummy, we'd like to start a dolls' hospital…' she began.

'… So, can we please have it in the small room down the hall?' Vera butted in.

Lily shot her a look of annoyance. '*I* was going to ask. I'm older than you and remember the hospital was *my* idea.'

'Well, *I* thought of using that room!' Vera waved an arm in the direction of the hallway to emphasise her point. An avalanche of dolls and dolls' clothes tumbled to the floor. She glared at Lily. 'Now look what you've made me do!'

'Girls, calm down,' Grace said. 'Both of you have great ideas.' She smiled at each of them. 'And it's fine for you to use the room.'

'So, we can set up our hospital and leave it there?' Lily asked.

'Yes, of course. Have fun.'

'Thank you Mummy,' both girls said in unison, their argument forgotten. Vera scrambled to pick up the things that had fallen on the floor and followed Lily down the hall.

'Let's line the dolls' beds against the wall here,' Lily suggested.

'Good. We can see them from the doorway then, Lily,' Vera said.

'Nurse Vera, remember to call me Matron because I'm in charge,' Lily said.

'Yes, Matron.' Vera giggled.

For the next few minutes the girls were busy tucking their patients into beds and making sure they were comfortable.

'We'll need to make charts to record their temperatures,' Lily said when they'd finished. 'I'll go and get some paper and pencils.'

'Shall I ask my friend Dorothy to be a nurse too?' Vera asked when Lily returned.

'Yes, that would be good. Go and get her,' Lily said, after considering it. 'Connie's too small to play nurses.'

The three girls worked hard caring for the dolls. Tiny medicine bottles were clustered on a shelf next to neat rolls of bandages cut from an old sheet. Several of the dolls had dressings.

'They'll be alright now,' Lily said as Dorothy left near teatime. 'Let's all check them again tomorrow morning.'

It was later than the girls had intended when they finally met to care for the dolls again the next day.

They stood in the doorway to the little hospital, staring in surprise.

The dolls were still in bed but they were all standing on their heads.

Vera let out a wail of protest and burst into tears. 'Who would do that to them? They'll be really sick now.'

Dorothy began to sniff. 'The poor things. All their temperatures will go up,' she complained.

Lily stood there, her face grim. 'Where's that brother of mine?' she demanded.

'Here!' Frank's voice came from down the hall. He and a friend burst into laughter. 'We thought your silly dolls looked better like that. You never know, it might cure their headaches.'

Laughing, they raced outside with three angry girls in indignant pursuit.

Chapter 13

Training for the Chamar Teenagers

About the time the McMillans returned to India in 1919, Grace's brother Harry arrived back in Calcutta. After the war ended, he'd settled back in England and began improving and expanding his printing business. It wasn't long before the YMCA General Secretary for India and Ceylon contacted him while visiting London.

He offered Harry the position of Association Press Secretary at the YMCA Bookroom in Calcutta. Harry loved India. Keen to return, he and his wife Helen prayed for God to guide them. After a lot of consideration, they believed the right decision was to go.

In 1919, most passenger ships needed to be reconditioned after being used as austere troop transports. Like the McMillans, Helen had to wait until a ship was ready for women passengers. Harry organised a manager for his London business and went ahead of her.

He worked in the YMCA press bookshop and promoted stock by attending conferences, establishing agencies in many areas, and interviewing heads of colleges.

For part of the time, Harry and Helen were down in Mysore on the west side of the country. The manager of the Wesleyan Mission Press was on furlough in London and the mission asked the YMCA if Harry could help them out.

While they were there, the first plane to fly over Mysore almost caused a riot. Amazed crowds stared into the sky, shouting in disbelief at the enormous bird.

When it landed on the Maharajah's racecourse and the pilot came out, a roar from thousands of people rolled through the crowd like peals of thunder:

'WHY, IT'S A MAN!'

On another occasion, Harry and Helen heard that some English people living close by had seen a tigress walking along their verandah. It padded into their dining room looking for food. Shutting the door on it, the people sent a message to keepers from the Maharajah's zoo. Somehow, they caged it and carried it away.

The zoo was founded in 1892 for the exclusive enjoyment of the Maharajah's family. He often travelled abroad, collecting rare animals from different countries and bringing them to the zoo in exchange for animals from the Mysore forests.

By 1920 the public was allowed entry. Years later, when India became independent, the Maharajah at the time presented the zoo to the Department of Parks and Gardens of the Mysore State Government.

Harry and Helen returned to Calcutta when the manager of the Wesleyan Mission Press came back to Mysore. With urgent matters in their London business needing attention, they sailed back to England.

Harry grieved for India.

He wrote:

My spirit was still with Mother India – her sunshine and sadness, her palaces and poverty, her learning and ignorance, her opulence and need. For there is an indefinable something, which thousands have experienced who have left her shores, which holds one as if with an iron vice.

When one has seen India's vast expanses, all else seems small; beside her matchless lustre day and night, all else seems drab; beside her needy millions, one's own little soul seems hardly worth a thought.

For months I had a heavy heart – a soul agony. My friends could not understand me. As a matter of fact I was looking at things English with Indian eyes.

※

During summer at Kachhwa, Archie felt discouraged. It was now August and the two weeks in June with his family in Nainital seemed a long time ago.

Philemon, his helper in Bahoranpur, had continued causing strife with Indians and missionaries alike. With his unpredictable hot temper, he took offence at imagined slights that were never intended. Some people were afraid of him.

God's Holy Spirit produces patience and kindness in a believer, and as Philemon was exhibiting neither and was refusing to work at his problem, the Benares District Board gave him his notice while Archie was in Nainital.

Another disappointment for Archie was that the YMCA worker with the Chamars left to go back to Almora.

The YMCA, established in India in the late 1800s, encouraged young men to develop a healthy mind, body, and spirit through Christian principles. In India they were now also helping in practical ways among the poor in rural villages.

In 1916, the first Indian National General Secretary, K. T. Paul, started cooperatives and credit societies to encourage cottage industries and teach improved agricultural techniques. These societies encouraged the villagers to unite, help each other, and free themselves from borrowing from loan sharks.

Now the worker had gone.

Archie poured out his problems in a letter to his friend Frank Lenwood in the London LMS Board. Frank and his wife had been missionaries in Benares when the McMillans first came to Gopiganj. Archie knew he'd understand.

There was also some encouraging news to tell the LMS Board.

Dhani Ram, an Indian Christian worker, agreed to take over the work in Bahoranpur. Archie would stay there with him for the first month to help settle him in.

Ramswarup was coming to stay with Archie for a few days soon. He was a great encourager and Archie was looking forward to seeing him.

In Kachhwa, several 12 to 17-year-old Chamar boys had been attending the farming school since April. Archie and two capable instructors were running it.

The boys' parents provided food, but Archie paid the boys a small amount for their work. They were doing well, learning to read and write Hindi as well as working on the farm.

They'd be planting wheat soon. People passing by watched Archie ploughing the fields near the road, using a new plough designed for Indian conditions.

Archie taught the boys Christian bhajans, held Bible lessons and organised games and sports for the boys. He was also keen for them to learn to care for poultry, make mud bricks and learn building skills. They'd already worked on the roof of their hostel, clearing out the snakes and rats which had been the previous tenants.

It was an all-round programme that gave the boys the opportunity for a better life. Archie hoped they would also turn from the Hindu gods and give their lives to the God who loved them.

In October there would be a new influx of boys for another six months' course.

A new motorbike for Archie arrived from England in June. Friends back home had contributed much of the cost. Before the rains started, he rode it along the pathways to some of the villages. It meant he no longer arrived dehydrated and tired from cycling in the heat and dust, battling against the wind.

It saved time too.

※

In autumn, Archie travelled to Nainital to escort Grace and two of the children home to Kachhwa. This time, Frank and Lily would be staying on until December, boarding at school for the last few months of the school year.

Crates of luggage were piled next to the four McMillans as they waited for their train at Bareilly Junction. Their hens, cooped up in a crate, needed a reprieve.

'Vera and Connie, let the hens out for a while over there in the grass,' Grace said. 'But keep an eye on them please.'

'Yes, Mummy,' they chorused. They watched for a while but crowds of people from different nationalities and tribes were coming and going, carrying all kinds of interesting things.

Ignored, the delighted hens wandered away…

Angry shouts jerked the girls back to their responsibility. Waving a stick, a man chased the indignant hens away from his drying grain.

A frantic few minutes later, with a flurry of feathers and apologies, all the hens were back in their crates for the journey home.

Doctor Ashton arrived back in Kachhwa in December after six months' leave. The rest of his family was still in Edinburgh, where his wife was caring for their teenage children who were attending school or university. Loneliness and financial difficulty were often the way of life for the missionaries.

While he was in Britain, a consignment of surgical equipment had arrived at Kachhwa Hospital. Kind people had organised for it to go to the mission as surplus from the Army Medical Board now that World War I was over.

None of it would go to Gopiganj. Doctor Ashton had needed to close the clinic before he left. It had helped several thousand people every year but now there was no one to run it. Lack of funds was no doubt a big factor too.

※

By December 1920 unrest against the British was spreading through India. People refused to pay tax, and school boys on strike filled the Kachhwa bazaar.

'The boys are angry that the headmaster is eligible to vote and the majority of Indians aren't,' Archie told Grace after he found out about the strike. 'They've declared they won't return to school until he resigns or withdraws his vote.'

'It's no wonder that many don't dare to vote, the way things are now,' Grace commented. 'I believe it will continue to get worse.'

Problems had slowly been building up over the years. Back in 1600 the East India Company was granted a Royal Charter by Queen Elizabeth 1 to trade with India. They traded mainly in cotton, silk, indigo dye, salt, tea and opium. Wealthy merchants and aristocrats owned shares in the company.

The British Government had only indirect control but the East India Company gradually began to gain power over many parts of India. They had their own armies to protect their interests from other European countries which vied for trade with India.

In 1756 the tragic incident of the Black Hole of Calcutta took place. Indians captured some British and held them in a dungeon where many died of heat exhaustion, dehydration and suffocation.

In response, the East India Company took over the administration of the country in 1757 after defeating Indian troops and their French allies at the Battle of Plassey. Company rule lasted until another Indian rebellion in 1857. The following year, the British Parliament passed the Government of India Act, legislating that the British Crown was now in control of India.

Indians had practically no say, either in central government or at a local level. In 1885, educated middle-class Indians founded the Indian National Conference to push for a much greater say.

There seemed to be a political standstill until 1909 when reforms were pushed through by Lord Morley, the Secretary of State for India, and Lord Minto, the Governor-General of India. Wealthy and influential Indians could now be on councils to advise British governors.

Ten years later in 1919, another Government of India Act was passed, creating a national parliament with two houses. About five million of the wealthiest Indians could now vote but this was only a tiny fraction of the population.

Indians could hold positions as provincial ministers of education, health and public works, but law and taxes were still under British control. The British decided to re-evaluate the situation in 1929 to see if India was ready for further reforms, but many

Indians were angry. The changes were coming too slowly and gave too little to the people. The scene was set for the tragedy known as the Amritsar massacre.

The British officer, Colonel Reginald Dyer,* had banned all gatherings to prevent riots but on Sunday 13 April 1919, thousands of Sikhs, including women, children and the elderly, gathered at Jallianwala Bagh, a large walled area in Amritsar, Punjab, in the far north of India. Dyer arrived with a large group of riflemen and commanded them to shoot at the crowd. They continued firing for over ten minutes, killing 379 unarmed protesters and injuring more than 1,000. This was shocking enough but what made things even worse was that Colonel Dyer wasn't charged, only forced to resign his position after an inquiry found him guilty. His soldiers weren't charged either.

February 1921 saw Archie's concern for his family's safety growing by the day.

'There are anti-government addresses every day at the bazaar, Grace,' he told her. 'Indians in British employ are encouraged to leave their jobs, too.'

'I hope our employees don't leave. They are our friends,' Grace answered.

'No, I don't think they will,' Archie said, sounding far more positive than he felt. He knew he'd feel relief only after Grace and the children were safe in Nainital by the end of March.

Reports from Lucknow told of an angry mob throwing stones at the district magistrate, knocked out three of his teeth.

It was a difficult balance for the police. They were trying to keep law and order without incurring complaints of repression. It was a losing battle.

---

*   Promoted to temporary brigadier general in 1916.

Added to this, there was sad news from Gopiganj. Reverend Murphy's wife had died suddenly and he had left to settle his children in England.

While Reverend Murphy was away, Archie took on the men's work at Gopiganj in addition to his own work in Kachhwa.

No women missionaries had been in Gopiganj in 1920 but now Albenia Waitt was there again. Dorothy Sibree joined her, and two years later in 1923, she married Reverend Murphy.

Each day Grace and Archie prayed for protection, guidance, wisdom and encouragement. They were certain God had plans for their family. But right now, they weren't sure what to do.

Later it would all unfold at the right time, but they could never have guessed how it would be.

※

Letters from England took weeks to arrive, and when one came from Grandpa John for the children towards the end of 1921, they were excited.

> My dear Grandchildren, Frank, Lily, Vera, Constance, he wrote. I am very much obliged to you for your good wishes to me on my 82nd birthday. Your letter, Frank, is very well written; your picture book, Lily, is well drawn and coloured; your poem, Vera, is beautiful, and Constance, yours also and the photo reminds me of Vera at your age.
>
> How very nice you all join in cheering up an 'old disciple'. Accept my best thanks. I feel like taking you all out to tea and having a good time with cakes and buns!
>
> I am glad to say I am fairly well – the cold has come on us rather severely. I keep indoors more.

Aunty Jessie also keeps fairly well, and goes to meetings. She is now (3.00 p.m.) at an afternoon missionary meeting.

Christmas is drawing near and we will not forget you all.

With much love, from Grandpa.

'I wish we could go to a tea shop with Grandpa and eat cakes,' Vera said.

'Never mind,' Grace told her. 'It won't be long till Christmas and we'll be going away.'

The McMillan family travelled to Baihar to meet up with missionary friends Grace and Archie hadn't seen for years.

At Christmas, Archie dressed up as Santa, handing out gifts. When it was Connie's turn to receive her gift, she reached up and kissed him, not realising who he was.

When she ran back to Grace, she said, 'Father Christmas has eyes just like Dadda.'

'That's interesting, love,' Grace said, keeping in with the fun. 'Tell Dadda when you see him.'

'Yes, I will,' Connie nodded, and she ran over to join the other missionaries' children.

In the following days the McMillans travelled with the missionary family through the jungle tracks to villages Grace and Archie remembered well.

As they lurched along in the bullock cart, a girl sitting next to Vera leaned close to speak to her.

'Tigers leap out of the jungle and kill people along here,' she said, pronouncing each word slowly for effect. 'And I reckon they'll pick you!'

Terrified, Vera's eyes grew round in fear. Was it better to scan the jungle for large striped cats slinking through the undergrowth or was it better not to look at all? She huddled down lower in the cart.

'You scared?' taunted the girl. 'Look, there's a tiger coming to get you right now.'

Too frightened to scream or say anything to her at all, Vera sat in silent misery for the rest of the journey.

All she wanted was to go home to Kachhwa.

Chapter 14

Good Times and Sad Times

During the winter at Kachhwa the children looked for different activities to entertain each other.

The older three had played tennis and badminton with other missionaries' families in Nainital and Frank was learning the violin there. He had taken up photography and was experimenting with different techniques, with pleasing results in spite of the limited technology available in the early 1920s.

The family played tennis at Kachhwa too, and for indoor activities they had a thick book filled with activities and games.

It was fun to think of original creative ideas.

'Let's write a home newspaper,' Lily suggested. 'It will cheer you up.'

Vera was recovering from influenza. 'Yes, let's!' she said, excited at the idea. 'We could put news items, recipes and stories in it. You could draw pictures too. You're good at art.'

They sat down together at the table with pens and paper.

'First, I'll put in the date,' Lily said. She printed it neatly: Tuesday 16 Jan. 1922. 'I'll put "Editor: Lily McMillan" too.'

'Write about the influenza first,' Vera suggested.

'Okay.' Lily talked as she wrote. 'Last week Rev A. W. McMillan fell ill with the hateful influenza. His two smaller daughters and his only son and heir…'

Vera snorted. 'Son and heir,' she said, mimicking a plummy English accent.

'Be quiet, this is serious. It's supposed to sound official.' Lily took a breath and began again. 'Right ... son and heir caught it from their worthy father.'

She added news about two other missionaries who'd been ill. 'Miss Sibree and Miss Waitt went to Kachhwa for a little while, but they were kept there much longer because Miss Sibree fell seriously ill. Miss Waitt returned last week to her work and Miss Sibree is greatly improving though she is very weak. She has been nursed by a nurse from Allahabad.' Lily stopped writing and looked up at Vera. 'What now?'

'What about the badminton game? Put "AN EXTRAORDINARY BADMINTON GAME" as the heading.'

'Hmm ... I guess we can exaggerate quite a bit, can't we? Make it more interesting, won't it?'

'Exactly! Write this down, Lily.' Vera's eyes danced in fun. 'A few nights ago, in Kachhwa there was an extraordinary badminton player who sent one shuttlecock to the other side of the Ganges, another right over the big mango tree.'

'So far as my knowledge goes, he must be the world's champion player in tennis and badminton,' Lily continued their story. 'I'm sure all my readers will congratulate the Rev Doctor Ashton of Kachhwa who also has a hospital and is doing numbers of cataract operations. Patients come to him from hundreds of miles around.'

'That's great! Shall we put a recipe in now?'

'Sure. What crazy thing shall we think up?'

'I know! GINGER BISCUITS WHICH TURN OUT PUTTY.' Vera looked at Lily and they both burst out laughing.

Both now well into the mood for fun, their imaginations ran wild.

'This is going to turn out to be really awful.' Lily thought for a moment. 'Alright. Ingredients: 3 cups water, 1 cup flour, 3 cups ginger, 1 and 2/17ths teaspoons sugar, 1 cup water…'

'You said water before.'

'Too bad, I've already written it down. Now what else? 1 quart castor oil, 1 ounce quinine.'

Vera screwed up her face. 'Oooh! That's disgusting!'

'Delightfully disgusting, isn't it?' Lily was looking forward to watching other people's reactions too. 'Now for the method,' she said, continuing to write. 'Mix it all together and get a thick pole and bang it out on a rolling board until it becomes rubber.'

'Add this,' Vera said, bouncing up and down on her chair. 'Owing to the ginger it is very good for stomach aches.'

'Oh no, I've got one now from laughing so much.'

Vera began sliding off her chair. 'Shall I make up the recipe for you now then?' A cheeky grin lit her face.

'No way,' Lily reached over and gave Vera a hug. 'I'm so glad my cheeky sister is back,' she said. 'I missed that when you were sick.'

❧

It wasn't long before Connie recovered too.

She loved teasing Doctor Ashton by hiding his walking stick. He pretended to be worried, hunting around the garden and behind chairs in the drawing room, talking as he went.

'Oh, no, I've lost my stick. Where can it be? Connie, do you know where I put my stick?'

Dancing from one foot to the other, Connie bubbled with laughter until he found it.

The other children teased him too. He played along, enjoying the fun.

Knowing he didn't want a cushion behind him when he sat down in the drawing room, the children invented a new game.

'Doctor Ashton, look at your shoes!' Frank said.

As he leaned forward, Lily slipped a cushion behind his back.

Hiding a smile, he ignored it.

'Oh, Doctor Ashton, look! There's a mouse under the table over there,' this time from Vera.

Another cushion joined the first.

'Doctor Ashton, can you see the hairclip I dropped?' Lily asked.

By now there were three cushions bunched behind him. He grabbed them and threw them at the laughing children.

It was the start of a grand pillow fight.

※

Several issues were raised at the BDC meeting in January.

Insurance forms sent from the London LMS Board for mission property needed filling out.

'There's cover for fire damage but what about civil disturbance?' someone asked.

A chorus of concern filled the room. Rumours of a blacksmith in the area making 200 knives for potential looters weren't comforting.

Each time the BDC met, they prayed for provision and guidance at the beginning of their meeting. Now they were also praying for protection.

They committed the meeting into God's hands as they continued discussing the business at hand.

Everyone voted that Mr Mukerji, the Indian pastor on the committee, should be instated as a fulltime LMS missionary. They suggested he should visit England to meet the Board of Directors, but some of the directors were planning to travel to India in a few months anyway. They came every few years to see the mission situation first hand.

The BDC was changing its structure at the end of March to become the Benares LMS District Church Council.

Three Indian members from the churches in Benares and Mirzapur and one member from the smaller churches in Gopiganj and Kachhwa could join the missionaries.

Archie was all for it. When the British had to leave India, the indigenous church would need to stand on its own. This way, leaders would grow in faith and ability as they learned to take charge.

There were several Indians at the church in Gopiganj but Ramswarup was the only Brahmin who'd dared to be baptised. Death threats and the fear of being ostracised prevented others from taking that step of faith.

Ramswarup continued to share the gospel with many people. The missionaries believed many more Chamars would soon have faith in God.

※

Archie heard more reports of unrest sweeping through the country. The military had taken control of Bareilly, the city where the McMillans changed trains to travel to Nainital or Almora. A number of areas in the state of Bihar northwest of Calcutta were under military control and there were riots in Agra too.

It was no longer safe for women and children, or in fact any of the British now.

After checking the prices of fares on P&O liners to London and Sydney, Archie wrote to Frank Lenwood at the London LMS Board. He asked what course the board expected him to take if they had to evacuate fast.

Before the humid heat of the summer months arrived, the missionaries settled their wives and children at the hill stations in the Himalayas as usual. Archie's family was in Nainital but Mrs Grant and her two children, Barbara and little Colin, were in Snow View, Almora.

Colin was a happy child. He chatted to everybody and porters stopped to talk to him – he was everyone's friend and they loved him.

In the middle of July, not long before his third birthday, Colin became ill with dysentery.

His mother was frantic. The Grants had already lost their other son, Kenneth, to dysentery in India so she'd been extra careful trying to protect her other children from infection.

Her husband John was in Bahoranpur when the message arrived, alerting him to come to Almora.

It took him five days to reach his family. The monsoon rains swelled into floods, and the hill roads were almost impassable. A landslide of rocks and mud came charging down the hillside straight at him. He leapt out of the way as it swept past, crushing everything in its path.

For those five days as he struggled on, John thought of his wife facing fear and exhaustion without him.

After he arrived, they nursed Colin night and day.

It was not enough.

Good Times and Sad Times

On Saturday 29 July their beautiful little boy slipped away into eternity. They buried him that day in the small cemetery on the hillside as the sun's rays flashed farewell as they slid behind the mountains.

Consumed with grief, the Grants knew they had to leave India. John resigned. It was a further grief for him leaving his work with the Chamar people he loved but caring for his family needed to come first.

Heartbroken, they made a booking to sail to England in October.

❧

Archie wasn't well. Doctor Ashton had invited him to stay in his home to see if he could help with diet and medication but after a brief improvement, Archie continued to have diarrhoea. It had been like that for more than a month.

'I think you should spend time in Nainital,' the doctor told him. 'Hopefully with the cooler climate, better food, and Grace's loving nursing, you will recover well.'

For a few days the change seemed to do him good but then Archie was ill yet again. By now he had lost a lot of weight and was weak and lethargic.

When he was admitted to the Ramsey Hospital in Nainital, tests showed he had a bacterial infection. Antibiotics weren't discovered until 1928 by Alexander Fleming, so weren't available. The surgeon prescribed medication he said would help if Archie continued to take it for quite a while.

His physical health improved and he headed back to Kachhwa in the beginning of September. But he was tired and depressed.

Grace and the young McMillans were staying in Nainital until the end of the school year and wouldn't be back until the beginning of December.

The house felt hollow without their happy chatter and activity. It seemed to reflect how Archie felt in himself – hollowed out, burnt out with nothing left to give.

Doctor Ashton and other members of the Benares Church Council agreed Archie needed a rest away from India.

They knew he'd been exhausted when he came back to England from France in 1919. Archie had then travelled through England promoting the LMS, before arriving back in India.

Since then he'd worked hard, taking on three other missionaries' work as well as his own when they went on furlough. He was disheartened; it was hard hearing of the rapid spread of Christianity in South India when most of the Hindus in the North were opposed to the gospel.

Grace and Archie had long talks together after the family was reunited in Kachhwa, and they continued praying for God to guide them.

'I think with everything taken into consideration,' Grace said, 'it will soon be the right time for our family to leave. As well as the increasing unrest, we need to consider options for further education for the children.'

Archie nodded. 'I agree Frank would benefit from a good technical school next year,' he said. 'The others don't need to go yet. After a good rest I'll be ready to come back.'

'I know your heart is here with the Indian people, Archie. So is mine,' Grace countered. 'But we both know our children can't stay and we made the decision not to divide our family between countries. As I said, I believe it's God's timing for us to go.'

'I don't believe so. Not yet, Grace.' The thought of leaving

India permanently was too hard to take. 'You and the girls will be safe in Nainital while I'm away. I could take Frank with me when I go to London and find a suitable technical school.'

'But is London right for us? If we settle there again, Vera's health will suffer.'

'What about Australia then?' Archie asked. 'The climate would suit her there. Your sister Lilian and her husband Jesse have been happy living in Sydney since they emigrated, and you'd be near them.'

'That's a better option…' Grace began. She stopped, then looking straight at Archie she continued, ' If we do go there, I may never see Mother again or you see your father, until we all meet in heaven.'

They were silent for a moment, Archie thinking of his father and sisters and Grace thinking of her mother and sisters still in London. What would they feel if Archie, Grace and the children settled in Australia?

Grace sighed. She longed to see her mother Elizabeth again. There was sadness in her voice when she spoke. 'Mother's 83 … and … I miss her a great deal. Like you miss your father, Archie. They've been so supportive of our calling to India, they'd want us to make the right decision for our children now.'

After further discussion, prayer and letters to family and the LMS directors, Archie booked berths for Frank and himself on a ship sailing to Sydney.

When Grace and Archie prayed for God to guide them, they didn't know that their lives would soon have a total change of direction.

Chapter 15

Where Now, Lord?

Like a child in a fairground, Grace's brother Harry welcomed new experiences. He sold his business in London after accepting a position with the LMS as a superintendent in their printing works in Malua, Samoa, in 1922.

He'd had contact with the LMS most of his life. Like Archie, he'd helped raise funds as a child for one of the mission's ships named the *John Williams*. He knew John Williams was the first European missionary to Samoa, arriving in 1830.

As an adult, Harry had been an auxiliary secretary for the LMS for a while when he lived London. He was deeply impressed with their work throughout the world.

In India he'd seen their work first-hand. He lived at an LMS facility in Calcutta and always kept in contact with Grace and Archie, visiting them at Gopiganj, Baihar and Kachhwa.

Over the years, the Samoans had welcomed Jesus into their hearts and after Helen and Harry settled in, they learned there was a church in every village. The LMS had set up the printing works at Malua in 1900 with a staff of three. By 1922 there were between 25 and 30 male employees from Samoa and the Ellice Islands (Tuvalu).

They printed a monthly magazine, Christian literature, a Samoan/English dictionary, Samoan hymn books, textbooks and novels, and also did job work for the government and local businesses.

Supplies came by ship to Apia and the printing works' Model T Ford rumbled and lurched over the uneven roads to collect them.

Life in Samoa challenged Helen's Western way of running a household. For instance, was it really necessary to set out cutlery in a particular order?

Harry had already begun to appreciate the island way of living. 'When you come to think of it,' he said to Helen, 'there are many of our Western customs and habits which are unnecessary. Some are positively ludicrous.'

She laughed. 'I guess you're right when I think about it.'

They both soon loved the simpler, relaxing way of life.

On one occasion when Harry needed to get to Apia in a hurry, he found the rear tyres of his Model T completely flat.

'Stuff the inner tubes with hay,' he suggested to his staff, 'and then tuck them back into the tyres with hay.'

It worked well until he tried to cross a stream.

The parade in Apia for King George's birthday gave Harry an opportunity for his imagination to fly.

With the help of several of his staff, they detached the body of the car from the chassis. Then they constructed a giant pig by stretching canvas over a wooden frame and attaching it to the chassis. Large letters, painted white on each side on the black canvas pig stood out bold for all to see: 'Mo Siaosi V' – for King George V.

Several men hid inside the giant pig, just as they did in the Trojan horse. One drove the vehicle by peering through the pig's mouth; another grunted, using a gramophone horn like a megaphone, and others moved its legs and tail.

The crowd loved it, roaring with laughter as the pig lolloped down the street.

It wasn't surprising their float won first place.

There was more laughter when Harry purchased 15 instruments and two drums to start a brass band. As the group began to practise, all the cattle in the area started mooing.

※

Before Archie and Frank left India, the LMS London directors visited all the mission stations in North and South India in February 1923.

They encouraged the missionaries in the North by acknowledging all the love and effort they'd put into their work but also had tough news to impart. The society was still severely in debt and they had to cut back wherever they could. In fact, if there wasn't a large amount gifted in legacies soon, they'd have to pull out from North India.

This wasn't a new problem. In the past, God had always provided just enough at the last minute for them to keep going. Was it his will for them to continue to struggle on in an area where only a few were interested in the gospel? The missionaries in the Benares District Church Council all hoped so.

It was with these concerns that Archie and Frank sailed to Australia. When they arrived at Freemantle, they found word had gone ahead of them and a welcome was waiting. Several members of an LMS committee met them and drove them to Perth where they enjoyed a meal and company until it was time to be back on board again.

Encouraged, they sailed out of port knowing they had made new friends in a new land. There was a stopover at Melbourne on 25 April, and Archie and Frank attended an ANZAC service for the first time.

At Sydney, Grace's sister Lilian and brother-in-law Jesse Collyer welcomed them into their home.

Jesse, a manager of a chain store, loved to tell how he'd worked as an apprentice grocer in London in the mid-1880s.

'Half of the sugar came in large blocks,' Jesse explained to Frank. 'I cut it into pieces using a chopper and mallet and then diced it into cubes. It took a whole day to cut enough to supply our customers for a week.'

'That sounds like exacting work,' Frank said. 'You'd have to watch what you were doing all the time.'

Jesse nodded. 'Then I wrapped the sugar in cone-shaped bags made by hand in the store. They needed to be rolled tight so no sugar eased its way out.'

'That would take some practice.' Frank imagined the results if the sugar escaped. 'Apart from the sugar, what else did you do?'

'Oh, that was just the start of it. Rice, sago, tapioca and currants all needed tying into flat paper packets too.' Jesse leaned back in his comfortable armchair and continued, 'Most of the dried fruit sold in Britain arrived in large cases or barrels from Greece. It was full of tiny stalks. My fingertips felt raw after hours of rubbing the fruit over a sieve to extract all those stalks.'

'You must be pleased you're not doing that anymore, Uncle Jesse.'

'I certainly am, Frank. Blending tea wasn't much fun either. We used wooden spades, two of us mixing a large quantity on a wooden floor.' Jesse laughed at the distant memory. 'I was covered from head to toe in black dust after blending tea.'

Frank laughed too, but it must have been unpleasant being covered in tea dust, he thought. 'The grocery business sure isn't for me,' he said. He'd be staying with the Collyers while he attended Sydney Technical High School. 'After I finish school, I plan to take up an apprenticeship in electrical engineering.'

Archie had plans too. After he'd rested a while longer, he'd visit churches in Australia and New Zealand to promote the work of the LMS. Relaxed from the sea voyage, he was already putting on weight and feeling stronger.

Then the cablegram from the LMS London directors arrived. It was like a blow to the stomach.

They'd made the decision to close their North Indian missions.

꙳

The LMS decision meant all the LMS missionaries in Almora, Calcutta, Mirzapur and the Benares district including Gopiganj and Kachhwa would have to leave.

It hit the missionaries like a bombshell. The prospect had been looming for years but they'd believed and hoped there would be a miracle.

Now it was final.

In Almora 70 years before, no one had heard of the gospel at all. John Budden and his family had come there from the LMS mission in Mirzapur in 1850 and after a few years there was a school, orphanage, hospital, leper asylum and a church.

There were more than 700 Christians in the wider area now. Many of the lepers had accepted Jesus as Lord. Knowing him had made a huge difference to their lives – it gave them hope.

In Calcutta and Benares State the missionaries had established schools, hospitals, and clinics, and now they'd started the agricultural school to train Chamar teenagers. There were churches there too.

Was everything to close?

Was all their hard work and tenacity wasted?

Where was God in all this?

In Australia, Archie received a letter confirming the cablegram from the directors. After the initial shock, he thought through his options. He was 40 now and had many more years of life ahead.

God could still use him to spread the gospel.

He wrote to the LMS directors to discuss it all. One of the options was that he could transfer to an LMS mission in South India. It would mean he'd need to learn a new language – Telugu or Tamil – but he was sure he could do it.

He also suggested that if the Chamars in Benares State heard people from South India give their testimonies about how God had changed their lives, they would accept Jesus into their hearts as well. The missionaries had already sowed the gospel into the Chamars' lives and Archie felt there'd be an amazing breakthrough.

Another option was that after a few years' break he could return alone to South India. By then his family would be well settled in Australia. Grace had told him that if this option truly was God's will, she would accept the hardship and heartbreak of separation. It would mean a great sacrifice for both of them.

The third option Archie put forward was that he could resign from the LMS and join the American Methodist Episcopal Mission in India. They were the mission in Nainital where Grace and the girls were now.

At the end of the letter Archie asked the directors to send a copy of their reply to Grace. He knew it was an unsettling time for her, and he wanted her to know what was happening without further delays.

Archie received the sad news from England in mid-1923. His father, John, had died on 9 June.

It hit him and the whole family hard. Grandpa John was well-loved.

Archie's heart ached. The fact that he would never receive another letter from his father created a deep hollowness in his heart.

Jessie, Archie's sister was now alone. She had devoted 21 years to caring for their father since their mother Sarah had died. Their sister Elsie and her family were in London but Archie wanted to show his love and gratitude to Jessie by bringing her close to his family in a new land.

For three months he reached out to God, finding comfort for his pain in prayer. He was grieving for his father and also for his missionary work, first in Balaghat, then Gopiganj, and now Kachhwa.

In early September he wrote again to the LMS directors. He was visiting several centres in New Zealand on deputation, promoting the work of the mission in a number of churches. The presence of the Spirit of God touched people's hearts to spread the gospel, and two nurses in Wellington offered to go into the mission field.

Impressed by New Zealand, he liked the climate, the society, and the life style, preferring it all to Australia.

He conceded that Grace had been right; it was time to leave India for the children's sake, and now for Jessie's as well. He knew for certain Jessie would never cope in India.

Through letters, he and Grace decided to emigrate to New Zealand. Jessie wrote and confirmed she would come with them.

With sadness, Archie sent a letter of resignation to the LMS Board and advised them he'd booked to sail from Sydney on 27 October to Colombo. From there he'd travel to South India and visit three LMS mission stations before travelling north, arriving in Kachhwa on 30 November.

In the future, maybe after five years, he hoped to work in an LMS mission station in South India. If the LMS directors agreed, he could stay there for three months from January to March 1924. That way he'd learn how to pronounce one of the new languages and to read and write it as well. While away from India for those five years he could practise and refine his language skills until he was competent.

He loved India and always would.

His greatest desire was to serve God for the rest of his life, doing all he could to benefit India and her people.

He and Grace, thousands of kilometres apart, continued to commit it all to God.

God answered their prayers, his timing perfect.

While Archie was in New Zealand, he visited the YMCA. Doctor Datta, an Indian Christian and a National Secretary of the Indian and Ceylon YMCA like K. T. Paul, was visiting there as well.

Born in Lahore, Doctor Datta was well-known and respected by missionaries in India. He graduated in medicine in Edinburgh in 1908, lectured in biology at Lahore and was the government advisor for students leaving to study overseas.

He accompanied the Indian troops to France in the First World War as chief Secretary for the YMCA and it is highly likely Archie served with him there. Like Archie, Datta was mentioned in despatches twice. It is probable they received recognition for the same acts of service for the British Army.

Datta explained to Archie that he'd been invited to visit Australia and New Zealand, and Archie told him of the recent events that were changing his direction in life.

Datta smiled. 'I've just been saying I'm looking for someone from India to teach the Fijian Indians about moral living. The old village systems have broken down,' he said. 'Then *you* walked in the door! Would you consider working for the YMCA in Fiji among Indians there?'

Most of the Indians in Fiji had arrived in ships from India between 1879 and 1916 as indentured workers for the British-owned sugarcane plantations, or they were the descendants of those workers.

They were indentured for five years with low or spasmodic pay, and their living conditions were bad. Women were often molested in the fields by British or Indian overseers, and illegitimate births and women's suicides were common.

After five more years the workers were free to make the choice to return to India at their own expense or stay in Fiji. Most had no money to pay for the fare home. They started businesses in Suva or leased fields to grow their own cane.

After an outcry in Britain at the injustice and cruelty of it all, the indenture system was abolished in 1916.

The Indians had come from various parts of India. Different languages and dialects tumbled together in a mixing-pot of castes. Some English and Fijian words drifted in too, until their version of Hindustani gradually became unintelligible to Hindi speakers back in India.

Archie considered what Doctor Datta had said. 'My family will be based in Auckland. I obviously need to be sure that serving in Fiji is God's will,' he said. 'But this sounds an amazing opportunity to help these people. Tell me more.'

'Most certainly,' Datta said. 'The Fijian Indians – about 65,000 of them – need to be lifted from ill-treated labourers to citizenship. You'd be working in Fiji for eight months of the year and in New Zealand for four months visiting the YMCAs around the country. You could be of assistance to the 700 Indians living here too. The contract would be until the end of 1926. Would this suit you?'

Archie's eyes lit up. 'Yes, definitely. I feel all my work in Balaghat and North India and my understanding and love for the Indian people has prepared me for this new task,' he said. 'I'll consider the offer seriously, pray about it and come back to you with my decision.'

'Excellent,' Datta said. 'I'll be looking forward to hearing from you.'

Archie left the YMCA office with much to think about. He had hoped to spend more time with his family now they'd be settling in New Zealand. He discussed it with several ministers in the churches he visited and as they prayed together, they all believed God had opened this opportunity for him to make a difference in the Fijian Indians' lives.

Archie contacted Datta with the news that he would accept the position, starting in July 1924 after his family was settled in Auckland. He'd be on the staff of the YMCA National Council of India and Ceylon but the Methodist Mission in Fiji would give assistance where they could.

☙

After arriving in South India, Archie spent three days with LMS missions. Thrilled by the amazing work of God there, he spoke at several congregations of more than 1,000 Christians in Travancore, with the local missionaries interpreting.

Gladys Harries from Archie's own home church in London gave him a tour of her school, and showed him the lace and embroidery industries where a few thousand Christian women had employment.

He toured Scott Christian College at Nagercoil in Tamil Nadu where several hundred students studied.

He visited the LMS Neyyoor Medical Mission (now the C.S.I. Kanyakumari Medical Mission) where Doctor Pugh gave Archie a tour. The hospital, founded in 1838, was famous throughout India. They treated more than 100,000 patients each year.

He also saw a girls' boarding school, and a stamped-cloth factory that employed Christian women.

In the Cuddapah district (now Kadapa), there were already 250 village churches and they were still adding more.

Archie left the area encouraged. He could see the LMS needed strengthening in the south. The Spirit of God was sweeping across the land in an exciting way.

He arrived back in Kachhwa to a warm-hearted welcome. He hadn't seen his family for months and they'd missed each other a great deal. It was so good to be home.

They all missed Frank, wishing he could be with them too. Still in Sydney, he would be sailing to New Zealand in January to begin the school year at a technical college in Auckland. Archie had arranged for friends to meet him and he would board with them until the rest of the family arrived.

It was going to be strange having Christmas without him.

Archie's sister, Jessie, was with them for Christmas though. She'd sailed from England in mid-November and arrived in

Bombay on 7 December. Archie travelled to meet her and was away from Kachhwa for several days.

Grace and the girls settled down at night, comfortable in the knowledge the night watchman was keeping guard.

A crash jerked them awake.

Burglars had crept into the house, stepping over the sleeping watchman. Two of them targeted the heavy medicine chest, thinking the sahib must keep his jewels in it, and another collected some brass bowls. They began carrying them across the room.

Just then, the clock chimed. They had never heard one before.

Crying out in fright, they dropped the chest, smashing many of the glass bottles, and ran from the unknown terror.

The startled watchman leapt after them, dodging brass bowls scattered over the garden.

'Stay in bed, girls,' Grace called. 'I'll find out what's going on.'

Vera and Connie shared a room. Sitting up in bed, they chatted in excitement until Grace came back and told them what had happened.

'Wow, it's just like an adventure story!' Vera said delighted.

Connie was wriggling with anticipation. 'Won't it be fun telling Aunty Jessie?'

'No, you must definitely *not* tell Aunty Jessie.' Grace's tone was firm. 'She will be frightened. She was worried enough just coming to India to be with us until we leave the country.' She stood up. 'Now I know this is exciting for you but settle down and try to sleep.'

The following morning, Grace sent an employee to the station to meet Archie and let him know what had happened. It was just as well Jessie didn't know a word of Hindi.

The welcome, when she arrived at the family bungalow, was

warm with affection. Jessie didn't realise anything was wrong until a British police officer arrived to interview the watchman.

Terrified he'd be punished for sleeping on the job, the attempted burglary, and the damage to the medical supplies, the Indian burst into tears.

'That poor man! What is he crying for?' Jessie asked, concerned.

'Ah, he's being blamed for something he hasn't done,' Grace answered her. 'Archie will make sure he won't be charged.'

Lily, Vera, and Connie looked at each other but managed to say nothing. It wasn't until later when they sailed from India on the SS *Manora* that Grace gave them permission to tell Jessie the story.

॥

After Archie had arrived back from New Zealand, he learned that several of the missionaries in the Benares district were either on furlough or ill. Another had to leave for England urgently and asked if Archie could take his place in Benares until March when he returned.

Archie agreed, moving his family there for three months. They found it an interesting experience, never having lived in an Indian city before.

During winter a well-known evangelist held meetings supported by the five different missions in the area.

The people soaked up the gospel message for over an hour. Some of the men joined Bible study classes afterwards.

Archie felt a deep satisfaction.

'Now there are educated men devoted to Jesus and learning about his teachings in this city full of Hindu pilgrims,' he said to Grace. 'It's not happened like this before!'

'It's a wonderful encouragement,' she agreed. 'We can add this to all the other special memories we have of India and we can bring them with us when we leave.'

'Yes, that's true,' Archie said, 'but we'll leave behind many great friends. I'll visit Ramswarup when we go back to Kachhwa to pack everything, and tell him I'll write.'

'Never feel disappointed that no other Brahmins accepted Jesus and were baptised, Archie,' Grace said with insight. 'God has used that one man in a mighty way and he will continue to influence so many for good.'

'You are so right, dear. And the work with the Chamar people will continue at Kachhwa. I'm so relieved that our mission here won't be closed but transferred to other missions. They will reap what we have sown.'

Grace nodded. 'It's all in God's hands.'

'It certainly is. I know I've made the right decision to work with the YMCA in Fiji but I still feel I'm deserting the LMS, especially Robert Ashton.'

'I can understand why you feel that way, and I love you for it,' Grace said. She looked at Archie with her lovely brown eyes, filled with compassion but with confidence too. 'I am sure you are following God's will,' she said with conviction. 'We can keep in touch with our friends to see how they are, and they'll write back to us.'

Archie smiled at her. Grace was right. Their ties to India weren't broken. They'd just be growing longer.

Chapter 16

To New Zealand and Fiji

The McMillan family sailed from Calcutta on 3 April 1924 on the SS *Manora*. They expected to reach Sydney about 1 May, and stay a month with the Collyers. Grace hadn't seen her sister Lilian for 16 years. It would be wonderful to see her again.

During May an LMS exhibition was going to be held in Sydney and Archie had offered to help before he continued on to Auckland.

On board ship, the three girls had schoolwork each day to keep up with their studies but they also played quoits and other games on the deck.

Archie found extra work for Vera. 'Here, I expect you to finish these before we reach Sydney,' he said, handing her a pile of classics he'd selected from the ship's library. 'I had to leave school at the age of 12, only a year older than you are, Vera. So it's very important to me to ensure you have a good education.'

Vera bit back her disappointment. The books weren't easy reading, and at 11 years old she wanted to join in the games as often as the other girls. Throwing the books on her bunk, she stormed around the cabin to work off her frustration before she began to read.

There were things to look forward to, though. A highlight on board the *Manora* was the traditional fancy-dress party held each voyage. The family discussed it one evening at dinner.

'It'll be great fun,' Vera said, her eyes shining. 'I don't know what I'll dress up as, though.'

'You've done so well with your reading,' Grace commented. 'What about a character from a book?'

'Red Riding Hood!' It was the first thing Connie thought of.

'No. That's babyish.'

'What about a character from history?' Lily suggested.

'That's an idea.' Vera considered it for a while. 'But which one?'

Archie set his knife and fork on his empty plate and concentrated on Vera. 'Like Mother, I've noticed that you've progressed well with your reading,' he said. 'What about a character from one of Rudyard Kipling's books?'

'The *Jungle Book* stories?'

'No. Remember our home in Gopiganj on the Grand Trunk Road?'

'Yes?' Vera answered, puzzled, not sure where this was leading.

'In Kipling's story of Kim, he and the Buddhist priest walked long distances together along that road. The priest was looking for a sacred river. Kim was actually an orphaned Irish boy brought up by Indians. He was dark and spoke Hindi fluently so no one realised he wasn't an Indian until he was older. Then the British used him to spy against the Russians.'

Vera sat forward, interested. 'That's a great story.'

'Yes, one of the best.' Archie smiled at her. 'If you dress up as Kim, I could be the Buddhist priest. We could go as a pair.'

'Yes, I would like that.' Vera still felt it was unfair demanding she plough through the pile of classics but this sounded like fun. She smiled back. 'I'd like that a lot.'

The fancy-dress evening finally arrived. The McMillan family paraded in their chosen costumes with all the other passengers.

The evening was extra special for Vera when she and Archie won first place.

※

Winter fog smothered Auckland harbour. As the ship eased towards land, it grazed against a submerged rock, frightening the passengers.

The city was close now. Relieved passengers clustered the decks, peering into the mist.

To Connie, it held hidden adventures just waiting to be discovered. Grace and Archie had told her about New Zealand. It was so different from India. She'd miss the excitement of travelling into the Himalayas, her school in Nainital, and her friends.

She wouldn't miss the snakes or scorpions though. It had meant wearing shoes all the time because she might tread on one. Her face lit up at the realisation. 'May I have bare feet on now?' she asked.

Grace laughed. 'It's a bit cold for that, love. In New Zealand it's coming into winter at this time of year, opposite to where we were in India.'

'Oh.' Connie wasn't disappointed for long. The ship was swarming with activity as people prepared to step onto a new land.

Arriving at Auckland was full of new experiences and the joy of being with Frank again. He had settled into his new school and had been attending the Mount Eden Congregational Church with the family he'd been boarding with. He was even a Sunday school teacher.

The McMillans bought a house in Epsom, naming it *Satpura* after the hill range running through Madhya Pradesh where Grace and Archie had first spread the gospel.

The girls enrolled at local schools. Lily headed for Epsom Girls' Grammar School which Vera would attend later.

Epsom Primary School had been burnt down in 1923. Vera's class met at the racecourse on Greenlane Road while Connie joined the younger children at a church hall.

'Wait for Lily and Vera at lunchtime so you can all come home together. They'll show you the way back at the end of the lunch break too,' Grace told Connie when she walked with her to school on her first day. 'Otherwise you might get lost.'

'Yes Mummy,' Connie promised.

At lunchtime when Lily and Vera arrived at the hall, Connie wasn't there. After searching everywhere, they raced home in tears.

Lily told Grace, Archie and Aunty Jessie what had happened. 'No one knows where she's gone,' she said, finishing her story. 'The headmaster's rung the police.'

'She's just disappeared into thin air,' Vera sobbed. Her sometimes annoying seven-year-old little sister suddenly seemed irreplaceably precious. 'Lily and I prayed we'd find her but we didn't.'

'Don't give up yet,' Grace said. 'God knows where she is.'

'Girls, stay here with Aunty Jessie and eat your lunch then head back to your schools,' Archie decided. 'Mother and I will go to the hall and start a search. We'll be praying too as we go.'

At the hall, Grace and Archie met with the school principal and a police officer who were organising a search party.

Grace stared down the empty street, a silent prayer on her heart. 'Please help us find my little girl, Lord.' At that moment, two little girls rounded the corner heading back towards the hall. 'Look, there she is!'

In tears, Connie ran into Grace's arms. 'Mummy, we got lost,' she blurted out. 'My new friend said she knew the way home but she didn't.'

'Well, you're found now,' Grace said.

'Remember to wait for Lily and Vera in the future,' Archie told her firmly, indicating the police officer and the principal. 'We were just going out to search for you.'

'I'm s-s-sorry.'

Walking home with Grace and Archie for a belated lunch, Connie began to smile a little. A warm, safe feeling seemed to float inside her chest. When they reached home, she began skipping along the pathway and ran up the steps to the door.

In her memory, the first day at Epsom Primary would always be an adventure.

※

'What are those pretty colours on the road?' Connie asked Vera a few days later as they walked to school. It was raining and Connie had never seen rainbows on a road in India.

'Well,' Vera said, thinking for a moment. She wasn't sure either but she didn't want Connie to know that. 'A little old man comes from fairyland and paints their sunsets on our roads so we can see them too.'

'Wow,' Connie was fascinated. In her mind, she could picture the little old man with a paintbrush in his hand.

In class the teacher asked the same question Connie had asked Vera earlier. 'Does anyone know what causes the rainbow colours on the road?'

Connie's hand shot up first. Excited, she told the class Vera's story.

She couldn't understand why everyone laughed.

※

In Suva, Archie was battling against racism.

He was disgusted.

The European members of the YMCA in Suva flatly refused entry to Indians. It didn't matter if the Indians were educated, successful Christian businessmen or not. Fijians weren't accepted either. The word 'Christian' in Young Men's Christian Association didn't seem to mean anything to them at all.

The Indians started their own branch in Dilkusha about 19 kilometres away and the Young Fijian Society had a large membership, but the three groups wouldn't unite.

Under the umbrella of the Indian YMCA, Archie published a newspaper, *Bharat Putra* (Son of India) which soon gained popularity among the Indians.

He initiated the Indian Reform League along with educated Indians, government clerks and interpreters. Most of the members were Christians but some were Hindus or Muslims. A women's wing was formed ten years later.

The league's purpose was to advocate for social reforms. One of the changes needed was to update the marriage laws. Traditional Indian marriages weren't required to be registered with the Fijian Government and Archie was concerned at the number of underage girls forced into marriage. After much consultation, the law was later changed.

The league gave practical help as well. During an outbreak of typhoid in 1925, the organisation provided nurses to care for the sick.

The YMCA encouraged sports: cricket, hockey, lawn tennis and football. The Suva Football Association was formed through help from the league. In India the year before, the YMCA had organised India's first sports team to the 1924 Olympics in Paris.

Archie felt satisfaction in his achievements despite the opposition at times.

In 1926 a government commission reviewed the education system in Fiji. The Indian population totalled 70,000 by then and 20,000 of those were school-aged children. The commission recognised Archie's extensive knowledge of the Indian people and mission schools in India. They asked for his views on how they could best meet the students' needs.

His report was added to the commission's printed findings.

Archie had continued to keep in touch with missionaries in the Balaghat Mission to the Gonds, and the LMS.

Change was underway. In 1926, the American Methodist Episcopal Mission (later the Methodist Church in Southern Asia) took over the Almora mission.

By 1928 most of the LMS mission centres in North India, including Kachhwa, had been handed over to the Bible Churchmen's Missionary Society (BCMS). No one could know then that the BCMS would also leave after India gained independence.

Archie often wrote to his family and they wrote in return to let him know about life in their Epsom home in Auckland.

One winter evening, a knock at the door alerted Grace. 'I'll go and see who it is,' she said, getting up from her chair by the fire.

'Careful, it might be a burglar,' Jessie warned, thinking of the episode in India. 'You never know.'

Grace returned, followed by a middle-aged stranger. 'This is Mr McIntosh,' she said. 'Pull up another chair by the fire, Frank, please. He has a heavy cold.'

Grace hurried about in the kitchen making hot drinks and slicing cake for everyone, and Lily got some eucalyptus for his cold.

In between bouts of coughing and sneezing into a large handkerchief, he told them his story.

'I've just come from England,' he said. 'It's so hard to find work these days.'

'Yes, it can be quite a problem,' Grace agreed.

'My four motherless daughters are coming on another ship that arrives in Wellington next week,' he went on, mentioning the date and time. 'There's no one to meet them or care for them, not unless I can get there in time. I have no money for a train fare.'

'Can we give you something towards your fare?' Grace asked. 'We'd be glad to help.'

'No, no,' Mr McIntosh said, waving his hand in refusal. 'I will walk there.'

'But it's about 400 miles!' Vera was shocked.

'Well, then, do you know anyone there who could meet their ship and let the girls stay a few days until I can arrange something?' he asked, his sad eyes appealing to each of them. 'I go to the Congregational church too,' he added.

'I'll see what I can do,' Grace said.

'Thank you so much.' With a final sneeze and cough, Mr McIntosh left the house.

'That poor man,' Grace sympathised. 'Imagine being stuck in a situation like that.'

'I'm still not sure about him,' Jessie said. 'Something about his tale doesn't ring true.'

She was proved right.

Later, a visiting Congregational minister from Wellington told Grace that when the girls' ship arrived, several ministers from various denominations were all waiting on the wharf with offers of hospitality.

No unaccompanied girls were on board.

It was a hoax.

※

At the end of 1926 Archie completed his YMCA contract and returned to Auckland to reunite with the family.

The following year, he was ordained the minister of Greenlane Congregational Church which Grace and the four young McMillans had attended since they arrived in Auckland.

One of the families at the church would later play a significant role in their lives, particularly for Vera.

The Potter family was well-known and loved at Greenlane Congregational. Back in 1910, Harry Potter and his wife Annie, along with their five children, had set up a mission. Several other families joined them to open a Sunday school.

About a year later the mission was recognised as a church. Harry Potter was the secretary. Land was purchased and a building was moved to the new site on a large cart pulled in style by a steam engine.

Three of Annie and Harry's adult children attended the church in 1927. Charlie was the organist and Mamie taught the preschool children. Ray and his wife Eileen attended too.

Mamie lived with her widowed mother and aunt, caring

for them both. On Christmas Day the whole family gathered together, including Eileen and Ray's new baby daughter.

Archie arrived to offer congratulations for the birth. At the doorway of the bedroom where baby Kathleen slept, he slipped off his shoes.

'This place is hallowed ground,' he said, awed by the miracle of new life. He didn't put his shoes on again until he was ready to leave.

Family was so important to Archie.

Over the years he'd missed out on many special moments in his children's lives. He'd missed the everyday little things, often taken for granted, that weave the fabric of family life.

Now was his opportunity to make up for lost time.

At home, he listened to Lily and Vera sing different parts of the melody in a song they had learned at school. Connie joined in as the three girls washed and dried the dishes.

He took Vera's bike apart and cleaned and painted it. She and Aunty Jessie went outside to see the transformation.

Vera was thrilled. 'Thanks a million. I think you've got a halo and sprouted wings, Dad.'

'He's my clever brother,' Jessie laughed. 'He can put his hand to fix most things around the place. I'm impressed by what you young people are doing too.'

Frank was now a trained electrician and Vera had started at Epsom Girls' Grammar. Lily had won a book as a prize for art at school.

At the end of the year, some of Vera's drawings and poetry were included in the school magazine, *Te Korero*.

Chapter 17

Serving God in Fiji

Harry and Helen Waller's story had continued to parallel Grace and Archie's in many ways. They had left Samoa in 1924, moved to New Zealand, and bought a printing business in Hamilton. Their son Henry and his family and their daughter Helen and two small girls lived there too.

Now that Archie and Grace had a car – a Ford that someone named Blackbird – the family all piled in for a drive to visit them all.

'It'll be wonderful to see them again,' Grace's joy was contagious. 'And our friends, the Clarks, have been in Hamilton a few years now. Let's visit them as well.'

'Splendid idea,' Archie agreed.

Gulielma Clark had attended Bible College with Grace back in 1902. Both women had served in missions in India; Gulielma with the Friends' Foreign Missionary Association* in the Hoshangabad district in Madhya Pradesh. That's where she'd met George Clark. Their three children, Elizabeth (Elzeth), Gulielma (Elma) and Stephen had all been born in India. While

---

* The same mission as Archie's Sunday-school teacher J. D. Maynard served.

everyone was enjoying afternoon tea, Elzeth mentioned she was soon starting a Karitane nursing course in Auckland.

'What kind of nursing is that?' Grace asked.

'It's learning to care for babies from new-borns to two-year-olds,' Elzeth explained. 'The course lasts for sixteen months.'

'I've heard of Plunket nurses,' Grace said. 'Is it something like that?'

'Well,' Elzeth thought for a moment. 'Plunket nurses have more training than I'll have. They're already registered nurses before they go on for further training.' She paused to hand around a plate of cakes. 'Both Karitane and Plunket were started in Karitane, near Dunedin, by Dr Truby King in 1907. He was so concerned about the high infant mortality rate he was determined to make a difference.'

'That is so encouraging. A real blessing that something's being done to save babies' lives.' Grace told her about her brother and sisters who'd died in infancy.

Gulielma Clark entered the conversation. 'Some of my siblings died very young too. I think it is wonderful Elzeth's doing this training.'

'Yes, a great service to others. Will you work in a hospital after you're trained, Elzeth?' Grace asked.

'I could, but I'd rather work in private homes helping new mothers. We can take charge of a household if the parents are away or if the mother is in hospital.'

'While you're doing your training, you must come and visit us in Epsom when you're not on duty,' Grace offered. 'Come for a meal.'

Elzeth smiled. 'Yes, thank you. I will.'

She came often, enjoying their hospitality, and a growing friendship with Frank blossomed into love.

They were engaged in 1928 after Elzeth finished her training. She moved back home to Hamilton and took on private Karitane cases. In between their frequent letters, Frank rode down to see her on his motorbike.

※

A number of months after Archie completed his contract with the YMCA in Fiji, Grace's brother Harry accepted the same position. He and Helen moved to Suva in 1927 after selling their business.

He soon discovered the European division of the YMCA was more interested in holding dances than anything else. They informed him that if he invited Indians to join them, they'd walk out. Like Archie, Harry was deeply disappointed in them.

The Indian group's activities at Dilkusha were interesting and varied. They had their own football team and gym, held lectures and socials, and read the literature made available to them. The Methodist missionaries invited them to use their schoolrooms and playing fields whenever they needed them.

The Young Fijian Society members also came to lectures and classes Harry ran, and they gave him a whale's tooth in appreciation.

Harry was elected a director of the Indian Reform League Archie had started. He was the secretary of the Fijian Scouts as well and wrote reports on activities in the local newspaper.

In 1928 the depression began to squeeze New Zealand and, to a lesser extent, Fiji. Funds for the YMCA began to shrink.

To help raise some cash, Harry hit on the idea of holding a carnival on King George V's birthday. Memories of the success of the pig float in Samoa inspired him to greater heights.

The local news reported the event:

> The YMCA may be given the credit for having organised one of the finest carnivals ever held in Suva. Early in the afternoon a procession, finer than anything Suva has ever seen, passed through the town and later, children's sports and amusements for everybody were provided in the Botanical Gardens.

The carnival's success boosted funds for a short time but Harry knew he needed to resign to save the organisation money. An owner of a new printing company in Suva invited Harry to take up the position of editor-manager.

They published a newspaper and magazines, mainly for Fijian Indians. In his book, *Harry: The Unknown Man*, Harry wrote:

> This afforded me greater scope in extending Christian influence amongst Indians than my work in the YMCA had done.

It was the kind of work Harry loved.

He also taught a Bible study group and they sponsored an orphan girl at the Balaghat Mission to the Gonds.

Harry, Grace, and their sister Lilian hadn't seen their mother Elizabeth for a long time. When she died, their grief was sharp. Harry remembered her loving prayer, and how she read the 23rd Psalm to him before he left for Samoa. Memories were precious.

Now Elizabeth was gone, there was a gaping hole in sisters Florence and Louise's lives back in London. They had cared for her for years and missed her deeply. They emigrated to Sydney in 1928 to be close to Lilian and Jesse.

Archie came hurrying into the sitting room holding a letter, his face alight with enthusiasm. 'Grace, John Caughley has written and asked if I'd be interested in the position of school inspector in Fiji, starting in August.'

Grace looked up from darning her stockings. 'School inspector?' she asked, surprised. 'John Caughley – isn't he the Director of Education here in New Zealand?'

'He was when I met him some time back. But now he's the Director of Education in Fiji.'

'And he's offered you a position there?'

'Yes. If I accept this offer, I'd be his assistant.'

'I can see that you would like to.' Grace tied the final knot in her darning and put the needle next to the reel of thread on the little table beside her. 'Tell me more about this, Archie,' she said.

'I want to continue to work for the equality and recognition of Indians in Fiji.' Archie settled down on the chair across from Grace. 'When I was with the YMCA there, and started the Indian Reform League, I knew it would take a long time to change attitudes. I could continue to make a difference in the education field.'

'How is the school system set up in Fiji?'

'Sad to say, racial discrimination means there are separate schools for Europeans, Fijians and Indians. The New Zealand Education Department supplies the European schools with teachers and they conduct examinations.' As Archie continued, his voice became more animated. 'Two years ago, the Fijian Government created the Indian Department. They want to improve things for Indian school children.'

'There are quite a few mission schools in Fiji, aren't there?'

Archie nodded. 'Most of the schools are mission schools. Until a year ago, there was only one government elementary school for Indians there. The rest, about thirty or forty of them, are mission schools or run by groups of Indians.'

'This position of school inspector would really suit you with all your experience of mission schools in India,' Grace commented. 'And it sounds as if the Fiji Government is beginning to make changes for the better.'

Archie nodded again and smiled. 'Yes, on both counts. Lately, the Fiji Government has opened an Indian teachers' training college near Levuka. They expect many new teachers, and the number of government schools will increase rapidly in the next few years.' Archie's voice filled with dedication and purpose. 'I'd love to be part of it.'

'I can understand. Your heart will always be with the Indian people wherever they are. But what about our family, Archie? And does God want us in Fiji? That's the most important thing of all.'

'We'll need to pray earnestly about it,' Archie said. 'If I do accept the position, I want you to come with me to live in Fiji this time. As for our family, Frank now has a good job. He and Elzeth will be setting up their own home when they're married.'

'And Connie could go to school in Fiji,' Grace said, thinking things through. 'Maybe Lily would come. She could do nursing training there. But Vera? She's in the fifth form, so she'll be sitting her matriculation exam at the end of the year. She couldn't change schools now.'

'No, you're right. We both want her to continue her education and go to university. I've always wanted at least one of our children to get a degree.'

'You're suggesting she stay here while we four live in Suva? But where would she stay?' Scenes flashed through her mind: Vera making a birthday cake for someone she didn't even know;

Vera concentrating on her Latin homework; and Vera pacing the kitchen floor, pouring out her frustrations, needing reassurance and understanding only Grace could give. 'She'd feel so alone.'

'Neither of us would want to leave her behind, dear, but we could find some kind family at church she can board with. And she could come over for the summer holidays.'

Grace bit her lip. Summer holidays would fly by all too fast. If God directed them to Fiji it would mean sacrifice. 'We'll need to commit this to God, and ask others to pray with us too.'

'Yes, we need to know God's will in this.' Archie stood up. 'I'll write to John and let him know we are considering the position seriously and will let him know shortly.'

❧

Early in June, Elzeth Clark ripped open the envelope, eager to read Frank's latest letter. His note was brief. Disbelieving, she stared at the words on the page, reading them again to be sure. There was no mistake. He needed her answer soon.

'Frank's parents are moving to Fiji in August,' she explained, still incredulous as she showed the letter to her parents. 'And Frank's asking if our wedding can be in six weeks' time so Reverend McMillan can officiate at the ceremony before they leave.'

'What? Did you say in *six weeks*?' her mother asked.

'Yes.'

'Do you want to?' her father asked.

'Oh yes, Dad, but Frank and I are still saving. We haven't enough to set up our first home yet.'

'God will provide. You'll see.'

Elzeth talked to her friends at church too. Excited, they

gathered around her. 'Take the plunge,' they all told her. 'How romantic.'

After weeks of flurried activity and arrangements, Elzeth and Frank were married on 24 July 1929 in the Hamilton Baptist Church on a rainy winter's day.

God did provide for them. Frank accepted a friend's offer of a job as an electrician in his business in Wellington.

Vera moved in to board with Mamie Potter and her mother and aunt, members of the Greenlane Congregational Church. Soon she was enfolded into the warm circle of their family.

It was just what Vera needed. Separated from her own family, particularly Grace, she felt abandoned and lonely. Mamie treated her like the daughter she'd never had.

They both shared a love of reading. When Vera began studying at university for her Bachelor of Arts degree, Mamie loved to hear about it. She in turn talked about the treasures she found in the books she read.

Mamie's real name was Mary but no one called her that. A story floated around the family about Mamie's boyfriend who had gone away to fight in the First World War and never returned. If it were true, Mamie was never bitter.

Vera lived with the Potters for five years. All through her life she never forgot their kindness.

The year sped by for the family in Fiji. Archie was so pleased to show the others the many interesting things to see, do and try.

They ate mangoes, the juice rolling down their chins, and enjoyed fresh sugarcane, guavas and coconuts.

They watched Fijian dancers and fire-walkers and listened to the Fiji Defence Force Band.

They swam in the sea and ate picnics under the shady trees along the shore. They sailed on ferries to explore little coral islands and bought coral at the wharf where tourists swarmed from the overseas passenger ships.

They went on day trips, admiring the scenery and watching workers loading sugarcane on a little train headed for the factory.

They also spent time with new friends and Harry and Helen. Harry now owned the printing works in Suva where he'd worked as editor-manager. He re-named it The Pacific Printery.

Archie was working on writing a Hindustani handbook with a Hindustani/English dictionary in Devanagari and Roman scripts.

He included lessons in grammar and exercises to practise. There were lists of useful sentences in Hindustani with the English translation and lists of idiomatic Hindustani sentences with their English meanings. Another section of the book dealt with information about Indian religions, customs, festivals and languages.

It was published in 1931.

That same year, Lily moved into the nurses' accommodation at the Colonial War Memorial Hospital in Suva. She had loved nursing from early childhood, telling the family she wanted to be a missionary nurse.

Connie, at 14, was the only young person at home now. The house seemed to echo her feeling of loneliness. 'It's too quiet. I miss the others and the fun we all had together,' she said at dinner one evening.

'I miss them too,' Archie said. 'Maybe things will change in the future and they'll be close by. For now, why not join Girl Guides? You'll make some new friends.'

Connie's face brightened. 'Yes, I'd really like that,' she said. The news she was now an aunt cheered her too. Frank and Elzeth's baby son Peter was born in October 1931.

Lily graduated as a nurse in 1933 – another reason for the family to celebrate at their home *Almora* at Lami, Suva.

'Congratulations,' Archie said. He put his arm around Lily's shoulders, giving her a squeeze. 'Well done, our Lily.'

'My clever big sister,' Connie put in. 'You know, you've inspired me to train as a nurse when I leave school.'

'Really?' Lily was surprised. 'I'm just ordinary me.'

'Yes, you do inspire us, dear! You are a wonderful nurse,' Grace said, hugging her. 'I can vouch for it myself. In April, the week after I had my left kidney removed because of that cyst, you were the only nurse in the hospital who could get me into a comfortable lying position.'

'She still tells everyone you have a magic touch,' Archie said, laughing.

'I'm just so pleased I could do something to help you, Mother.' Lily kissed her on the cheek then stood back a little. Her beautiful brown eyes filled with sympathy. 'You'd been through a really tough week.'

'I had, but I was so grateful to finally be well enough to go out on the hospital verandah in my bed. I was lying out there thinking I had nothing to do. I was being so lazy.'

'Lazy? You'd just had a major operation to remove a kidney with a large cyst, and septicaemia into the bargain,' Lily remarked. 'You're the only one I know who'd say that.'

There was silence for a moment then Archie said quietly,

'We were so worried we'd lose you Grace. But the Lord is good. You are so well now.' He grinned suddenly. 'Remember Vera's response to that telegram I sent telling her that you were recovering and felt lazy?'

Grace smiled too then. 'Yes, she wrote me that little song. It did cheer me up. Trouble was, it hurt to laugh when you and Connie sang it to me in the ward.'

'Vera's clever,' Connie said. 'She wrote it so the words infer the exact opposite to what they say.'

'That's what makes it funny.' Lily began singing to the tune of 'My Bonnie Lies over the Ocean'. Archie and Connie joined in:

> She lies there and says she is lazy,
> And lazy she must be of course,
> For Mother's ideas and opinions
> I always entirely endorse.
>
> Bring her, bring her
> Bring her some stockings to darn, to darn
> Bring her, bring her
> Bring her some stockings to darn.

By the time they finished, everyone was laughing.

'That song cheered all of us,' Lily remembered. 'And, Dad, didn't you send some odd telegram message to Vera to tell her Mother was finally leaving hospital?'

'Yes, "Happy Toes".' He stood up. 'Let's play a game of Ludo,' Archie suggested, pulling it out of the cupboard. It was his favourite board game.

Everyone was pleased when Lily won.

She sat back and took a deep breath. 'While everyone's here I want to share with you what I've been praying about lately. I believe God is calling me to the mission field in Papua.'

'That's a wild place to go,' Grace commented, 'although perhaps no wilder than the jungles of India where Dad and I were before you were born. You can be sure we will be constantly praying for God to guide and protect you.'

'Thank you.' Lily smiled at her. 'Don't worry. The mission's been there since 1874. I'm sure it's not so wild in Port Moresby.'

'I hope not.'

'And I won't go for a few years; I'll need more nursing experience and Bible training. Then I'll apply to the LMS. Pray they'll accept me,' she added.

'If God wants you there, it will happen,' Archie advised. 'They need gifted nurses like you in Papua. We'll all be supporting you and praying for God to lead you.'

'Dad and I have been praying for guidance lately too,' Grace said. 'A few months ago, he received a letter from a missionary in Benares. He's retiring through ill-health soon and wondered if Dad would take on the work. The LMS in London also wrote and asked him if he'd be willing to re-join the mission, but in South India.'

'Benares! South India! Will you go back to India?' Connie asked, wide-eyed.

Archie shook his head. 'No. Even though preaching the gospel among the Hindu pilgrims draws me like a giant magnet to Benares, we are not going, nor to South India.'

'But why, Dad?' Lily wanted to know. 'You would love that.'

'Yes, we both would, but it isn't the right place for us now. The political situation is still very unsettled in India and I believe God wants us here.'

'He's worried about my health,' Grace explained.

'That played a great part of our decision,' Archie agreed. 'It was our twenty-eighth wedding anniversary when your mother was in hospital.' He turned to Grace, smiling. 'I want to celebrate twenty-eight more years with you, dear.'

Grace's smile lit her face. She glanced at the gold watch on her left wrist, the anniversary gift Archie had given her in hospital. He'd been delighted he could at last afford to give it to her. 'I pray we will,' she said.

※

In New Zealand the sharp fangs of the Depression bit deeper. With insufficient income to pay Frank's wages, his boss had to let him go.

Frank found work digging drains, but he earned barely enough to provide for his little family.

Over the months, Archie and Grace read their son's letters with increasing concern. Archie wrote, suggesting Frank apply for work in Suva. They needed electricians in Fiji.

Frank's family arrived in 1934 and Frank found steady employment in Suva. Elzeth soon began helping the Fijian mothers with her Karitane skills.

Vera graduated from Auckland University in May, and Grace and Archie travelled to Auckland to attend her capping for Bachelor of Arts. It was a proud moment for them all.

Chapter 18

Mission Ships and a Cruise Ship

In Archie's spare time, he and Grace's brother, Harry, served on the committee for the LMS' ship *John Williams V* which was based in Suva when it wasn't taking provisions to other Pacific Islands.

The ship was a three-masted auxiliary engine schooner of 500 tons. Captain Evans-Hope and his wife attended the same Presbyterian Church as Harry and Helen, and they were all in the choir.

The McMillans went to the Dudley Memorial Church. Their Sunday school held a picnic on the ship. Little Peter, Grace and Archie's grandson, loved talking to the captain.

Back in New Zealand, Vera was now attending teachers' training college for a two-year course. During the long summer holidays, she was in Fiji with Grace and Archie.

Methodist missionary teachers from the Dudley House School for Indian girls attended the same church as the McMillans and often visited. Vera laughed as they told her some of the unusual answers some of the pupils wrote to questions on island history. She noted some of them down:

John Williams was a missionary at Tahiti. The name of his religion was the LMS.

John Williams was the man that took charge of the Pilgrim Fathers' ship.

John Williams was the 'Primeministear' who send from LMS to Pacific.

John Williams who was English man was the first man to start the Methodist Church in the world. It was very difficult.

After the *John Williams V*, there would only be two more ships named after this missionary. The sixth ship was dedicated in 1948 and the last one sailed between 1962 and 1968.

These days, Mercy Ships bring healing, hope, and the love of Jesus to many countries. Don Stephens founded the faith-based organisation in 1978 to send a floating hospital to the poorest people in the world.

❧

So often in the past, the McMillans had travelled by ship because they needed to. Now, early in 1935, Grace, Archie, Lily and Connie booked to sail to Sydney on the *Aorangi* for the first leg of an overseas holiday.

Connie was on edge. The matriculation exam results hadn't yet appeared in the *New Zealand Herald*.

'I won't know if I've passed or not until I get home.' She was almost in tears as she told Vera. 'And that will be months away.'

'I'll watch out for the results in the paper,' Vera said, understanding how stressed Connie was. 'And I'll send you a telegram to let you know.'

Mission Ships and a Cruise Ship

The telegram reached Connie in Sydney with good news; she had passed. In joyful relief she showed it to Archie and Grace. The whole family celebrated. The news brightened the five days they were trapped in quarantine because of a smallpox outbreak.

Given the all-clear from quarantine, the McMillans visited Grace's sisters and brother-in-law. Grace and Connie were staying for several weeks. Lily had already returned to New Zealand to start maternity training and Archie had sailed ahead of Grace and Connie to spend time in India.

He visited the Methodist missionaries who had taken charge of the mission in Baihar. John Lampard, who had started the Balaghat Mission to the Gonds, died in London that year.

Archie also visited his great friend Ramswarup in Gopiganj; they had continued to keep in touch through the 11 years since Archie had left India.

In April, Grace and Connie boarded the P&O passenger liner, SS *Strathaird* in Sydney. They would meet up with Archie again when they reached Bombay.

'I'm going to keep a diary of our trip,' Connie told Grace. 'I'll start when we get to Ceylon.'

'Great idea. We're going to meet up with friends of your father's there,' Grace told her.

When they arrived at Colombo, Ceylon (Sri Lanka), their Sinhalese friends met them on the wharf and escorted them to their chauffeur-driven car.

The tropical scenery was alive with colour. The brilliant green of banana palms contrasted with the darker green of coconut palms. Trees smothered with red, orange, mauve, or yellow flowers were everywhere.

Reaching their friends' home, the chauffeur swerved round

the drive, stopping under a covered entryway. Welcome glasses of iced lemonade in cool rooms with high stone archways refreshed them after the intense heat outside.

'Would you like a drive to see Mount Lavinia?' their hostess asked when they'd rested a while. 'It's a beautiful beach and not far away.'

Keen to go, they crowded back into the car.

The chauffeur drove them past well-designed stone houses set into lush gardens glowing with colour. Open-fronted shops crowded with goods brought back childhood memories for Connie. Shop owners hovered outside, ready to lure people in, just like in North India.

At Mount Lavinia, coconut palms clustered the shore, nearly obscuring the view of the waves sparkling in the sunshine as they rolled onto the beach. Shops selling lace and other souvenirs were everywhere.

'I'd like to buy some lace,' Grace said heading towards a shop. 'Ceylon is famous for it.' She found a little model cart complete with wooden bullocks at another stall. 'Oh, this brings back so many memories of our time in India,' she said in delight. 'I've got to buy this too.'

Later, the chauffeur dropped them off at the shopping area not far from the wharf.

Shopkeepers swarmed at them from all directions, holding their goods up close.

'Real moonstone necklace with real silver chain, only one shilling, madam.'

'Ebony elephants. Look, madam.'

'Look, moonstone necklace!'

'Look, madam!'

'No, no, we don't want anything,' Grace repeated again and again.

'Never mind, we don't charge anything for showing you our goods,' they chanted one after the other.

Rickshaws were lined up nearby, the drivers pestering for passengers.

The standard price for an hour's ride was sixpence halfpenny. It would only take seven minutes to reach the Strathaird.

'The fare is nine pennies, definitely,' the rickshaw owners insisted. They refused to bargain.

'In that case, we'll walk. It's not that far.' Grace and Connie set off down the road.

Two rickshaws chased after them. 'Alright, we take you for sixpence,' the drivers called.

Grace and Connie agreed but on arriving at the wharf, the men demanded one shilling each. They soon realised they weren't making any headway and left, pocketing sixpences.

That evening when the ship set sail, Connie watched fascinated as the lights of Colombo drifted away as the *Strathaird* chugged out to sea.

On 13 April they arrived at Bombay. Archie, waiting for them in the mass of people on the wharf, whistled a few sharp notes. It was a signal all the family knew.

'Whistle like this if ever any of you are lost in a crowd,' he'd told them, 'and I will find you.'

Someone called it the 'polly-whistle' and the name stuck.

Now both Grace and Connie heard it. Trying to pinpoint the location of the sound, they scanned the crowd.

'There he is!' Connie shouted. 'Let's go.'

An epidemic of smallpox in Bombay meant that only the passengers who had a certificate of proof for vaccination within the last three years were allowed ashore.

Clutching their certificates, Grace and Connie hurried from the deck and down the gangplank. They could see three Indians – a man and two women – standing next to Archie. As they drew closer Grace recognised them as friends from Bombay – two sisters and their brother – whom she hadn't seen for many years. They had come with Archie to meet her.

Before the Indians left, they gave them a box of Bombay sweets. Connie couldn't resist trying one.

Later she wrote in her diary:

> I think I'll like (them) very much after I've acquired a taste for them.

Another friend arrived at the wharf to take them for a tour of the city – the town hall, the Gateway of India arched monument, the hanging gardens and the governor's house – they saw them all.

They passed the Parsi* Towers of Silence, the high walls hiding the gruesome scene inside. 'Parsis believe their dead should not be buried but laid to rest in the open,' Archie explained to Connie. 'Men are placed in the outer circle nearest to the walls, women in the next circle and children in the very centre.'

Connie shivered as she saw the vultures circling over the building.

They drove on through street after street of massive buildings. 'It doesn't look as Eastern as Colombo,' Connie said. 'It's much drier, it doesn't look as fresh and there aren't many trees or brilliant flowers about.' It was obvious which city she preferred.

---

*   Parsee is the older spelling.

Mission Ships and a Cruise Ship

Back at the wharf, the McMillans thanked their friend for the tour.

'It makes visiting different places so much more meaningful when we're spending time with friends,' Grace said.

Archie agreed. He was joining Grace and Connie on the *Strathaird* for the rest of the voyage.

※

From Bombay, the ship sailed to Aden where the passengers disembarked to crowd along the scorching hot road. Men driving camel-drawn carts competed with taxis. A man carrying a goatskin water-bag attempted to cool down the path, while others swept up the dust and carried it away in kerosene cans.

Up on a hill, a square clock tower with a steepled roof dominated the view.

Arriving back on the wharf, the McMillans found hawkers in lots of little boats having great success selling melons and oranges. Sandals, matches, carpets and silks were for sale too.

'Where did all that produce come from in this arid land, Mother?' Connie asked.

Grace shook her head. 'No idea,' she said.

They reached Port Sudan on 19 April. Connie learned it was a new seaport for exporting goods railed from Khartoum. As she looked around, shading her eyes from the glaring sun, the dry, dusty land seemed to ache for a splatter of rain that hardly ever came.

A few Arabs spread out their wares – ivory elephants, models of crocodiles, necklaces and little figures, leather goods and postcards.

Two days later at Suez, many of the passengers left the

Strathaird to travel to Jerusalem or Gallipoli. Others were travelling through Cairo and would meet up with the ship again at Port Said later in the evening. The McMillans stayed on board to sail along the canal.

Partway through, the ship reached the Bitter Lakes. Before the canal was built, these were dry salt valleys among the sandhills. The lakes were created so that ships could pass on the wide stretch of salt water between the northern and southern parts of the canal.

Seagulls hovered around the ship. Underneath, their feathers were a soft pastel blue-green as if reflecting the colour of the sea.

Port Said seemed to boast importance.

Impressed, the McMillans took in the scene. Along with the *Strathaird*, many other ships dotted the harbour and masses of tall buildings clustered along the shore.

The family hurried ashore after dinner. Their ship wasn't moored next to the wharf but was connected to land by a long, extendable, jointed bridge that allowed the ship to move with the current.

Partway along the bridge, the family turned, looking back at the ship.

'It looks like a fairy boat,' Connie said with delight.

Lights twinkled from every deck and many of the portholes, illuminating the white boat against the surrounding darkness. The three yellow funnels, lit from the base, stood out too.

'I agree with the ship's designer that it looks impressive with three funnels,' Archie commented. 'But it's rather pointless because only the centre one works. The others are just for show.'

'Maybe that's what makes it more like a fairy boat,' Connie said.

Across the road from the wharf, the large Simon Arzt department store dominated the waterfront. The shop had good lighting and the stock was set out in neat aisles.

Grace was pleased. 'You know, I could be in any department store in Australia or New Zealand,' she said, looking around.

There the similarity ended. Staff dressed in white outfits with red tarbushes (similar to a Turkish fez) were on hand for many hours while ships were in port. Fixed prices meant there were no hassles with bargaining.

They sold embroidery, leather goods, ivory, lace, postcards, stamps and boots. Connie loved the beautiful designs and rich dyes woven into the eastern carpets and shimmering silks. Also on display were lightweight tropical clothes and sun helmets – those bowl-like hats Archie used to wear in India.

Leaving the store, the McMillans wandered through the streets. Hawkers pestered them from all directions, clamouring for attention.

'Mrs McPherson! Sea pearl necklaces only seven shillings. Real bargain.'

The salesman followed them down the street, bargaining as he went. The price of the 'real pearl necklace' dropped to only one shilling and sixpence before he gave up.

Other salesmen picked up the chant. They called out every Scottish surname beginning with 'Mc' they knew of. One of them called out, 'Lady Asquith!'

Grateful none of them had heard the name McMillan, the family kept walking. They passed stalls selling Turkish delight, silks, scent, and pretty little models.

Frustrated salesmen called out after them, 'Oh, you're so

Scotch!' But when Grace stopped to buy a Japanese kimono as a dressing gown for herself, other salesmen leapt into action.

'Turkish Delight' and 'Real Pearls' badgered them all the way down the street towards the wharf.

⁂

Connie's diary ends at this point but photos and postcards show the family cruised on through the Mediterranean to Malta and then to Naples in Italy. They went on a fascinating tour to Pompeii before boarding again to continue to Tangier, Gibraltar and the south of France.

They'd soon be in England. It was 16 years since the McMillans had left in 1919 after the First World War, and they were looking forward to seeing Archie's sister Elsie and her family again.

It was King George and Queen Mary's Silver Jubilee that year (1935). Grace remembered that in 1910 when Edward VII died, the printing firm Harry managed in Calcutta had to put black borders on all the official papers. It had been a difficult year in Gopiganj too, or at least the first half of it had been.

Now it was a year of celebration.

Grace and Archie were keen to show Connie the country where she was born. After exploring London, they travelled by train to Chester and into Wales.

'I want to show you Rhyl,' Archie said. 'Our family used to go there for seaside holidays.'

They visited Tintern Abbey and Conway Castle, travelled on the Ffestiniog Railway and tried to pronounce the longest place name in Britain.

'Lianfairpwll…' At each attempt, they all ended up laughing.

They visited places in England too – Stratford-upon-Avon,

Brighton, Hampton Court – but soon it was time to sail back home.

Archie and Grace now had another little grandson. Peter's little brother Bruce had been born on 19 August 1935.

Before going to Fiji, they stopped in Auckland, spending time with Vera and Archie's sister Jessie. Vera told them about her teacher's training course, enthusiastic about everything she was doing.

'After your course is finished, why not teach at Dudley House School in Suva?' Archie suggested.

'No, I can't, even though I'd love to. I need to do a compulsory year teaching at a New Zealand school the year after my course,' Vera explained. 'I don't get my New Zealand teaching certificate until I've completed that year.'

'Well, I wonder if you could delay that compulsory year,' Grace suggested.

'Maybe. I could ask, anyway. I'd certainly like to apply in 1937 if there's a position available.'

'I do hope so.' Grace was pleased just thinking about it. 'It would be so lovely to have you at home for a full year, rather than for just the summer break.'

Connie couldn't stop smiling. 'And then all our family will be together in Fiji.'

'Excellent,' Archie said. 'I'll keep an ear open towards the end of 1936 to see if there's a position opening up for you.'

It was hard to say goodbye again when the three McMillans returned to Suva, leaving Vera behind. This time they hoped she would be living in Fiji in 1937.

Over the summer holidays in January 1936 Vera stayed with the family in Suva again. Along with the teachers from Dudley House School, Archie often talked of the heartbreaks and challenges of teaching in Fiji. Legislation needed a forceful change to protect young girls.

Vera believed teachers in New Zealand also needed to be aware of the problems. But what was the best way to inform them?

At the end of the year, her story, 'Jasoda' appeared in the Auckland Training College magazine *Manuka*. It was a fictional story, but typical of the heartache for Indian girls as young as 12 who were pulled out of school to be married.

Chapter 19

Papua, Pakistan and Fiji

A teaching position at the Dudley House School for Indian girls was available in 1937. The New Zealand authorities reluctantly agreed that Vera could delay the compulsory year teaching in New Zealand. She sailed to Fiji, thrilled to be reunited with her family.

She moved with her parents and Connie into their newly-built home in Suva.

Grace and Archie named their home *Oneata* after the Fijian island where John Williams had sent missionaries to in 1835. The first Bible written in Fijian was printed in 1853 and a year later, King Cakobau* gave his life to God. Later, other missionaries brought the gospel to the Fijian Islands. The Baker Memorial Hall at the Methodist Mission at Davuilevu was built in memory of Thomas Baker who was killed by cannibals in 1867.

By the 1930s God had changed many lives in the islands for good.

On Bau Island, a hollowed-out log drum, or lali, summoned people to worship God, not for a cannibal feast. The stone pillar once used for smashing victim's heads against was now a baptismal font.

---

* Pronounced 'Thakombau'.

Vera knew Dudley House School was named after Hannah Dudley, a Methodist missionary from Australia. Even though Hannah had little education herself, she started teaching a small group of Indian girls in 1897.

Having a caring heart, she adopted 11 orphans and did whatever she could to help the Indian indentured women labourers and their children. They affectionately called her 'Hamari Mataji', Our Honoured Mother.

She died in 1931 in Auckland. Three years later the Methodists built the Dudley Memorial Church in Suva.

A plaque read:

> TO THE GLORY OF GOD
> FOR WHOSE KINGDOM
> HANNAH DUDLEY
> LABOURED IN SUVA WITH ZEAL AND
> DEVOTION FROM 1897-1913

The school had moved to larger grounds and buildings in 1927, not far from the McMillans' home.

Vera's pupils soaked up knowledge and kindness like deserts crying out for water. It was a punishment to send them home early. At home, they had no rights at all. Along with the other teachers at the school, Vera ached with concern and frustrated helplessness, praying that one day soon things would change.

The school is now coeducational and the name has changed to Dudley High School. On Wikipedia it states:

> With more than 1,000 students enrolling annually, Dudley High School has become one of Fiji's largest secondary schools with an estimated 12,000 old-scholars [alumni]. A Methodist

chapel close by is also named after Hannah Dudley and is attended by the Indian division of the Methodist Church.*

※

Lily left for Port Moresby, Papua, to join the LMS as a nurse. The mission ran a school and a hospital and they'd built a church and homes for missionary families.

At the hospital, there were cases of tuberculosis, malaria, leprosy, and yaws – a tropical bacterial disease which affects skin, cartilage and bones, often leading to tragic disfigurement.

Lily gave all her patients comfort and gentle care but it was the babies' clinic she loved the most. Thirty to forty friendly mothers brought their babies for a checkup, weigh-in and advice. Lily handed prizes to mothers who attended regularly and cared well for their babies.

She taught first aid and hygiene classes to the older children at the school. The Papuan Government held examinations at the end of the year and Lily was pleased when all the children passed.

The government was also paying for all the school children to have cod liver oil capsules three to four times a week, depending on the need of the child.

They were busy days for Lily. In the evening she was either studying for a language examination, or running a Girl Guides group. Full of fun and enthusiasm, the older girls practised living by the guide law and invited Jesus into their lives. The younger girls were beginning to learn about God, hearing beliefs so different from their tribal customs.

One of the missionaries, Mr Chatterton, led the Scout troop,

---

* en.wikipedia.org/wiki/Dudley_High_School

and the mission held church services for Scouts and Guides on Sunday afternoons.

Lily prayed from deep in her heart that the children would accept God as their Father and know his love.

※

Grace's brother Harry had retired in 1936 and he and Helen moved back to New Zealand. The sad news of Harry's sudden death in May 1938 hit the McMillans hard. He'd just come back from a holiday in England and India.

Memories of him were precious and the family supported each other in faith and love.

A visit from the McMillans' long-time friends, and now extended family, Gulielma and George Clark and their daughter Elma cheered them. They arrived in Fiji for a holiday and to visit the McMillans before Elma sailed to India as a missionary. Like Lily, Elma was a trained nurse.

Laughter filled the days as the Clarks joined the whole McMillan clan on a ferry trip to Nukulau, a little coral island on the reef. Back on Viti Levu, Frank, Elzeth, Vera and Elma drove around by car, exploring the island.

The Clarks returned to New Zealand with warm memories of tropical islands, fresh coconuts enjoyed on the beach, shady picnics, friendly people and the love of their family.

Some months later, Elma left her parents' home in Hamilton to sail to India, arriving in Bombay on 11 November. A long journey across India took her to visit Madhya Pradesh where she was born, before she headed to the city of Kasur. She was joining the Zenana Bible and Medical Mission (now Interserve) and she needed to learn to speak Punjabi.

Unknown to her, another missionary, Jack Ringer, arrived in India from England on the very same day. He was serving with the Central Asian Mission at Mardan in the North-West Frontier Province near Afghanistan.

Elma and Jack didn't meet until four years later at a Christian convention. After they married, she joined Jack in Mardan among Sunni Muslims. It was sometimes dangerous work.

Over the next few years, Jack and Elma were thrilled with the arrival of two baby boys. The savage turmoil of India's independence and the creation of Pakistan in 1947 would be a traumatic time for them. Later on, two baby girls were added to the family.

When the boys were old enough, they went to a boarding school in England. Years later, the girls had to leave for England too. The searing pain of long separation ripped at all their hearts, but it wasn't safe for the children to stay. There'd been a death threat against one of the boys and a planned kidnapping for the girls. Elma and Jack couldn't bear to risk their children's lives.

Many years later when Elma was a widow in her mid-80s, she lived in the little cottage her parents had owned in Hamilton. She loved sharing with people how God had intervened to save their lives and provide for all their needs.* The McMillans hadn't had to face years of separation from their children in their missionary work. The number of times Archie was separated from the rest of the family when the children were little was hard enough but it was only for a few months. They were still in India

---

* Jack and Elma's mission stories are found in two books and a booklet: L.T. Daniels, *Frontier Challenge* (Penistone, England: Bridge Publications, 1987), a short autobiography by John Ringer, *From the Kings Guards to the Khyer Hills* (Institute Press), and Donna Huggard with Elma Clark Ringer, *My Life*.

Ripple Effect

and if he needed to get to them, he could. Now in 1938 all his family was close together in Fiji except for Lily in Papua.

※

When the 1938 school year ended, Vera set out on a bus tour of Viti Levu. From Suva, they travelled up the west coast as far as Ba* in the north. But as they were leaving, a storm hit. Wind whipped the trees into a frenzy and rain poured from the sky in a thrashing waterfall. Water began lapping across the road.

Further along, the bus pushed its way through knee-deep water but they continued on to Rakiraki at the top of the island.

'The concrete bridge further ahead is submerged,' the villagers warned the bus driver. 'The water roaring across it is strong enough to roll a small car.'

'The bus will make it.' The driver seemed confident but he suggested all the male passengers stay behind while he drove on with Vera. 'I'll get the lady through to where she wants to go,' he asserted. 'No problem.'

'Are you sure?' Vera asked, uncertain. 'I think maybe we should stop here too.'

'You'll be fine. Sit on the right-hand side and I'll open the door in case you need to leap out.'

Vera still enjoyed exciting stories and now she was living her own adventure.

She stayed on the bus.

A torrent of floodwater rushed inside, soaking her luggage.

Continuing on, the bus ploughed its way through another stretch of water.

---

* Pronounced 'Mba'.

'It looks about knee-deep and rising fast,' she said to the driver.

He just kept on driving. Several kilometres south of the village of Matawailevu he had to admit defeat.

A wide expanse of water lay ahead of them and somewhere beneath the depths was a submerged bridge; or there used to be. There was no way to tell.

Behind them, the flood would now be too deep to attempt to cross. The driver managed to turn the bus and headed back to the village.

'We will be safe there. It is on high ground,' the driver told her. 'The name Matawailevu means invincible over floods.'

Vera was relieved, but when they arrived at the village, she realised the higher altitude was exposing them to the full force of the gale.

Uprooted trees and amputated branches lay scattered in the lashing rain.

The driver found shelter for her in a family home. Vera knew only a few words of Fijian. Feeling awkward and not knowing what else to do, she sat down and took out her crochet work.

The family burst into excited, nervous chatter.

Vera looked up, puzzled. 'What's wrong?' she asked the driver.

'They say you had better keep standing,' he explained, coming over to her. 'The house might fall any minute.'

'Oh.' This was not good news.

'We will find you a safer house very soon.'

After another short dash through the pouring rain, Vera found herself in a smaller bure with a friendly hospitable family who offered refreshment.

'Vinaka vaka levu, thank you very much,' Vera repeated, smiling at their kindness.

Village men brought in strong supports to prop up the rafters on the windward side of the building. Other families from unstable bures crowded in for the night.

The following morning, the storm had moved on, but the road south was still blocked.

In the early afternoon the driver came to suggest to Vera that they return the way they'd come. He'd swum 60 metres across the flood to find someone with a radio to hear updated reports on the situation.

'They are mending the last bridge that we crossed before we got here,' he said. 'It broke after we arrived.'

'Just as well we weren't on it when it did,' Vera commented.

The driver smiled. 'Do not worry. It is alright now.'

As they travelled back, Vera could see devastation along the way. 'It's amazing,' she said. 'The roads are dry now but they must have been six feet under water yesterday judging from the debris in the trees.'

They stopped at Rakiraki, but when they reached Tavua in the north of the island, they found floodwaters again. It meant another night in a village.

By 6.30 a.m. the following day the bus set off, heading back to Ba. Everyone was looking forward to breakfast.

Hope faded about one and a half kilometres before they reached their destination. A huge expanse of waist-deep water blocked any further progress.

'We will wait for the water to subside,' the driver said. 'It shouldn't be too long.'

Six hours later, they were still waiting.

Several kind Indian lads waded through to Ba to buy lunch for them while the passengers continued to wait.

A couple of hours later, a taxi driver told them about the news broadcast from the Suva radio station. The headlines announced rates of exchange, and bomb shelters in Britain, but there was no mention of the floods in Fiji at all.

At last the bus crept forward through the flood. At the highest point, water sloshed across the floor.

It was nearly midnight when they finally reached Suva.

Vera decided to write about her experiences in an article for *The Fiji Times & Herald*.

> My chief impression of this experience is the great kindness we received everywhere, she wrote, and the happy camaraderie which we found everywhere on the road.

By viewing it that way, her adventure always remained a highlight.

In 1938 Vera had returned to New Zealand for her compulsory teaching year to gain her certificate from the Auckland Training College for Teachers. She was placed at Okaihau, near Kerikeri in Northland and taught Primers 1, 2 and 3.

※

In Port Moresby, Lily was still nursing at the LMS hospital. Concerned about the number of patients with tuberculosis returning home and infecting others, she suggested they move to a ward at the hospital. They could receive treatment there and hopefully a cure. Most patients refused. They didn't want to leave their families.

The baby clinic stopped running when their scales broke. A donation of new scales from Sydney would arrive soon. Lily was looking forward to starting the clinic again, but world events soon altered everything.

Chapter 20

World War II: A Fijian Perspective

On 1 September 1939, war broke out in Europe, and Japan signed a pact with Germany and Italy on 27 September 1940, forming the Axis.

Like a deadly plague, war spread across Europe, the Middle East, North Africa, and the Pacific.

The LMS decided to evacuate their missionaries from Papua. It was to prove a wise move. Lily returned to Fiji, recording her homecoming in the family visitors' book on 29 February 1940.

Things had changed since she had left home. Connie was training to be a nurse at the Colonial War Memorial Hospital in Suva. Soon Lily was back on the nursing staff there too.

Archie was still the school inspector but he'd begun working on an idea for a small dictionary, the *Nurses' and Students' Guide to Hindustani*. It dealt with pronunciation, how to give instructions, how to ask for information from new patients, questions and advice for inpatients and information for relatives. It was published in 1943.

The surprising news was that Vera had left teaching and was now working for the Chief Censor for the Fiji Government in an upstairs office in the Post Office building.

At first, she'd been appointed as a temporary clerk for postal censorship work. Her performance was so satisfactory that the government increased her duties by giving her highly confidential and sensitive work for the Chief Censor in addition to her other duties.

Among other tasks she was decoding war messages and had taken a vow of secrecy.

On 19 November 1940, New Zealand troops arrived for training in Fiji, including the Medical Corps 7th Field Ambulance. Most of the soldiers had never been overseas before.

For Private Harold Jamieson, there were so many new experiences: the ship, his first sight of tropical islands, and walking ashore in a new land. He was looking forward to training.

As a Christian, Harold had attended church with his family back in Whanganui. Hearing about a social night called the Fellowship at the Greenery, organised by the Methodist Mission in Suva, he decided to go.

The Fellowship was for Christian soldiers and local church families and they met on Saturday nights at Reverend Green's, the Methodist minister's house. There was laughter, a great supper and pretty girls.

The Fellowship held a picnic by the sea on New Year's Day 1941. The Methodist Mission hired two buses to transport everyone to the picnic – one for civilians and the other for soldiers. Harold was sitting in his bus laughing and chatting with his friends when they stopped at a pickup point by the Post Office.

A young woman got on the bus. Whatever she said to the driver was drowned out by the soldiers' cheering.

Harold could see she wasn't sure where to sit. He also noticed her soft green eyes and that her bouncing, light brown hair, parted in the centre, was held back in a thick bob with clips on each side. She looked pretty in her light summer dress and sandals.

Patting the empty seat next to him, he said, 'Here, come and sit next to me.'

She paused, looking into the blue eyes smiling up at her. She saw in them kindness and a sense of fun. 'Yes, thank you,' she said. 'The civilian bus was full. By the way, I'm Vera McMillan.'

'Private Harold Jamieson,' he said. 'Glad to meet you, Vera.'

It was the beginning of their friendship. On Saturday evenings they met at the Greenery. Sometimes he walked with her along the beach, laughing and talking, sometimes stopping to pick up an interesting shell or piece of coral. Gradually, they got to know each other better.

He told her about his early childhood on a farm near Otaki and his family's life in Whanganui. In turn, Vera told him about her family.

Months passed, nudging and jostling each other in a rush of activity. One Sunday Harold trudged his way up Holland Street to see Vera, his first visit to her family home, *Oneata*.

Grace and Archie gave him a warm welcome. 'Come and sign our visitors' book,' Archie said.

Harold wrote '7th Field Ambulance' and signed his name. It was 18 May 1941.

In August Harold returned to New Zealand for leave before sailing to the Middle East.

Before he left Fiji, he and Vera met to say goodbye. Each moment together would be held and treasured in their memories.

They wouldn't meet again for three and a half long years. Vera and Harold continued to write the whole time Harold was in Egypt, Palestine, North Africa and Italy in the New Zealand

6th Field Ambulance. Their letters, checked by censor, arrived in spasmodic bursts. Sometimes they waited weeks for a letter, then several arrived all at once.

Included with one of his letters was a booklet on Psalm 23, complete with photos of shepherds tending their sheep in the Palestinian (now Israeli) hills.

'That's lovely,' Grace said when Vera showed it to her. 'Can I borrow it when I visit a Fijian woman I know who's in jail?'

'Of course,' Vera said.

Grace didn't speak enough Fijian to translate the Psalm, and Fatima, an Indian friend who went with her, couldn't read much English. Together they helped each other. Grace translated it into Hindi and Fatima translated it into Fijian.

All through the war, Vera attended the Fellowship at the Greenery. They met each week without a break. The group prayed for each soldier who'd attended and left for the battlefield. By the end of the war, not one soldier who'd attended regularly had died in combat or been seriously wounded.

After the Japanese attack on the American naval base at Pearl Harbour, Fiji became a strategic location in the war of the Pacific. United States troops were stationed there.

Some of the soldiers came to the Greenery. At Christmas the McMillans and other church members joined the Green family to give the soldiers a sense of family and normality.

By 1942, Japanese plans to sweep across the Pacific were succeeding. In March they bombed northwestern towns in Australia, including Darwin. Submarines lurked in Sydney Harbour.

Australian and New Zealand troops entered the Pacific War. Fijian soldiers fought alongside the Allies against the Japanese in Bougainville in the Solomon Islands.

Fiji was also in the firing line.

At the McMillans' home, Archie had construction workers build a secret air raid hideaway he'd designed beneath the house in case of a Japanese invasion. Under the upstairs verandah was a storage room. To anyone who didn't know, it appeared uninteresting. But in a panelled wall, a concealed secret door slid back to reveal a tunnel to an underground room. There was another entrance from a trapdoor in Archie's study.

Archie and Grace trained as air raid wardens. For Grace, the experience brought back unsettling memories of bombing in London in the First World War. Like so many others, they prayed the war would end.

'Come and see the air raid shelter, it's finished,' Archie called to Grace and Vera. 'Come on Leo. Here boy!' Their black and white Labrador Cross was terrified of the dark shelter. No one – not Grace, Archie or Vera – could coax him to enter.

To everyone's relief, including Leo's, the air raid shelter remained unused throughout the war. As wardens, Grace and Archie would be out and about in the event of an air attack. Lily and Connie would be on duty at the hospital and Vera would be taking calls on the emergency phone.

※

On 13 May 1943 the German and Italian forces in Tunisia surrendered to General Freyberg. The triumphant but weary Allies travelled the long journey back across North Africa to Egypt.

Believing he would soon be home, Harold wrote to Vera asking her to marry him. He hadn't received a reply by October when he was drafted to Italy, along with all the other soldiers of the 2nd New Zealand Division.

Finally, in mid-November a telegram came. Vera had sent it

three weeks earlier. She had finally received his proposal. It had arrived on 18 October, five months after Harold had posted it. On the telegram was a message of just three words he had waited so long to see.

GLADLY AGREE LOVE.

He replied at the first opportunity with an airgraph letter.
Vera's next letter arrived, dated 17 November 1943:

> Wherever did my cable get to?? she wrote. I dispatched it on Oct 18, and was told you'd get it in three days, and instead it took over three weeks! Well my dear if you had to wait all that extra time, after already having waited four months, then I'm very, very sorry. I expect you've been wondering and wondering why ever my answer didn't come. If only we could be nearer! Either my cable got lost or else you have been shifted to some inaccessible place where such things were never heard of. Anyway Harold it is a great relief your long wait is over, five months of it; but you didn't really have any doubts did you?

Harold also received a letter from Grace. In it she wrote:

> I believe that you both have been engaged <u>in heart</u> all these two years and have been wise for allowing a time for testing your love for each other before actual engagement. God bless you Harold, and bring you safely home again.

The savagery of war continued through 1944.

Connie graduated as a fully qualified nurse. Unlike Lily, she felt she wasn't in the right profession and was unsure of her ability. Career choices for women were limited in the 1940s, though, so she struggled on, coping with continual headaches.

Lily left Fiji to move to Tauranga, taking up a position as a Plunket nurse. It was a real joy – her favourite aspect of nursing. A friend introduced her to Edwin (Ted) Williamson, and Lily joined the Tauranga Baptist Church choir with him.

They announced their engagement to family and friends and made plans to celebrate their wedding on 13 January 1945.

Harold sent Vera an airgraph from Italy in July 1944, suggesting she sail from Fiji to New Zealand and stay with his parents, Ethel and Andrew, in Whanganui.

The New Zealand Government was sending replacement soldiers to release men who had been in combat for years. Harold was certain he'd be home before Vera arrived, knowing it would be difficult for her to book a ship in wartime. Delays in troop transportation meant she was there for many months before him, finding work in a department store cafeteria.

Waiting was hard. She thought of Harold enduring another Italian winter in the snow and prayed each day for his safety.

※

It was Grace and Archie's 40th wedding anniversary on 12 April 1945. Vera sailed back to Fiji for a brief visit to celebrate.

Dinner at the Grand Pacific Hotel in Suva was a special occasion. Built by the Union Steamship Company in 1914, the hotel's stately elegance was the pride of Fiji. In December 1953,

Queen Elizabeth and Prince Philip stayed there during their visit to the island.

Years later, tourism concentrated on island resorts leaving the hotel vacant and neglected by 1992, a crumbling eyesore on the waterfront. These days, the hotel's magnificence has been recaptured after extensive repair and refurbishing. A grand re-opening was celebrated in 2014 to mark her centenary.

Now in 1945 this would all be in the future. The McMillans – Grace, Archie, Vera, Connie, Frank, Elzeth and their two sons Peter and Bruce – all crowded around a large table and ordered from the menu. Everyone had made their choice but Bruce couldn't decide on anything.

Vera and Connie made some suggestions but Bruce shook his head.

He looked around at the family, a helpless expression on his face. 'Please may I have a piece of toast?' he asked.

❧

Harold didn't arrive back in New Zealand until 21 April 1945. After a whirlwind of preparation, he and Vera were married on the cool autumn morning of 10 May at the Whanganui Central Baptist Church.

Lily was Vera's matron of honour. Grace and Archie had wanted to be present but it wasn't possible. They'd come over to New Zealand for Lily's wedding in January and thought they'd be attending Vera's wedding as well. Everyone had expected Harold to be home by Christmas.

But he was home at last, and their wedding was a day to celebrate. In fact, Vera and Harold felt the whole town was celebrating with them. Flags and bunting were everywhere, decorating streets and buildings after Victory in Europe Day just two days before.

Then, on 15 August they celebrated Victory in Japan Day. The war was over.

Chapter 21

India 1947:
The Political Earthquake

Vera and Harold's baby daughter Margaret was born on 17 February 1947. She was Grace and Archie's first granddaughter.

Frank and Elzeth had moved back to New Zealand and were living in New Plymouth. Elzeth was pregnant again and the baby was due in June. In Tauranga, Lily and Ted's baby was due in July.

They were all joys for the family after the long years of war. Archie and Grace were delighted.

Now aged 64, Archie wasn't slowing down in retirement. He was planning an overseas trip alone to India and several other countries, but his first destination was Whanganui to see his new granddaughter in July.

He talked it over with Grace. 'I know you don't think it's safe to travel to India in the present unrest, dear, but would you like to just come with me to Whanganui then return to Fiji?' he asked.

Grace looked up from the photos of baby Margaret she was holding. 'I'd love to, but I think I'd better be patient and wait,' she said. She was 71, seven years older than Archie, and felt she needed to take life at a steadier pace. 'I could meet you in Sydney at the end of your trip and together we can visit my sisters for

Christmas. Then we can go on to New Zealand and see all our grandchildren, new babies and all.'

'And it will be a lot warmer then too.' Archie was pleased. 'It will be a joy. Then at the end of 1948 when we move to New Zealand, we'll see the families far more often.'

The move was something else to look forward to, although shifting from Fiji after 19 years would mean many changes. It would take a while to adjust back to a Kiwi lifestyle, but Grace felt it would be a change for the best. 'God is *so* good to us, isn't he?' she said.

There was more good news for Grace and Archie. Frank and Elzeth's third son, David, was born on 23 June. A month later, while Archie was staying with Vera and Harold in Whanganui, Lily and Ted's baby, Laurence, arrived on 25 July.

'Three new grandchildren in just over six months,' Archie told everyone he met.

Rocking little Margaret in his arms, he smiled down at her. 'You have two new little cousins,' he said. His heart filled with love and pride as her baby face dimpled into a smile in return.

'You're getting to know your granddad, aren't you?'

The memory lightened his journey as he travelled to Sydney and on to Mount Kosciuszko where he stayed at the hotel. On 13 August, snow blown by a bitter wind stung his face and ears.

The weather cleared two days later and Archie tramped around taking photos. 'It's grand being back on a mountain in the snow,' he told some of the skiers. 'The last time was 36 years ago in the Himalayas.' Memories of his trek to the Pindari Glacier in 1911 rekindled fresh in his mind.

It would soon be a different India from the country he had known. As he was taking photos on the mountain in Australia, he thought about how India would be celebrating independence from the British in just a few hours. He wondered what he would find when he arrived there.

He didn't know that Elma Ringer and her two small boys were taking a break from the intense heat, staying at Chakrata, a beautiful hill station north of New Delhi.

At midnight on 15 August, Indian independence coincided with the creation of the Muslim state of Pakistan.

The political upheaval fueled fear and wholesale slaughter.

Elma's husband Jack was in Pakistan on the other side of the new border.

Millions of refugees stampeded across the border in each direction. Hindus fled for their lives from northwest India, and Muslims escaping from India hoped to reach the safety of Pakistan before they were murdered. Trains overloaded beyond capacity slowly hauled their way across the border. British troops and civilians were leaving en masse.

There was no hope of a message from Elma ever reaching Jack.

Both India and Pakistan seethed in turmoil.

Praying for his family's safety, Jack caught a train to India. Two people on the train were killed on the way. Later, Jack was told a lot more people lost their lives on those train journeys.

Somehow, he reached Chakrata.

The train back into Pakistan was also crowded with terrified people. Forty people jammed into compartments meant for ten. On the Indian side of the border, Sikhs and Hindus roamed the platforms, hunting down Muslims. On the Pakistani side the terror was reversed; Muslims attacked any Sikhs and Hindus they could find.

Finally, the Ringers reached Peshawar where there was military protection.

※

Archie visited Ceylon and Burma (Myanmar) before travelling to India.

He sailed from Australia on SS *Eastern*, an Eastern & Australian Steamship Company cargo steamer with accommodation for 36 first-class passengers. Archie was impressed that the journey from Fremantle to Colombo only took eight and a half days.

Keen to go sightseeing, he travelled inland to Mihintale. This was where Mahinda, an Indian Buddhist monk, had lived in a cave from around 250 to 220 BC. Mahinda, the son of Emperor Asoka of India, persuaded King Tissa of Ceylon to convert to Buddhism. A temple now marked the place, and behind it, hundreds of steps led up a steep, rocky pinnacle.

Archie climbed the 775 steps, the last hundred in his socks on the bare rock by Buddhist decree, clinging to a cable until he reached the summit.

Far below, jungle spread across the land, the home of elephants, leopards and crocodiles.

Not far away were the ancient ruins of the Sinhalese city of Anuradhapura. Archie wanted to explore those too.

Later, he noted in his photo album:

Among the ruins of Anuradhapura in the heart of Ceylon where 2,000 years ago a great city flourished covering 16 square miles. For many centuries it remained buried by dense jungle.

He was intrigued by the ruins of a Buddhist hospital. Close by was a stone bath that was used to immerse patients in medicated water.

At the entrance of the hospital, sculptures lined the steps. On one side was a leopard with a deer and on the other, a snake next to a mongoose. Archie thought they possibly represented the Buddhist belief that all living creatures are equal and natural enemies should live in peace.

From Ceylon, Archie travelled to Rangoon (now Yangon) in Burma. He explored the city, finding a YMCA in a building previously used by the Baptist Mission Press before the Japanese invasion in World War II.

The 26th Indian Infantry Division, as part of the British Army, had freed Rangoon from the Japanese on 3 May 1945. Destruction from the war was still evident. All that was left of the Immanuel Baptist Church was a bombed-out shell, although still visible on the wall behind the pulpit were the words:

LET THE PEOPLE PRAISE THEE O GOD
LET ALL THE PEOPLE PRAISE THEE
BLESSED IS HE WHOSE TRANSGRESSION IS FORGIVEN
WHOSE SIN IS COVERED

Archie wondered whether God's message would still be preached in this turbulent country in the future. Burma had been under British rule since the 1820s but gained independence on 4 January 1948.

A sudden heavy downpour sent him running for cover. A man pedalling a rickshaw swished his way along the flooded street past the ruins.

Not far away was the Jubilee Hall. Inside, lying in state, were the bodies of Aung San, the Prime Minister, six cabinet ministers and two others who had all been assassinated in a cabinet meeting on 19 July 1947.

The large Secretariat Building where the shooting had taken place covered a whole city block. In addition to the iron railing, two high barbed wire fences lined the perimeter, and rolled barbed wire edged the footpath. Armed guards patrolled the area.

Archie learned that the new Prime Minister's residence was similarly fortified and guarded 24 hours a day. A curfew restricted anyone from approaching his residence, the Secretariat or the Jubilee Hall during the hours of darkness.

As Archie reached the wharf to board his ship, the sole Union Jack he'd seen in the city fluttered halfway down its pole at the harbourmaster's office.

⁂

It was now 21 October. Archie timed his arrival in India to be in autumn after the rainy season and two months after India gained independence.

In Calcutta, he watched a parade to commemorate the fourth anniversary of the Provisional Government of Free India. It was first set up in Singapore by Subhas Chandra Bose in 1943, aided by the Japanese.

Archie heard that Bose had been a wanted man in British India. Stories still circulated of how he'd escaped through the northwestern border, dressed as a sadhu, bribing the sentry with his gold watch. How he got to Singapore was a mystery.

British Indian troops captured by Japanese in Singapore had joined the Axis countries, forming the Indian National Army

(INA). They fought alongside the Japanese on the Assam Front in Burma. In return, they expected Japan to help the INA free India from British rule.

In August 1945, Japanese propaganda announced Bose had died in a plane crash, but the information was regarded as unreliable. Stories hovered around the Allies' intelligence organisations that he had defected to the USSR but no one really knew.

Archie continued to watch as the procession of the Azad Hind Dal (Free Indian Army), a branch of the INA, marched past. It was formed to take over civil administration to replace the British Civil Service in India. Afterwards, Bose's brother Sarat spoke at a meeting, stating that his political party was pushing for a Union of Socialist States of India.

He wasn't successful; the first Indian democratic election was held from October 1951 to February 1952.

A huge picture of Bose mounted on the front of a truck was in the street where he had lived. Alive or dead, he was considered a national hero.

Continuing on his journey, Archie spent a few days in Darjeeling where he had recuperated from blackwater fever back in 1903. He then headed to Gopiganj.

At first it seemed nothing had changed since his family left India in 1924. People still pushed along the crowded streets in the centre of the town, eddying around a camel at the crossroads. Stalls at the side of the street still sold sweets, open to swirling dust and flies.

Then he noticed some things *had* changed.

The mission compound he had spent many hours developing was now overrun with self-sown trees. No one lived there anymore. He could just see part of the roof and verandah of their former family home. The LMS had handed over most of their mission centres in North India, including the medical mission in Kachhwa, to the Bible Churchmen's Missionary Society in 1928 while Archie was the minister of Greenlane Congregational Church. The BCMS was going to leave soon too but it looked like no one had cared for the mission compound in Gopiganj for years.

Disappointed, Archie turned away.

Outside the town, the Musahar people still lived in poverty, dressed in rags as they sat outside their low grass huts. Now that there was no mission at Gopiganj, Archie wondered who would help them.

His reunion with his friend Ramswarup, who was now in his 80s, lifted Archie's spirits for the rest of the day. Although it was more than 12 years since they'd met in 1935, the years seemed to roll away as they talked. It didn't seem like 32 years had passed since the day Ramswarup made his stand for Yishu and was baptised in 1915.

He was still strong in his faith in God.

Encouraged, Archie travelled to Benares, visiting places he remembered well and seeing new ones.

There were wide views of the city from the minaret of a mosque built by Emperor Aurangzeb in the 17th century to replace the temple of Vishnu he'd destroyed; there were baskets suspended on bamboo poles to hold lights for the Diwali Festival along the banks of the Ganges River; and there was a large marble relief map of India on the floor of the Bharat Mata, Mother of India Temple.

Archie saw the new Buddhist temple at Sarnath where Buddha had spoken his first message 2,500 years ago; close by were the ruins of a 2,000-year-old Buddhist monastery.

His sightseeing tour over, Archie headed for the Benares railway station. Cattle roamed free and unrestrained along the platforms and railway lines. He caught a train to Lamta in the Balaghat area, thrilled to be heading for Baihar where he and Grace were married more than 40 years before.

On the road between Lamta and Baihar, the remains of a bullock lay in the morning sun, abandoned by a satisfied tiger. It had attacked the bullock about 32 hours before, dragging it from its harness and feasting on it right there on the road.

That tiger won't be too far away. It will be resting after two nights of feasting, Archie thought. It was a sharp reminder that he was now in the jungle. Survival meant staying alert at all times.

A Methodist Mission was now in Baihar at the compound where John Lampard had started the Balaghat mission to the Gonds.

A large WELCOME sign strung across the road between two trees greeted Archie as he arrived.

He visited the mission's middle school where the Stephen Lampard Memorial Hall was dedicated to the Lampards' son Stephen. Archie and Grace had known him as a baby at the beginning of the century. In 1918 he'd left England to fight on the Western Front in France and had died on the battlefield.

Early the following morning Archie hiked along a pretty jungle road. Memories flooded back, but his senses stayed on tiptoe. About nine kilometres down the road he noticed the fresh paw prints of a leopard in the dust.

It made good sense to return to the mission. He had no intention of becoming a leopard's breakfast and he had a busy day ahead of him.

Later, hiring a covered bullock cart and driver to take him and three others to Khursipar, he soon realised that bullock carts in 1947 were built the same as they had been 46 years before. They still didn't have springs.

The track was pockmarked by hundreds of deep hoof prints sunk into the mud by cattle during the rains. Now in the dry autumn months the broken surface had set like concrete. Seated in the cart, the passengers bumped and lurched along the track.

'Stop please!' Archie called to the driver. 'I'll get out and walk.'

At Khursipar he saw the house where he and Grace had set up their first home, so different from their present home in Fiji.

Maha Singh, the pastor of the church in Khursipar offered hospitality. His daughter had recently won a scholarship – one of 25 out of 200 from all over India – for a free medical course at the Christian Medical College at Vellore in South India.

It was a wonderful achievement. Archie thought of the children he and Grace had taught in the village. It was a small start that had led to much bigger things.

At the village of Palera he met a group of Christians. Their pastor, Nand Lal and his wife Hiriya Bai, now grey-haired, had both been taught by Grace and Archie as schoolchildren.

Archie was filled with joy. God had answered so many of his prayers.

Travelling on to Nikkum where the Williams had been missionaries many years before, the group crossed the Banjar River. Archie remembered crossing it in 1902 at the end of the rainy season when the river had flooded. He'd started to go under but a Gond managed to reach him through the torrent and helped him to shore.

Memories were everywhere in India for Archie.

They were now passing a sugarcane field surrounded by a high bamboo fence to keep out wild pigs and deer. The owner had a high machan platform where he kept watch at night to prevent break-ins.

'How different it is from growing sugarcane in Fiji,' Archie commented.

He thought of the nights he'd spent on a machan waiting to shoot a man-eating predator. Life here in the jungle was still precarious.

Archie travelled south from Baihar to Coonoor by the Nilgiri Mountains in the Tamil Nadu State of South India. On the way, the bus passed betel nut palms and countless tea plantations.

Udhagamandalam, otherwise known as Ootacamund or just Ooty, is the capital of the Nilgiris district and a beautiful hill station. Known for its subtropical highland climate, mountains, lakes and birds, it has been a popular tourist area since the mid-1800s when the British fled there from the southern summer heat.

Archie walked through the botanical gardens admiring the bandstand, many varieties of Australian eucalyptus trees, flowers, and pools. In an open area, a sign by a young tree indicated it was planted to celebrate India's Independence Day.

In the centre of town the British had inappropriately named an intersection Charing Cross. The name was misprinted in Archie's bus timetable to read 'Charming Cross'.

It's a more suitable name, with the rolling hills in the background, Archie thought.

From Coonoor he caught a bus to the city of Coimbatore, taking in the beauty as the winding road angled down the hills.

It was now 16 November and he was on the first stage of his journey home.

He left Coimbatore by train for Madras (Chennai) where he stayed for several days, and on 25 November he boarded the SS *Rajula*. It was crowded with Hindu refugees from the Sindh province of India, which was now part of Pakistan.

Hundreds of the refugees disembarked at Penang and later Singapore. Many of them were wives and daughters of merchants already in Malaysia and Java, Indonesia.

Archie disembarked in Singapore as well. He boarded SS *Marella* on 29 November, arriving in Melbourne on 19 December. He continued on to Sydney.

Grace was there to meet him and they celebrated Christmas together with her sisters. It was wonderful to be together again. He had so much to tell her; letters and postcards conveyed only a keyhole view of his experiences.

They sailed on 8 January 1948, arriving in Wellington four days later, then travelled to Whanganui for a joyful reunion with Vera. Grace and Archie stayed several days with her and Harold and 11-month-old Margaret. They stayed with Frank and his family in New Plymouth too for a few days before returning to Fiji.

Chapter 22

Grace

News of Gandhi's assassination shook the world. The title Mahatma, meaning 'great soul', suited him well. Archie had held great respect for Gandhi.

Born on 2 October 1869, Mahondas Gandhi graduated in law in London and later lived in South Africa for 20 years, defending the rights of the many Indians living there. In 1915 he returned to India to take up politics and fight in non-violent ways for Indian independence.

By 1921 he was the leader of the Indian National Congress. As the years passed, Gandhi was jailed periodically for his resistance to British rule. He called Indians to civil disobedience because of the British monopoly and tax on salt.

During World War II he made a stand once again, demanding the British leave but he was against Subhas Chandra Bose, the leader who'd joined the Japanese to fight the British.

Gandhi longed for peace.

When Elma and Jack Ringer and their boys had been trying to cross the newly created border between India and Pakistan in 1947, Gandhi was working to stop the violence.

Early evening on 30 January 1948, a young Hindu stepped forward and bowed to Gandhi as he was walking with supporters.

Gandhi bowed in return. Then the young man pulled out a gun and shot him.

India lost a great leader.

Archie and Grace wondered who would follow in Gandhi's footsteps; India's vast population needed someone to legislate for good.

※

On 30 December 1948 Grace and Archie moved from Suva to live in Tauranga, New Zealand, to be close to Lily and her family.

Their new home *Goffs Oak*, named after the village where Grace grew up and where Archie met her, was designed by the same architect as *Oneata* in Suva.

The house, with extensive views, was built on a sloping section with the garage underneath. There were 14 steps up to the front door and it soon became too tiring for Grace; her health and energy were declining.

They moved two years later to a house on a flat section. This time they named their home *Clapton*, after the area in London where Archie had lived as a child.

A bedroom was built on the end of the garage for Archie's sister Jessie. She had remained in Auckland after Grace and Archie moved to Fiji, but now she was coming to live with them.

Connie moved in to care for them all.

On 18 May 1951, Vera and Harold had another daughter – Grace and Archie's last grandchild. Harold sent a telegram to let them know.

After sending a reply telegram of congratulations, Grace sat down to write a letter:

> My Darling Vera, how glad we are to receive Harold's wire (telegram) today with the important news. I said, 'Oh I hope it will be a dear baby Vera.' I don't mean in name but in looks etc with downy fair hair which later curled. Still, I know she must be lovely and sweet.
>
> We are longing to see her and you. We wonder if you have chosen a name yet.

She finished the letter with,

> God bless you darling. We are just going to thank Him in our family worship. Much love from Mother.

Three days later, Archie wrote. He was surprised a letter from Vera had arrived already and wrote to tell her so. Then he added,

> Please accept our apologies for referring to Shirley Faye as 'Bridget' in the telegram which we hope you received Friday evening. It was Connie's idea. I suggested Sarah!

He added,

> On Sunday at Te Puke I called on an Indian family – Sikhs – and had a very interesting time chatting in Hindustani. Last evening I took Connie to the pictures to see The Song of India – plenty of jungle thrills, tigers, panthers etc.

India was never far from Archie's thoughts.

That same year, Frank's family moved from New Plymouth to Hamilton. They built a new brick house on the land in front of Elzeth's parents' cottage, *Meadowcroft*. Now that they were closer to Grace and Archie, they could visit more often. It was a well-timed move.

Towards the end of the year, Grace slipped off the eiderdown quilt on their bed, landing hard and twisting her leg, fracturing her left femur. It didn't heal properly. When Grace came out of hospital, she used a wheelchair at first but soon graduated to crutches, using them both inside and outside the house.

Grateful that Connie was living with them, Grace and Archie relied on her nursing skills and practical help. Grace's memory for present-day events was slipping, but she recalled much from the past. She quoted Bible verses and remembered friends and family.

Her sense of humour and sweet, cheerful personality remained intact.

In April 1955 Archie and Grace celebrated their golden wedding anniversary at home. All the family were there except their grandsons Peter and Bruce.

Each member of the family wrote down a Bible verse to commemorate Grace and Archie's 50 years together and to encourage them in the years ahead.

Archie wrote in his small clear handwriting:

For I know whom I have believed, and am persuaded that he is able to keep that which I have committed unto him. (2 Timothy 1:12 KJV)

Below it, Grace wrote Psalm 40:5 from the KJV in her larger rounded hand. (It is quoted here from the CEV to make the meaning clearer.)

You, LORD God, have done many wonderful things, and you have planned marvellous things for us. No one is like you! I would never be able to tell all you have done.

Family members wrote verses that spoke of triumphs in life because of Jesus and thankfulness to God for his guidance, protection, goodness and care.

The result was a snapshot of Grace and Archie's lives together. God had protected them throughout the years in India, through two world wars and their many journeys overseas. He had given them purpose, provided for them, guided them and given them hope in the tough times. They had seen many of their prayers answered, and they had faith they would be in heaven one day with their Lord and Saviour.

❀

Two years later on 9 July 1957, Archie's sister Jessie passed away peacefully in Tauranga Hospital. She was 84.

Now that Connie was no longer caring for her aunt as well as Grace and Archie, she was able to accept a part-time position as organising secretary for the New Zealand Nurses' Christian Fellowship (NCF). Sometimes she travelled to hospitals around the country, helping to support existing groups, encouraging nurses, and forming new groups.

In August 1958 she visited Fijian nurses.

The journey begins, not just as a holiday trip, but as a mission sent by the Lord and by the NCF of NZ, she wrote. *Until the last few minutes before leaving, assurances of prayer sup-*

port kept arriving, earnest claiming of the blessing of God on the venture.

She hadn't been to Fiji since leaving by boat in the 1940s for maternity training in Rotorua Hospital. Now she'd be flying. It was a new experience to write about:

> A swift five hours' journey at 18,000 feet, instead of three days by sea brought me almost in a flash to these fair islands with their change of people, climate, and scenery. Here I was to meet many old friends of different nationalities, and make many new ones.

She believed nurses needed to support and encourage each other in their work and faith in God.

Connie was encouraged in her travels too. The Methodist Mission Baker Memorial Centre, built where an early missionary had been killed, was now the Fijian ministers' training centre.

At Dilkusha, where Archie and Harry had worked at the Indian YMCA, Connie met a pastor and spent time with him and his family. He travelled a lot, working among 300 youth groups involving 10,000 young people.

Connie arrived back in Suva grateful to God for the work he was doing in people's lives in the islands she loved and remembered.

She visited the Colonial War Memorial (CWM) Hospital where she and Lily had trained and worked as nurses. She walked past her family's old home, *Oneata*, and went aboard the mission ship the *John Williams VI* moored at the wharf.

Memories of life in Fiji swirled back – Uncle Harry at his printing works; Grace in hospital; Vera coming to teach at

Dudley House School; Leo, the family dog. Fiji would always hold a special spot in her heart. Now as she visited various places and met new people, more warm memories were created.

The nursing school at Tamavua Hospital was a few kilometres from Suva. The trainee nurses worked at both the local tuberculosis hospital and the CWM Hospital in Suva. A bus brought them into Suva for duty.

The medical school at Tamavua held a five-year course for about 100 students from many of the western Pacific islands as well as Fijians. It seemed unfair to Connie that at the end of the course they weren't counted as doctors but only as assistant medical officers.

Since Connie's visit, the nursing school and medical school have combined and are now on the campus of the Fiji National University. These days, medical students can become fully qualified doctors, attaining a Bachelor of Medicine or Bachelor of Surgery. Other students can qualify in health science disciplines including: medicine, nursing, dentistry, pharmacy, physiotherapy, radiography, laboratory technology, public health, dietetics and environmental health.

Connie would be pleased if she knew.

> How great is their need of training, she'd noted in the photo album of her trip. How important also that they have God's Word in their hearts and lives. Local Christian doctors and ministers hold a fellowship for them.

Like her parents, Connie's heart was in missions. Often suffering from headaches and generally feeling unwell, she still felt privileged that she could work for God in the NCF. Meeting new groups of nurses was inspiring.

Travelling by bus, she reached Ba at the north of the island of Viti Levu. Typical of many buses in Fiji, it had no glass in the windows. Rolled up canvas could be pulled down if it rained. Connie thought of Vera's bus trip around the island in 1938 and hoped she wouldn't end up in a flood too.

The bus broke down instead.

Taking advantage of the unexpected stop, Connie visited the tiny hospital in a village close by. Two nurses came outside for her to take their photo. Connie also took a photo of what she called the Nurses' Home. The small hut built of native materials had a peaked thatched roof and a low doorway at the front. It was a total contrast to the Nurses' Homes in New Zealand.

At Ba, Connie visited the Methodist Mission Hospital, enjoying a tour and talking to patients. The Australian sisters were training Indian nurses in the same CWM Hospital course held at Tamavua.

There was an Indian church near the hospital, but mission staff also held a service in the wards for staff and patients.

Cotton bedcovers sent from Australia had Bible verses embroidered on them in English or Hindi. Some had signatures stitched on in friendship.

'That's a lovely idea. Maybe other Christian hospitals could do something like that too,' Connie said.

Continuing her journey, she stopped at the Lautoka government hospital further down the island on the northwest coast. A nurses' training school was there too. Connie held an NCF meeting at the hospital in the evening, with the Fijian women wearing short white dresses over long black skirts.

Connie's three weeks had slipped past. It was now time to leave Fiji. Flying back to New Zealand from Nadi International

Airport, memories of the places she'd visited and the people she had met filled her mind.

One Australian nurse she'd met had come to Fiji to work in the government hospital for two years but had stayed for nine because of her keen interest in NCF and love for the Fijian people.

> Many more (like her) are needed, Connie wrote on the last page of her NCF Fiji album. Nurses, teachers, bank clerks showing Christ in their daily lives and serving the people in their leisure hours. Jesus said, 'I am the light of the world'.

She believed with all her heart that shining God's love by living a life of love and forgiveness drew people from the darkness of hate.

She had seen the transformation in the lives of the nurses.

If only the first missionaries to Fiji could also see what she had seen.

※

'When are we going to church?' Grace asked.

It was a Sunday in September 1961. Connie was preparing the midday meal. 'We've already been to church, Mother,' she explained gently. 'It's lunchtime now.'

'Oh, dear, I can't remember. Never mind, I'm sure it was a blessing to be there.'

'You're wonderful – always so cheerful despite the circumstances.' Connie turned to smile at her.

Grace's face lit up in an impish smile. She began to sing:

> Always cheerful, never disagreeable
> Sunshine all around I see;
> Full of beauty is the path of duty
> Cheerful I must always BE!

'I've never heard you sing that chorus before.'
'Nor have I,' Archie said, coming into the room.
'Oh, I learnt it many, many years ago,' Grace said.

She had mixed up some of the words of Fanny Crosby's chorus for the hymn 'Let Our Hearts Be Always Cheerful'. It always brightened Connie and Archie's day when they heard her sing it.

No doubt it lost its appeal when Grace sang it after a coughing fit at 3.00 in the morning.

Grace decided to stay in bed for the next few days. On 27 September she died peacefully at home.

Shortly afterwards, Archie wrote a letter which he copied to their many friends across the world:

> We are thankful that our dear one suffered no lingering illness or painful ending. On 27th September following a happy evening meal together in the bedroom – she had been in bed for several days – we began our usual family worship.
>   While the Bible was being read, our dear one quickly and quietly slipped away – a beautiful ending to a long and fruitful life.

He included a brief account of her life, then added,

> Through all, her cheerfulness and serenity were undiminished. Over the many years as wife and mother her influence has been immeasurable and she has been the soul of hospitality.

Now nearing her 86th birthday, she has gone to be with her beloved Lord.

Our dear one's life has illustrated the truth of the words: 'In quietness and in confidence shall be your strength; and that faith results in victorious living through our Lord and Saviour Jesus Christ'.

He and Connie contacted family members the evening of Grace's death, telling them how she had slipped into heaven – a serene entrance for a faithful woman of God.

After hearing the news, Vera wrote to Archie, telling him what she and Harold had read in the Bible together that evening:

> Harold read the first part of John 14 to me and stressed verse 3, pointing out that Jesus comes for us Himself to take us home. It is wonderful to think of His standing there when you were reading the Bible, and then of His tenderness in taking her so gently and quickly.

Grace's death was a double blow for Lily; her husband Ted had died on 7 August, the day before her birthday. She joined other family members and friends gathering for Grace's funeral at the Tauranga Wesley Methodist Church.

They all remembered her with love.

> We cannot grieve for Mother, though we miss her, for God has given her long years, which if extended further, would only mean extended frailty, Frank wrote. She certainly had a lovely disposition. I can never remember her cross or angry except when her indignation was roused over some evil or injustice.

Grace's favourite Bible verse was Isaiah 26:3,

> Thou wilt keep him in perfect peace whose mind is stayed on thee because he trusteth in thee. (KJV)

Her life was evidence of that truth.

Floods of sympathetic messages arrived to give comfort to the family and they meant a great deal, particularly to Archie.

※

Archie had booked to leave for India on 9 October to attend the Assembly of the World Council of Churches in New Delhi from 18 November to 6 December. He'd intended visiting Baihar and Gopiganj before the assembly.

'I'm so thankful I was with Grace when she passed away and that it didn't happen after I left,' Archie told family and friends. 'I think I'll cancel the whole trip.'

'Can you transfer your booking to a later date?' many of his friends suggested, knowing how much he looked forward to it. 'You could still go. Maybe being in India again would be a comfort.'

After consideration, Archie made a decision. He talked about it to Connie. 'If I go a fortnight later than planned and visit Baihar after the assembly instead of beforehand, will you be alright on your own?'

'Yes, you go, Dad.' Connie was sure. 'I'll manage. Lily is close by – we can comfort each other – and I have so many kind friends to talk to.' She paused for a moment then added, 'Mother was so pleased you had the opportunity to visit India again. She'd want you to go.'

'Thank you for your understanding,' Archie said. A large part of his heart had never left India and he longed to be there again.

He re-booked to leave on 23 October and wrote to friends and family to let them know.

A letter arrived from Frank Ashton at the LMS Hospital in Hong Kong. His father, Robert Ashton, had been Grace and Archie's missionary colleague in Kachhwa.

> Our sincere sympathy to you all. Though Mrs McMillan's passing must have been a great shock, you must be glad she was spared a long troublesome illness. We are glad you feel able to take your trip to India. The two knitted garments Mrs McMillan so kindly knitted arrived a day or so ago.

For years, Grace had continued to knit for people suffering from leprosy in hospitals. Both she and Archie supported the Mission to Lepers (renamed The Leprosy Mission in 1965) as well as the Bible Society.

Grace's death was going to leave a huge gap in Archie's life. He had loved her since he was a teenager in Goffs Oak while working on the farm and they'd shared so many experiences together over the 56 years they'd been married.

Those memories were close to him as he said goodbye to friends and family at Tauranga Airport on the first stage of his journey.

This time he'd be flying to India instead of travelling for weeks on a passenger ship.

After staying in Sydney for a few days, he flew to Calcutta and explored the city.

He found the building where Sir Ronald Ross, back in 1897, had discovered that malaria is caused by a parasite in the anopheles mosquito.

Archie was interested in the doctor's work, having studied tropical medicine in London and experienced malaria himself along with its near-fatal complication, blackwater fever. He was also interested Sir Ronald had been born in Almora; his father had been in the British Indian Army.

Wherever Archie went in India many connections and memories sprang to life.

Leaving Calcutta, he travelled to Benares, visiting the palace of the Maharajah. It was here that Lily had handed the Maharajah her doll.

Was that really 50 years ago? He could picture the scene as if it were yesterday. Archie hid a smile.

At Gopiganj it saddened him to find that his friend Ramswarup's gravestone was lying forgotten in a shed. He had died in 1949, two years after Archie had last seen him. A missionary had written to tell Archie the news.

'Tell sahib I am going home,' Ramswarup had said.

Archie took a photo of the gravestone and organised an appropriate place for it to be set up.

The Hindi inscription translated:

GOPIGANJ
PANDIT RAMSWARUP
MASIHI (FOLLOWER OF JESUS)
BAPTISED 1915
25 AUGUST 1949

Archie was sure he'd see Ramswarup in heaven one day, as well as Grace, his parents, and others he knew who had gone before him.

He would see his Lord Jesus too – the most amazing experience of all.

Just thinking about it gave him hope to go on.

Leaving the Benares district, he set off across Uttar Pradesh to various places including the Leprosy Mission (TLM) Hospital in Naini, Allahabad. Impressed by their dedicated work and compassion, he decided he must visit it again one day. The Leprosy Mission was worth supporting. They made an inestimable difference to people's lives

From there, Archie's journey took him to Agra and Landour. He and Grace had stayed in both places on their honeymoon. Again, the years drifted away…

Archie wished he could have stayed longer but it was now time to head to New Delhi for the World Council of Churches Assembly. He stayed at the New Delhi residence of the High Commissioner of Ceylon and travelled to the conference centre each day.

The contrast between the High Commissioner's residence and Baihar was dramatic. Like Gopiganj and Kachhwa, Baihar was where Archie's heart held the strongest attachment to the Indian people. He arrived in the jungle town for the golden jubilee of the opening of the Methodist church on 10 December.

A photo shows him with several local Christians he had known for many years. One of them was Manna Bai, Hira Singh's wife.

Hira was the first man in the area Archie had led to Jesus. When Hira was looking for a wife, he'd told Archie, 'One who is to be my wife must be a woman who will treat guests and visitors with every respect and must be a real help to me in my work for God.'

Now an elderly widow, Manna Bai still had a strong faith in God.

The following morning, Archie joined a group of Christians outside the bungalow where he and Grace had had their wedding breakfast 56 years before. Close by was the chapel where they were married. It was the perfect place to share precious memories with friends who cared and gave comfort.

In the evening he went for a drive with friends along a jungle road.

'I'm hoping to see a leopard,' he told them

It was so different travelling through the jungle by car instead of an open bullock cart. The big cats were probably frightened by the motor vehicle because they all stayed hidden.

'Too bad, I will just have to wait until the next time I come,' Archie said.

After travelling to Madras (Chennai), he flew back to New Zealand.

It was wonderful to be among family again, but now he was home, Grace's absence seemed to echo through the house.

He and Connie had a new smaller home built with a more manageable garden.

Archie named their new home *Baihar*.

Chapter 23

Dispensing Hope

As promised, Archie visited India again, arriving in Calcutta in February 1964. His priority was to visit the Bible Society of India.

> Today, in whole or part, the Scriptures are available in 125 Indian languages or dialects, Archie wrote, making a note to remember it.

He decided when he returned home, he'd write a long circular letter to family and friends. That way, they could all join him in his experiences and imagine they'd been there too.

He felt excited; the gospel was spreading through India and he was sure it would bring change. He thought back to the hours he'd worked translating the Bible into Hindi with other LMS missionaries. He wanted his copy donated to the church in Baihar when he died.

Right now, he had plenty of things he planned to do. He caught a flight from Calcutta to Nepal, admiring the clear views of Mount Everest, Kangchenjunga and other majestic giants of the Himalayas.

He (and Grace) had supported mission hospitals and aid workers in Nepal and India for years and he was keen to see them.

A missionary met him at the airport and drove him to a leprosy and tuberculosis hospital at Bhatgaon, not far from Kathmandu.

Staff members from Germany, Scotland and Australia welcomed Archie and showed him around. Some of the patients were outside for occupational therapy, making things out of rice straw or bamboo baskets.

Late in the afternoon Dierdre Banks, the nursing superintendent from the Leprosy Mission's Anandaban Hospital, drove Archie there for a visit. The jeep bounced and lurched the whole way over the stony road but the rough ride was worth it. Anandaban means 'forest of joy' in Nepali.

Church on Sunday was a heart-warming experience for Archie. 'It's amazing to think that only last Sunday I was in a church in Auckland with family, and this Sunday I'm at a church near the city of Kathmandu!' he said.

It was cold in the mountains in February, a sharp contrast to the New Zealand summer Archie had left.

'No wonder you send out appeals for knitted scarves and patchwork quilts for your patients,' he said to Deidre the next morning. He thought of Almora where another TLM hospital was located. It was higher in the Himalayas than Kathmandu. He would visit it later.

Anandaban Leprosy Hospital continues to help many people. Their website states:

> The Anandaban Hospital staff have a strong connection with patients throughout their entire journey with leprosy. Whether they are in the hospital recovering from reconstructive surgery; undergoing intensive physiotherapy; or in Rosa House (the rehabilitation unit) preparing to return to their

community, staff provide a safe and caring relationship with the patients, every step of the way.*

Archie had been invited to have lunch with a member of the British Embassy, so he left the hospital late in the morning. At lunch, he chatted with other guests, including a mountain climber who'd been on the historic 1953 expedition to Mount Everest with Sir Edmund Hillary and Tenzing Norgay.

While he enjoyed himself there, he was looking forward to his next destination – the United Mission Hospital at Tansen in Nepal where he would stay with Doctors Robert and Bethel Fleming.

United Mission to Nepal (UMN) had begun in an amazing God-inspired way. The Flemings and Doctor Carl Fredericks visited Tansen in 1951 and 1952 on a birdwatching expedition. While there, they examined and treated a number of patients.

The local people asked them to come back, and in 1954 they returned with others as the newly formed UMN. The mission staff trained Nepali nurses, paramedics, occupational therapists and pharmacists.

By 1964 when Archie visited, there was an international team of men and women from the USA, Australia, UK, Norway, Sweden, Holland and Germany, all working together.

The hospital website shows it is still helping many Nepalis:

> At present the hospital has around 405 Nepali employees (including trainees) and 12 mission appointees from six different countries, who work mostly as senior doctors in a teaching

---

* leprosymission.org.nz/anandaban, accessed 12 July 2019.

role, or in other support roles. The staff are grouped under the major divisions: nursing, medical, administration, and the two newer divisions of community health and pastoral care.*

The following morning, Archie left for the airport on his way back to Baihar, Madhya Pradesh.

Before going there, he stopped at Jabalpur, the third largest city in Madhya Pradesh State. His passion for sharing the gospel and interest in educational and medical work in India was as strong as ever.

The Hawabagh Women's College was established in 1928 by the American Methodist Episcopal Mission to educate women. Marion Warner from the mission in Baihar gave Archie a tour.

'Back in 1901 when I came to Baihar, few women, if any, could read,' Archie said. He was thrilled at the progress. He would be delighted to know that in the 21st century women are gaining degrees in many different fields at the college.

At dinner there was a pleasant surprise for Archie. The three other guests were from Fiji – an Indian and his wife, and a Fijian. The men were attending the theological college in the city.

Louise Campbell from the college drove Archie to Baihar in her jeep the following day. On the way they visited Kanha National Park for a short while.

'Look at that lofty machan,' Archie said, pointing. 'It's about 30 feet high. We could have a great view of game from up there.'

They climbed up the steps, entering through a door to the lookout room with open sides all around.

'It's so different from the machans I used to have to build out of

---

* www.tansenhospital.org.np/about/, accessed 12 July 2019.

any odd thing I could find and attach it up in the branches,' Archie commented. Memories flooded back as he told Louise of nights spent on cramped machans waiting for a man-eater. 'I'd love to come to Kanha again another day and spend more time here.'

He and Louise arrived in Baihar after dark and he settled into the same bungalow where he and Grace had their wedding reception on 12 April 1905. He'd be staying two weeks and was looking forward to the joy of wandering about and letting memories dance through his days.

A few days into his stay, he talked with the local licensed shikari (hunter). Many years before, Archie had known the shikari's father who had worked in the government dispensary in Baihar.

'Man-eating tigers are still around here,' the man told him. 'In the last two weeks, two women have been killed and a man badly injured.' The shikari had shot all three tigers.

It was a tragic loss of life. The women had entered the jungle to gather berries or firewood. Nowadays the government has banned people from gathering wood from tiger hunting grounds, although poaching of tigers continues.

The conservation programme Project Tiger was launched in India in 1972 to save the tiger population from extinction. On the Kanha website it calls the park 'a wild hideout taken straight from the famous *Jungle Book*'.

On Archie's second visit to the park he met an enthusiastic conservationist, Doctor George Schaller, a German American scientist associated with the Department of Zoology at Calcutta University. He was doing important research work.

While they were talking together, George offered to take Archie with him on a ride along the Kanha jungle tracks.

The previous afternoon, a tiger had killed a langur black-faced monkey and the scientist picked up the skeleton for further study.

In the monsoon season Dr George S. Schaller remains alone (in a small house within the Park) for Kanha is cut off, Archie noted. His wife takes their small child elsewhere.

Later, after Archie had returned home to New Zealand, George's wife wrote to tell him a leopard had broken into George's barn and killed a lamb. George slept on his open verandah to observe the leopard the next night when it came back for a goat. George was so keen to gather data he didn't mind sacrificing his meat supply.

At the age of nearly 81, Archie could still preach fluently in Hindi, and he addressed many church meetings while he was at Baihar.

Back in 1901 when he had just arrived at Baihar, he wrote the following hymn on his 18th birthday. He composed a tune for it in tonic sol-fa, all four parts, but unfortunately it has been lost.

> Another year has passed away
> Into eternity.
> A new-born year brings me today
> Fresh opportunities.
>
> Lord Jesus I confess to thee
> My sins of bygone days;
> And ask thee now most earnestly
> Forgive my sinful ways.

And now throughout this coming year
Help me thy will to do,
That I may never shrink or fear,
Do thou my strength renew.

I've consecrated all to thee
For use while yet 'tis day,
I'm still quite willing Lord, to be
Or do as thou wilt say.

Shine thou on me that I may be
A light in this dark world,
That others may thy likeness see
And enter in thy fold.

Speak thou to me, that I may speak
Thy word and not my own;
And may my hearers learn to seek
A never-fading crown.

It became a reflection of his whole life. He was still sharing the gospel. Comfortable talking to most people, he was keen to keep in touch with all that was happening in India.

While in Baihar, I was fortunate to meet and listen to a man I have often heard of, Acharya Vinoba Bhave, a second Gandhi, he wrote. Since 1951 he spends his life walking thousands of miles and appealing to landowners to donate land to the peasants that the landless may have a few acres and grow food for their families. Since 1951 donations have totalled over four million acres. This swami* walks about eight miles a day between 3.00 a.m. and 6.00 a.m.

The problems for India's poor were overwhelming but Archie hoped that owning a little land would help many families have a better life.

He was sure, too, that if they had faith in Yishu, the power of God would change their lives in an amazing way.

He had seen the evidence of it, and he prayed many more people in Madhya Pradesh would come to accept Yishu as their Saviour in future.

His prayers have been answered.

Along with the growth of Indian Christian communities in many states in India, though, persecution is also rising. Churches and Bibles are burned; Christians are harassed, beaten, imprisoned and murdered.

Just as Archie and Grace's friends Hira Singh and Ramswarup were persecuted for their faith, Christian Indians today are in constant need of our support and prayers.

After leaving Baihar, Archie attended the National Christian Council in India for a few days. It was an international mix of Japanese, German, English and Indian Christians.

His tour of India held so many facets of his life. He had countless contacts, met hundreds of people, made dozens of friends and kept in touch with many of them.

At home he had the autobiography of Jawaharlal Nehru,

---

* Hindu title meaning master over one's self.

Gandhi's successor and the first Prime Minister of India in 1947. Archie could relate to places and events in the book.

At Allahabad, his memories slid back to 18 February 1911.

He and Grace had gone to see an industrial exhibition in the city and he had posted a letter to a friend in England that day. Unknown to Archie, Jawaharlal Nehru was studying law in London at the time, and his father sent him a letter from Allahabad that very same day.

Those two letters made history, along with about 6,500 other letters and postcards. They were the world's first official airmail, even if the flight only lasted 13 minutes.

Piloted by a 23-year-old Frenchman, Henri Pequet, a two-seater biplane carrying the mail took off from a polo field in Allahabad to fly to Naini, about eight kilometres away. The mail was then loaded onto the train for Bombay and went from there to England by ship.

India Post and the Indian Air Force re-enacted the flight in February 2011, but this time the plane flew from Allahabad's Bamrauli Airport.

Nehru died on 27 May 1964. World leaders placed wreaths outside his residence and nearly 500,000 Indians filed past, many of them saying, 'Nehru amar rahen – may Nehru remain immortal.'

> It is still hard to realise Nehru is no longer with us, Archie wrote later in his circular letter at home. Bearing no trace of resentment or bitterness for the past, he has always been our friend.

Archie knew the British had made many harmful decisions and caused many injustices in India, but he also knew they had done much good.

Ripple Effect

The British Empire had also been the vehicle to spread the gospel to many countries in the world.

Spreading the gospel was Archie's top priority on his 81st birthday on Saturday 7 March in Allahabad.

My heart was so full of thanksgiving to God for health and strength that I went to the Bible Society and bought 81 copies of the gospels in Hindi, he wrote.

Taking many of the gospels, he headed to the Triveni Sangam. Like Haridwar, this was another site for the Hindu gathering of Kumbh Mela. Here the Ganges, Yamuna, and the mythical Saraswati Rivers meet in a confluence the Hindus believe will wash away their sins and end the cycle of reincarnation. They believe the gods take human form and also dip in the water to take away their sins.

Archie longed for the pilgrims to know the holy loving God.

At or near the Sangam and then in the centre of the city, mingled with a few friendly words, I distributed 70 of these gospels, often reading out a few verses to awaken interest; this led to some interesting conversations, Archie continued writing. It was a happy morning.

He had already contacted his friends at the Leprosy Mission Hospital at Naini. He arrived there at lunchtime, and in the afternoon handed out the remaining 11 gospels to patients.

The staff, knowing it was his birthday, had baked a cake and organised a party for him.

Letters and telegrams from family and friends completed his happiness.

Dispensing Hope

He stayed overnight and preached the following morning in the hospital chapel.

It was a touching sight to see near the front a young man without fingers or toes and only one leg; but (the young man) is a radiant Christian, Archie wrote.

He was evidence of the power and love of God through hardship and difficulty.

Five women at the service wore brightly coloured scarves, the last few Grace had knitted in 1961 – some of her final gifts to the Indian people she loved.

※

When Archie visited Gopiganj in 1947 the mission station he'd built was overgrown and neglected. Now when he visited, it was a hive of activity as a leprosy clinic.

Patients crowded into the bungalow his family had lived in for seven years. It was a deep satisfaction for Archie to know the mission station was still used for God's work, and it was also deeply satisfying to meet friends in the town he had known for 50 years.

He learned that the hospital at Kachhwa that Robert Ashton had opened 70 years before was run by another mission with Doctor Neville Everard.

The hospital had expanded.

Archie thought back to the 1920s when the LMS made the sad decision to pull out from North India. God had brought in other workers to take their place.

Archie and Grace would be thrilled to know Kachhwa

Christian Hospital (KCH) is now one of 20 hospitals with many community health and development projects run by the Emmanuel Hospital Association (EHA). They have hospitals in several different states in north, northeast and central India and help the poorest people in the lowest castes.

EHA was established by Indian Christians and foreign missionaries in 1970 but since 1974 it has been under the sole leadership of Indian Christians.

Their website states their mission:

> EHA is a fellowship of Christian institutions and individuals that exists to transform communities through caring, with primary emphasis on the poor and the marginalized.

It adds,

> We serve people and communities regardless of race, caste, creed or religion with a geographical focus of north, northeast and central India. We do this in the name and spirit of Jesus Christ in word and deed.

A Kachhwa Christian Hospital website tells of the hospital's comprehensive service to the community. As well as holding medical clinics and performing surgeries, KCH clinics encourage community health and minister to people spiritually. They provide education and leadership development. KCH has a training centre to teach dental and eye technicians, sewing, air-conditioning installation, electrical work, and nursery school teaching. They also offer literacy training.

KCH reaches out to people from the 90 villages in the area, with a population of about 120,000.

Most likely one of those small towns is Gopiganj.

※

Continuing his journey, Archie arrived in Almora for Easter week at the end of March and visited the Leprosy Mission Hospital. He hadn't been to Almora for 50 years. Back then he trekked up to the mountain village, but in 1964 the hospital was on a bus route.

He met two Indian doctors who led teams to visit outpatients at clinics wherever their jeep could reach. Treatment for leprosy had progressed in an incredible way in 50 years and research was ongoing.

After the LMS had pulled out of North India, the American Methodist Episcopal Mission had taken over the work in Almora in 1925. Nearly 40 years later, Indian Christians were caring for their own people.

During Easter, Archie preached to a congregation of 400 at the Budden Memorial Church, built in remembrance of John Budden, the first missionary there in 1850. Archie's heart lifted, grateful God had used the LMS to bless the Indian people and that he'd been part of it.

Other missions – both Catholic and Protestant, with staff from many different countries – had also made a lasting impact for good in India.

One of those missions was in Vellore where the training hospital had been established by an American, Doctor Ida Scudder. After leaving Almora, Archie travelled to South India, keen to visit the hospital the pastor's daughter from Khursipar had attended in the late 1940s.

The hospital had an amazing story to tell.

Ida's grandfather was the first American medical missionary to India and his seven sons also became missionaries. One of them was Ida's father. She had no intention of being a missionary and was firmly against it but after leaving school in the United States, she visited her parents in Vellore.

One night, three different men came on separate occasions to her parents' home, pleading for help. In each case, the wife was in serious difficulty during labour. The men all refused her father's assistance; only a woman doctor could attend a birth. By morning all three women were dead.

Unable to help, Ida had poured out her heartbreak to God, praying much of the night. After hearing of the women's deaths she made a decision: she would dedicate her life to train as a doctor and return to Vellore.

She graduated from Cornell University Medical College, New York, in the first course open to women.

After returning to Vellore, she saw patients in her parents' home at first but then began raising money in the USA for a hospital which opened in 1902. Soon she was training Indian nurses, a first for India. A few years later she opened roadside dispensaries and in 1918 she opened a college to train Indian women doctors.

With increasing need for a larger hospital, the new facility was opened in 1923.

Ida died there in 1960 after a lifetime of making a real difference for the women in Vellore.

Archie wrote,

> The Christian Medical College and Hospital in Vellore (founded by that remarkable woman Doctor Ida Scudder) provides an outstanding example of how a great institution

has grown from a small beginning within 60 years. All over the world there are friends of Vellore helping by gifts and prayer. Patients come from distant parts of India and 282 came from foreign countries like USA, Canada, United Kingdom etc.

The hospital services have continued to expand over the years since Archie was there. As their vision statement says,

> The Christian Medical College in Vellore seeks to be a witness to the healing ministry of Christ, through excellence in education, service, and research.

About 20 kilometres from the hospital is the Schieffelin Institute of Health Research & Leprosy Centre (SIH-RL) at Karigiri. It was founded through the cooperation of The Leprosy Mission, the American Leprosy Missions and the Christian Medical College.

Doctor Ida Scudder turned the first sod of soil in 1952 and the centre was completed in 1955.

Archie wanted to see it too, impressed by the new research undertaken there. People with leprosy travelled great distances for treatment and transforming operations.

Thirteen years after Archie's visit, the centre became independent from the three founding organisations. It has seven objectives but the first is:

> To serve in the spirit of Christ as an instrument of God in the healing of persons suffering from leprosy.

While he was there, Archie thought back to when he and

Grace had first been missionaries in Gopiganj in 1909. There wasn't much they could do to help people with leprosy then. It was heartbreaking to see them.

Now there was encouraging news from the hospitals he'd seen in Nepal, Almora, Allahabad, and Karigiri; and he believed there would be great breakthroughs in the near future for a cure that would lead to eradicating leprosy altogether.

He thought of the dedicated work of the United Mission Hospital in Nepal, the hospital in Kachhwa and the Christian Medical College and Hospital in Vellore. They saved many people's lives and relieved so much suffering.

In 1901 when Archie arrived in Baihar, the idea of a college where Indian women could be educated in medicine and other careers had seemed impossible. Now, women at the Hawabagh Women's College in Jabalpur near Baihar are achieving exactly that.

The best thing about each of these institutions is that they are showing God's love and sharing the gospel with the people of Nepal, and in India from the north in Almora to the south in Vellore.

In September 1947, shortly after India achieved independence, several Protestant churches in South India united to form the Church of South India. It had taken years of talks and preparation, but now they demonstrated unity, a real witness to the nation.

Archie knew that in North India the churches were going through the same process but the Church of North India wouldn't be formed until 1970.

Changes in missionary societies took place soon after Archie's last visit. The LMS merged with the Colonial Missionary Society in 1966 to form the Congregational Council for World Mission (CCWM). Over the years, the mission merged with other mission societies and changed its name to the Council for World Mission (CWM).

Before he left South India, Archie visited Bangalore. On a Saturday evening he attended a recital by a visiting choir from Madras at St Mark's Cathedral. To his delight, the same choir was singing on Sunday morning at the church he chose to attend. Music had always flowed through his life. Now, the beautiful singing made a special finale to his trip.

After flying to Colombo, he boarded the P&O liner *Canberra*. It was a relaxed journey home to New Zealand.

> I have learned a lot from this tour, and made many new friends, he wrote, finishing his circular letter. It's been worthwhile and has enriched my life.

※

Archie settled down to suburban life with Connie in Tauranga, enjoying church life, family, friends and his pet pigeons, Raja and Rani, and their budgerigar Laddie.

India – with her diversity of people, languages and customs, jungles, mountains and plains – had been an inseparable part of his life for so long, and she remained on his mind and in his prayers.

Nearly five years after his last overseas trip and three days before he died on 6 January 1969, Archie called Connie to his bedside. His energy almost gone, he asked her to write a letter for him to friends and family as he told her what to say.

With great effort, he slowly began to speak:

'I thank you for the greetings you have sent me and for your friendship over the years. Christmas has passed, and as usual, it has been a happy one. In mid-November I developed clots in both legs, and since then I have kept to my bed – I am feeling very weak.'

Connie stopped writing and waited for Archie to gather his strength to carry on.

'While I lie in bed I remember the motto my dear Grace and I took on 12 April 1905, our wedding day – "That in all things Christ might have the pre-eminence".'

Memories were crowding around Archie. Scenes from the past floated through his mind. There was Grace, young and beautiful, who had willingly left family and a comfortable English village to live in the Indian jungle to be with him as they served God together. Now, Grace was departing to the Himalayas with the children for several months as he continued his mission work in the plains.

Yes, they'd sacrificed much and faced many hardships, frustrations and danger together, but it had all been worth it.

He felt privileged to have shared the gospel among the people he loved. It was a true blessing.

Another blessing close to his heart was his family.

He thought of the triumphs in his life. Clear memories came to mind of people who had given their lives to God because of his witness and caring. There was the satisfaction of working at the Gopiganj clinic and in Kachhwa, training young Chamar men in a variety of skills to better their lives.

Thoughts of many answers to prayer came to mind. God had provided for their family's needs and guided their steps. He had opened doors for them to live in New Zealand at the right time and to help Indians in Fiji. He had been able to return to his beloved India four times.

Archie smiled, remembering the time many years before

when he'd chatted to a blind man and his friend on a train journey in India.

The conversation had set off an argument between the two friends. The blind man was adamant Archie was an Indian despite everything his friend told him.

'No Englishman speaks Hindi like that,' he'd said.

Archie was delighted; it was a real compliment. God had given him the gift of speaking Hindi like a native so he could identify better with the people.

Through all his experiences, he knew he could trust God. He wanted everyone to know they could too.

When the LMS had to pull out of North India, Archie was concerned God's work there could end. But God had great plans for other missions and Indian nationals to establish Christian hospitals, colleges and missions.

Connie picked up her pen as Archie began speaking quietly again, a strong conviction in his words. 'Another verse that means a lot to me is: "I know whom I have believed and am persuaded that he is able to keep that which I have committed unto him against that day".'

He was confident that when he died, he had a home with God in heaven. The Bible told him it was a place of joy where he would meet Jesus face to face and reunite with loved ones who also had faith in God.

Heaven seemed so close to Archie now. Jesus' presence surrounded him, and family and friends who'd gone before him were not far away. He could almost see Grace. Pandit Ramswarup would be waiting for him too. Archie thought of his words now.

'A dear Brahmin friend said to a missionary many years ago, "Tell sahib I am going home." I feel the same as my dear old friend – I too am going home.'

He felt deep contentment.

It was wonderful to know God's love for India was, right now, giving hope and healing to hearts and lives across the land.

References

Books and articles

John Grant. *Ram Swarup*. London: London Missionary Society, 1925.

Vera Jamieson. 'Trapped in a Storm'. *The Fiji Times & Herald*. 28 December 1938.

Vera Jamieson, 'A Race with Death, in India'. Note: Vera's date of 1913 is incorrect. The incidents took place in 1914 as verified by her father's letter to the LMS Board, 17 June 1914.

A. W. McMillan. *Jungle Pioneering in Gondland*. London: Morgan & Scott, 1906.

A. W. McMillan. *Family Links*. A family tree and brief history of the McMillan family, 1960.

A. W. McMillan. *My Memories*, 1883-1909.

A. W. McMillan. Himalayan Trek Diary, November 1911.

Connie McMillan. *Laughs for Vera*. Compilation of anecdotes from Vera's life.

Connie McMillan. Diary on SS *Strathaird*, 1935.

Grace McMillan. *McMillan Children 1908-1924: Memories of our Children's Sayings and Doings*.

Harry Waller. *Harry: The Unknown Man. The autobiography of J H Waller.* Brown, Jones & Robinson, 1935.

Lily and Vera McMillan, *Home Newspaper.* Compiled 1922.

'Education in Fiji – Inspector of Schools – Auckland Man Chosen – Experience in India'. *New Zealand Herald.* 23 April, 1929, pg 12.

Letters, reports and albums

Letters and documents, 1909 to 1924. LMS archives. School of Oriental and African Studies Library, London University.

Jesse Collyer. Letter explaining how a grocery business was run about 120 years ago.

Archie and Connie McMillan. *Memories of Mother.* Compilation of extracts of letters of condolence.

Archie and Grace McMillan. Family letters.

Archie McMillan. Family photo albums.

Archie McMillan. Report on his journey to India, 1964.

Connie McMillan. Photo album about Nurses' Christian Fellowship, 1958.

Elzeth McMillan. A DVD compiled by her family on the story of her life.

John McMillan. Letter to his grandchildren.

Lily McMillan. LMS Reports on mission work in Papua.

References

Websites

Dudley High School, Suva www.schoolandcollegelistings.com/FJ/Suva/206677982711192/Dudley-High-School

Google maps. www.google.com/maps

Ida Scudder, an American missionary in South India, scudder.org/about/history/india-medical-missions/ida-scudder-story/

Kacchwa Hospital www.ehausa.org/hospitals/kacchwa.html

The Christian Medical College, Vellore www.cmch-vellore.edu/

The Leprosy Mission www.leprosymission.org, leprosymission.org.nz/anandaban

United Missions Hospital, Nepal www.tansenhospital.org.np/

Wikipedia. en.wikipedia.org Indian gods, rivers, mountains and cities.

www.ingramcontent.com/pod-product-compliance
Lightning Source LLC
Chambersburg PA
CBHW071343290426
44108CB00014B/1423